DOG TIONARY

DOROTHÉE SCHNEIDER

Wortschatz für den Hundefreund
Deutsch – Englisch
Englisch – Deutsch

animal Learn®
VERLAG

ISBN 3-936188-06-8

Illustrationen: Jürgen Zimmermann, Stuttgart
Satz & Layout: Annette Gevatter
Druck: Druckerei Mack GmbH, Schönaich

animal learn Verlag
email: animal.learn@t-online.de
www.animal-learn.de

Hinweis zur Benutzung

Dieses Wörterbuch ist für das schnelle Nachschlagen eines Begriffes gedacht und verzichtet deshalb auf grammatikalische Feinheiten. Die amerikanische Schreibweise weicht manchmal geringfügig von der englischen ab; nicht überall wurde das extra erwähnt (zum Beispiel: Verhalten amerikanisch: behavior/ englisch: behaviour oder Leine amerikanisch: leash/ englisch: lead usw.)

Maßgeblich für das Nachschlagen ist im Allgemeinen das Hauptwort eines Begriffes, also zum Beispiel im Deutschen: Bestätigung, konditionierte oder Entwicklungsphase, vegetative usw.

Bei vorwiegend fachsprachlichen Begriffen wurde der Bereich angefügt, aus dem sie stammen, wie zum Beispiel die Bereiche Agility, Jagd, Obedience, Schutzdienst u. a.

DEUTSCH – ENGLISCH

Pfote → paw

A

Aalstrich backtrace
Aas carrion
abbeißen bite off, snap at, tell off
abbiegen (nach) turn (off)
Abbildung picture
abblocken block
abbringen von etwas put someone off (doing) something
Abbruch (Sport) break-off (sport)
abdriften drift off
Abdruck (z.B. Fuß-) imprint
Abduktoren („Abziehmuskel“, Muskeln zur Bewegung eines Körperteils von der Medialachse weg) abductors (muscle)
Aberglaube superstition
abfallend slanted, slanting, sloping
Abführung the act of escorting away
Abgang start of tracking
Abgangsstelle start, starting point
abgearbeitet worn out
abgehärtet sein (gegen) inured (to)
abgekämpft exhausted
abgemagert emaciated
abgeschieden secluded
Abgeschiedenheit seclusion
abgeschlossen (z.B. Ausbildung) completed (e.g. training)
abgesehen von apart from
abgestumpft (z.B. Gefühle) blunted (e.g. feelings)
Abhandlung (wissenschaftliche) treatise
abhängig (von) dependent (on)
abhärten (gegen) toughen to
Abhärtung hardening
abheilen heal (up)
Abhilfe schaffen remedy things

abjagen (etwas) snatch something away from
abkanzeln give someone a dressing-down
abkaufen buy something from
Abkehr (von) turning away (from)
Ablassen (Schutzdienst) drop (protection work)
Ablassen auf Kommando (Schutzdienst) stop biting on command (protection work)
ablecken lick off
ablegen drop, down
Ablegen (lay) down and stay
Ablegen aus der Bewegung down while in motion
Ablegen nach Herankommen down after recall
ablehnen (im Sinne von missbilligen) disapprove of
ableinen release (from leash)
Ablenkung distraction
Ablenkung, Übung unter... (excercise) with distraction
Abmachung agreement
Abmagerungsdiät reducing diet
Abneigung (gegen) dislike (of, for)
Abpfiff final whistle
abrasieren shave off
Abreise departure
abrichten train, school
Abrichter trainer
Abrichtung training, schooling
Abrichtungskennzeichen working certificate, performance title
Abroll-Leine flexi-leash
Abruf, abrufen recall
Abrufübung recall exercise
abrutschen (von) slip off (from)
Absage cancellation
absäugen wean
Absäugen weaning, ablactation
abschaffen abolish
Abscheu (vor) abhorrence (of)
abscheulich dreadful
Abschied farewell
Abschiedsschmerz wrench
Abschiedsszene farewell scene
Abschiedsworte words of farewell
abschließbar lockable
Abschließen lock (up)
Abschlussgrundstellung finish
Abschlussgrundstellung (um Hundeführer herum) go-behind finish
abschmettern/ abschießen (den Ball) launch (the ball)
abschnappen snap at, tell off
abschnüren tie off
absetzen (Welpen von der Muttermilch) weaning
absichern cover

Absichern von Verhalten (Generalisieren) proofing, generalization
Absicht intention
Absitzen aus der Bewegung sit-in-motion
absorbieren absorb
absperren block off
Abstammung genealogy, (family) descent
Abstammungslehre theory of evolution
Abstammungsnachweis pedigree
Abstand space
abstecken (Gelände) mark out
abstimmen (über) vote (on)
Abstimmung voting
Abstrich (medizinisch) smear (medical)
abstumpfen make someone insensible
absuchen quarter
absuchen (einer Fährte) follow (or work) a track
abtasten feel, examine (with fingers), go over
Abteilung C, Schutzdienst protection work
abtrainieren retrain
Abtreibungsspritze mismating shot
abwägen (z.B. Worte) weigh (e.g. every word)
abwandeln modify
abwarten wait for
Abwärtstrend downward trend
Abwehrreaktion defensive reaction
Abwendeübung turn-away-exercise
Abwesenheit (eines Verhaltens) formen shaping the absence
Abwurfstange displaceable bar
Abzeichen markings
Abzeichen, Logo club insignia, logos
Achillessehne achilles tendon
Achselhöhle armpit
Acht, in Form einer... (z.B. beim bei Fuß gehen) figure eight (e.g. heelwork)
achtbar respectable
Achtbarkeit respectability
achten auf pay attention to
achtlos careless
Achtlosigkeit carelessness
Achtsamkeit carefulness
Achtung haben, voreinander respect for each other
achtungsvoll respectful
adäquat adequate
addieren add (up)
Addisonsche Krankheit addison's disease

Addition addition
Adduktoren („Anziehmuskel", Muskeln zur Bewegung eines Körperteils zur Medialachse) adductors (muscle)
Adel nobility
Adel, ohne... coarse, without refinement
Aderhaut (des Auges) choroid membrane
Adlernase aquiline nose
adoptieren adopt
Adoption adoption
Adrenalin adrenaline
Adressbuch directory
Adressenverzeichnis mailing list
Affenpinscher Affenpinscher
Afghane Afghan (Hound)
Afghanische Bulldogge Aryan Molossus
Afghanischer Windhund Afghan
Afrikanischer Elefantenhund African Elephant Dog
Afrikanischer Nackthund African Hairless Dog
Afrikanischer Sandhund African Sand Dog
After anus
Afterklaue (oder -kralle) dewclaw
Aftersack anal sac
Agalaktie agalactia, absence of milk
Aggression (gegenüber Personen) aggression (towards people)
Aggressionstrieb aggression drive
aggressiv aggressive
Aggressivität aggressiveness
Agility (Sport) agility (sport)
Agility-Kegel, nummerierte numbered agility cones
Agility-Parcours agility course
Agility-Prüfung agility test
Agility-Pylonen, nummerierte numbered agility cones
Agility-Reglement agility regulations
Agility-Turnier agility trial
Ägyptischer Schäferhund Armant, Egyptian Sheepdog
ähneln look like
Ahnentafel pedigree
ähnlich (mit) similar (to)
ähnlich klingende Kommandos similar sounding words for commands
Ähnlichkeit (mit) similarity (to)
Aichi Aichi
Aidi Aidi, Atlas Sheepdog
Ainou Ainou Dog
Ainu Hund Ainu Dog
Airedale-Terrier Airedale Terrier

Akarusräude follicular mange
Akbash Akbash Dog
Akita Inu Akita Inu
akrale Leckdermatitis acral lick dermatitis, acral lick granuloma
Akromegalie acromegaly
Aktion action
aktivieren activate
Aktivitäten, gemeinsame activities together with (the dog)
Akzeptanz acceptance
akzeptieren accept
Alano Alano
Alapaha Blue Blood Bulldog Alapaha Blue Blood Bulldog
Alaskan Husky Alaskan Husky
Alaskan Malamut Alaskan Malamute
Albinismus albinism
Albino albino
allbekannt well-known
Alleinbesitzer(in) sole owner
Alleinbleiben being left alone
Alleinfutter(mittel) complete and balanced food
Alleinjäger solitary hunter
Alleinsein loneliness
Alleinsein, Angst vor dem ... fear of being alone
Allergie allergy
alles everything
alles in allem all in all
allgegenwärtig omnipresent
allgemein general
Allgemeine Rassehunde-zuchtschau all-breed dog show
allgemeines Erscheinungsbild general appearance
Allgemeinheit general public
Allgemeinrichter(in) all-rounder judge
Allgemeinwissen general knowledge
alljährlich annually
allmählich gradually
Allround-Richter all-rounder (judge)
Allroundsportler(in) all-rounder
Alopezie alopecia
Alpenbracke Alpine Hound
Alpenländische Dachsbracke Alpine Basset Hound
Alpha-Figur alpha figure
Alphahund leader of the pack, top dog
Alpha-Hund alpha male
Alpha-Hündin alpha female
Alpha-Position alpha position
altbewährt well-tried
Altdänische Dogge Danish Broholmer
Altdänischer Hühnerhund (Vorstehhund) Old Danish Pointer

Altenglischer Rauhaarterrier Broken-Haired Black and Tan Terrier
Altenglischer Schäferhund Old English Sheepdog, Bobtail
Altenglischer Terrier Old English Terrier, Welsh-Terrier
Alter age
Alternativverhalten alternative behaviour
Altersbestimmung age determination
Alterserscheinung sign of old age
Altersfrische fitness of the old/ elder dog
Altersklasse veterans class
Altersschwäche infirmity (of old age)
altfarben traditionally coloured
altmodisch old-fashioned
Alunk Alunk, Sonangi
Ambition ambition
ambivalent ambivalent
American Staffordshire-(Bull)terrier American Staffordshire Terrier
Amerikanische Bulldogge American Bulldog
Amerikanischer Blauer Gascon Laufhund American Blue Gascon Hound
Amerikanischer Cockerspaniel American Cocker Spaniel
Amerikanischer Eskimo Hund American Eskimo Dog
Amerikanischer Fuchshund American Foxhound
Amerikanischer Nackterrier American Hairless Terrier
Amerikanischer Pitbull Terrier American Pitbull Terrier
Amerikanischer Wasserspaniel American Water Spaniel
Amerikanisch-Kanadischer Schäferhund American-Canadian White Shepherd
Amme foster mother
Ammenaufzucht foster mothering
amtlich official
Analbeutel anal sac
Analbeutelentzündung infected anal glands
Analdrüse, verstopfte impaction of the anal glands
Analkontrolle anal greeting
Anatolischer Hirtenhund Anatolian Karabash
Anatomie anatomy
anatomisch anatomical
Anbindehaken spiral stake
Anbindepflock peg, tie-out stake
anbrüllen yell

anders als different from
andersfarbig of other colour(s)
anerkannt durch recognized by
anerkennen accept
anerkennen, als Rasse recognize as a breed, accept as a breed
Anerkennung acceptance, recognition
Anfall attack
anfallen, angreifen attack, lunge at
anfällig (für eine Krankheit) susceptible (to an illness)
Anfänger(in) beginner
Anfänger-Team beginner team
anfassen touch
anfixieren, anstarren (etwas) focus on something
Anforderung requirement
Anforderung ändern criteria shifting
anfragen (bei jemandem ... wegen) inquire (of someone about something)
anfreunden become friends
angeboren inherited
angeboren (im Sinne von eingezüchtet) inbreed
angekört approved (by breed club) for breeding
angeleint leashed, on a leash
angenehm pleasant
angeschossen wounded
angesetzt (z.B. Ohren, Rute) set on (e.g. ears, tail), inserted (tail)
angewölft inborn
Anglo-Francais French-English Hound
Anglo-Russische Bracke Russian Parti-coloured Hound
Angorahund Maltese
Angriff, angreifen attack
Angriff oder Flucht fight or flight
Angriffslust aggressiveness
Angst (vor) fear (of)
Angst, panische ... vor be terrified of
Angst vor dem Alleinsein fear of being alone
Angstbeißen fear biting
Angstbeißer fear biter
Angst einflößen fill someone with fear
ängstigen, sich be afraid (of)
Angstneurose anxiety
Angstschrei cry of fear
angstvoll fearful
Angstzustand state of anxiety
Anhaltezone (Agility) pause area, pause box (agility)
anhänglich affectionate
ankämpfen gegen fight against
ankeifen bark at, yip at
anketten chain, put on a chain

anknabbern nibble (at)
ankommen arrive
ankören koerklassing
Ankörung examination as to suitability for breeding
anlächeln smile at
Anlass occasion
anlasten, jemandem etwas blame somebody for something
Anlegepflock peg, tie-out stake
anleinen put on a leash
anleiten instruct
Anleitung instructions
anmelden (einen Hund zur Prüfung) enter
anmelden bei (Wettkampf/ Körung) enter in (trial/ competition/ koerung)
Anmeldung entry
Anöstrus anoestrus
anpassen, sich adapt, adjust
Anpassung adaptation
anpassungsfähig an adaptable to
Anpassungsfähigkeit adaptability
anpirschen go stalking
Ansatz (z.B. Rute, Ohren etc.) insertion, set, set-on (e.g. tail, ear etc.)
Ansatzfährte original track
anschauen watch
anschlagen (im Sinne von bellen) barking, alert by barking
anschreien yell at, shout at
ansetzen (auf der Fährte) start (a dog) tracking
Ansicht (über) opinion (on)
Ansichtssache, das ist that's a matter of opinion
anspringen jump up (at a person)
anstarren stare at
anstecken, sich mit etwas to catch something
ansteckend infectious, contagious
Ansteckung infection, contagion
anstupsen nudge
Antiläufigkeitsspritze oestrus-prevention injection
Antirutsch-Bodenbelag rubber floor matting
Anti-Rutschspray für Hundepfoten firm grip spray
Anwärter(in) zum Richteramt apprentice judge
Anwartschaft certificate towards a title
anwendbar (auf) applicable (to)
anwenden apply
Anzahl number
Anzahlung deposit
Anzeichen für sign of

anzeigen (z.B. Rettungshunde-arbeit) alert
Anzeigetafel (Ergebnisse) scoreboard
anzweifeln doubt
Aorta aorta
Apathie apathy
apathisch apathetic, indifferent
Apotheke pharmacy
Appell immediate obedience, call
appellieren an make an appeal to
Appenzeller Sennenhund Appenzell Mountain Dog
Appetitlosigkeit inappetence, lack (or loss) of appetite
applaudieren applaud
Applaus applause
Apport delivery
Apportierb(l)ock dumbbell (stick)
Apportierdummy dummy
apportieren retrieve, bring
Apportieren auf ebener Erde retrieve on flat
Apportieren über die Hürde retrieve over jump
Apportiergegenstand dumpbell
Apportierhund retriever
Apportiersack retriever bag
Arbeit work
Arbeit nach dem Schuss (Jagd) retrieving killed and/ or wounded game (hunting)
Arbeit, geistige brainwork
Arbeit (wissenschaftliche Abhandlung) treatise
arbeiten work
Arbeitsfreude willingness to work
Arbeitshund working dog
Arbeitsleistung efficiency
Arbeitsprüfung field trial
Arbeitsweise (Schutzdienst) style and technique (protection work)
arbeitswilliger Hund willing worker
Ardenner Treibhund Ardennes Cattle Dog
Areal area
Ärger anger
ärgern, sich be (get) annoyed
Ärgernis annoyance
Argument argument
Argumentation argumentation
argumentieren argue
Ariege Laufhund Ariegeois
Arischer Molosser Aryan Molossus
Armant Armant, Egyptian Sheepdog
Armmanschette (Ringsport) arm cuff (mondioring)

Art (biologisch) species
Art (und Weise) manner
Artenschutz protection of species
artfremd alien
Arthritis arthritis
Arthrose arthrosis
Artikel (im Sinne von Text) article
Artois Laufhund Artois Hound
Arznei medicine
Arzt doctor
Arzt, zum ... gehen go to see the doctor
Askaridenbefall roundworm infestation
asozial antisocial
Asphaltplatz asphalt ground
Assistenzhund (für Behinderte) service dog
Assoziation association
assoziieren associate
Asternale Rippe false rib
Atem breath
Atlasschäferhund Atlas Sheepdog
atmen breathe
Atmosphäre atmosphere
Atmungstrakt respiratory tract
Atopie atopy
Atrophie atrophy
attackieren attack
Aufbaudiät stress diet
aufbauen stack (a dog in the show ring), build up
aufbegehren (gegen) rebel (against)
Aufbeißer dog with pincer bite
Aufbewahrungstasche für Zubehör article bag
Aufbiss pincer bite
aufblicken look up
aufbrausend quick-tempered
auffangen catch
Auffrischungsimpfung booster shot (or vaccination), revaccination
Auffrischungskurs refresher course
aufgebaut stacked, set up
aufgeknöchelt knuckled-up
aufgeregt excited
aufgestellt (Ohren) erect (ears)
aufgestülpt (Nase, Schnauze) upfaced, tip-tilted (nose, muzzle)
aufgeweckt alert
aufgeworfen (Nase, Schnauze) upfaced, tip-tilted (nose, muzzle)
aufgezogen drawn-up, tucked-up, cut-up
aufhören stop
auflauern, jemandem waylay someone
auflecken lap (up)
Auflösungswort release word
aufmerksam attentive

Aufmerksamkeit (während)
attention (during)
Aufmerksamkeit erregen/ fordern attract attention
Aufmunterungen rufen
cheerleading
aufnahmefähig (für)
receptive (to)
Aufnahmegebühr admission fee
aufnehmen take up
aufnehmen (z.B. Geruch oder Gegenstand) pick up (e.g. a scent or an article on the track)
aufrecht upright, erect
Aufregung excitement
aufreiten (auf) mount (of)
aufrichten (Ohren) prick (ears)
aufscheuchen flush
aufschreiben take a note of
aufspringen leap up, mount
aufstöbern flush
aufwachsen grow up
Aufwand expenditure (of)
Aufwand, großer Energie-
require a great deal of energy
Aufwandsentschädigung
expense allowance
aufwärmen (vor Sport)
limber up
Aufwärtsentwicklung
upward trend
aufziehen raise, rear, bring up
Aufzucht raising, rearing
aufzwingen, etwas
force something (upon)
Augapfel eyeball, orb
Auge eye
Augen, kugelförmige
bulging eyes
Augen, offene open eyes, haw eyes
Augen, schräg gestellte
slanting eyes
Augen, tiefliegende
deep-set eyes
Augenbraue eyebrow
Augenfleck eye mark
Augenhöhle eye socket, orbit
Augenlid eyelid
Augenlinie eye level
Augenmuskel eye muscle
Augentrübung cloudiness of the eye
Aujeszkysche Krankheit
Aujeszky's disease
Aus! (Hörzeichen zum Stillwerden) Quiet! (verbal command)
Aus! (Hörzeichen zum Ablassen) Out!, Drop it! (verbal command)
ausarbeiten (einer Fährte)
follow (or work) a track
ausbilden train, school
Ausbilder trainer
Ausbildung training, schooling

Ausbildungskennzeichen (AKZ) title, working certificate, performance title
Ausbildungskennzeichen (AKZ), anerkannte, zur Teilnahme an recognized titles for attendance at
Ausbildungsmethode, neue/ moderne new training method
Ausbreitung spreading
ausbürsten brush out
Ausdauer endurance
Ausdauer (im sportlichen Sinn) staying power
ausdiskutieren thresh out
Ausdruck expression
Ausdruck, orientalischer oriental expression
ausdrucksvoll expressive, full of expression
ausdünnen (Fell) thin (coat)
Ausfluss discharge
Ausgangsposition (Obedience) starting position, heel position (obedience)
ausgebucht booked-up
ausgedient useless
ausgedreht (Füße) turned out (feet)
ausgeglichen balanced
ausgeliefert sein be at someones mercy
ausgeprägt pronounced
ausgeschoren shaved
ausgewogen well-proportioned
Ausgewogenheit balance
ausgreifend with good reach
auskämmen brush out
Auskreuzung outbreeding
Auslassen (eine Sache) drop (an object)
Auslassen/ Ablassen out, release
Auslauf exercise
Auslaufplatz exercise run (or enclosure)
Auslöser trigger
Auslösereiz trigger
ausmerzen cull
Ausrichter, Veranstalter organizer, sponsor
Ausrichtung alignment
ausruhen, entspannen relax
ausrupfen pluck
Ausrüstung equipment
ausscheiden exclude, excrete
Ausscheidung elimination, excretion
Ausschlag (Krankheit) skin eruption, rash (disease)
Ausschleichen (z.B. Gebrauch des Haltis) fading (e.g. using the Halti)
Ausschlussfehler breed disqualification, disqualifying fault
Ausschreibung premium list

Aussehen appearance
Außenlinie silhouette
Außenseiter(in) outsider
außer Konkurrenz out of concurrence, not for competition
aussortieren (Vieh) sorting (live-stock)
ausstellen exhibit, show
Aussteller(in) exhibitor
Ausstellung exhibition, show
Ausstellungshund show dog
Ausstellungskalender events calendar, show schedule
Ausstellungsleine show lead
Ausstellungsordnung show regulations
Ausstellungsring show ring
Ausstellungsschur show clip
Ausstellungstraining show training
ausstopfen stuff
ausstrecken, darbieten hold out
Austausch replacement
Australian Cattle Dog Australian Cattle Dog
Australian Kelpie Australian Kelpie
Australian Shepherd Australian Shepherd
Australian Silky Terrier Australian Silky Terrier
Australischer Hütehund Australian Shepherd
Australischer Terrier Australian Terrier
Australischer Viehhund Australian Cattle Dog
Australischer Windhund Australian Greyhound, Kangaroo Dog
Austreibungsphase stage in labour
Austrocknung dehydration
Auswuchs (bei Knochen) outgrowth (from bone)
Auszeichnung award
Auszeit (in Trainingssequenz) time-out (in training)
Ausziehleine flexi-leash
Autoimmunerkrankung auto-immune disease
Auto-Belüftungsgitter air fence up
Autobox kennel, car crate
Auto-Hundeschutzgitter car safety fence
Auto-Hundeschutznetz car safety net
automatisches Sitzen automatic sit
Autor(in) author
autoritär authoritarian
Autorität authority
Autorität, natürliche/ echte natural authority
Auto-Schondecke car blanket

Auto-Sicherheitsgurt für Hunde safety belt for dogs
Auvergne Vorstehhund Auvergne Pointer
aversiv aversive
A-Wand (Agility) a-frame (agility)
Azawakh Azawakh

B

Bachblüten Bach flowers
Backe cheek
Backenzahn molar
baden bath, bathe
Baganda (Jagdhund) Baganda Hunting-Dog
Bagirmi (Jagdhund) Bagirmi Dog
Bahnbeobachter(in) (beim Hunderennen) foul judge
Bahnrennen track racing
Bakhund Old Danish Pointer
Balg skin, pelt
Bali Berghund Bali Mountain Dog
Balkanbracke Balkan Hound
Ball ball
Ballen (Pfote) pad (paw)
Balljagen chase a ball
Ballspiel ball game
Balz courting
balzen court
Balzzeit mating season
Band ribbon, tape, ligament
Bandscheibe intervertebral disc
Bandwurm tapeworm
Barbet Barbet
Bardino Canary Dog
Barsoi Borzoi, Russian Wolfhound
Bart beard, whiskers
Bas Rouge Beauceron, French Short-Haired Shepherd
Basenji Basenji, Congo Dog
Basisgeräte ground obstacles
Basis-Kontroll-Übungen basic control issues
Baskischer Schäferhund Basque Shepherd Dog
Basset Basset Hound, Basset, Short-Legged Hound
Basset Artésien-Normand Artesien Normand Basset
Basset Bleu de Gascogne Basset Bleu de Gascogne, Blue Gascony Basset

Basset d'Artois Basset d'Artois
Basset Fauve de Bretagne Basset Fauve de Bretagne
Basset Griffon Vendéen Basset Griffon Vendeen
Bastard mixture, bastard, crossbreed
Batakenhund Batak Dog, Sumatra Wild Dog
Bau den, nest
Bauch abdomen
Bauchfell peritoneum
Bauchhoden retained testicle
Bauchhöhle abdominal cavity
Bauchlinie bottom line
Bauchschlagader abdominal aorta
Bauchspeicheldrüse pancreas
Bauhund burrow dog, earth dog
Baumstamm (gefällter) log
Bayerischer Gebirgsschweißhund Bavarian Schweisshund, Bavarian Mountain Hound
beabsichtigen zu tun intend doing
beachten pay attention to
Beagle Beagle
Beagle Harrier Beagle Harrier
beängstigend worrying
beanstanden criticize
Bearded Collie Bearded Collie
Beardie Bearded Collie
Beauceron Beauceron
beben, zittern quiver, tremble
Becken pelvis
Beckenpfanne hip socket
Bedeutung von importance of, meaning of
Bedingungen im Ring (Wettkampf) ring conditions (competition)
Bedingungen, optimale optimum conditions
Bedlington Terrier Bedlington Terrier
bedrohen threaten
Beduinenhirtenhund Bedouin Shepherd Dog
Bedürfnis requirement
beeindrucken impress
Beeinflussung, beeinflussen influence
beeinträchtigen impair
Beeinträchtigung impairment
befedert (Ohren, Beine, Körper) feathered (ears, legs, body)
befedert (Rute) plumed (tail)
Befehl command
befürworten advocate
begegnen meet
Begegnung meeting
Begegnung, feindliche encounter
Begleithund companion dog

Begleithund, verkehrssicherer traffic-sure companion dog
Begleithundeprüfung companion dog test
Begleitumstände circumstances
Begriffsvermögen comprehension
Begrüßungszeremonie greeting ritual
behandeln treat
Behändigkeit agility
Behandlung treatment
Behandlungstisch examination table
Behang earage, pendulous ears, hanging ears
Behindertenbegleithund assistance dog
behost trousered
behutsam careful
Behutsamkeit gentleness
bei Fuß gehen heel
Bei Fuß! (Hörzeichen) Heel! (verbal command)
Beifall applause
Beifall klatschen applaud
Beinheben lift his leg
Beinmanschette (Ringsport) leg cuff (mondioring)
Beispiel example
Beißarm (Ringsport) bite arm (mondioring)
beißen bite
Beißerei dog fight
Beißhemmung bite inhibition
Beißkorb muzzle
Beißrolle, Beißwurst (Spielzeug) tug toy
Beißwurst (Schutzdienst) riot stick (protection work)
Bekanntgabe announcement
bekommen (z.B. Krankheit) develop (e.g. disease)
belächeln smile at
belegen (im Sinne von züchten) cover, breed
Belgische Bracke Belgian Short-Haired Pointer
Belgischer Griffon Belgian Griffon
Belgischer Karrenhund Belgian Mastiff
Belgischer Schäferhund Belgian Sheepdog
Belgischer Zughund Belgian Draught Dog, Belgian Mastiff
beliebt popular
bellen bark
bellfreudig talkative, vociferous
Bellfreudigkeit joy of barking
Belohnung, belohnen reward
Belohnung durch Übungen repertoire reinforcement
Belohnungen abbauen get rid of rewards

Belohnungsleckerli treat, snack, bait
Belohnungsspiel play as a reward
Belohnungsspiel als Auflösung einer Übung release reward
Belohnungstäschchen bait bag for the reward
Belüfter, Autoheck- trunk ventilator
Belüftungsgitter, Auto- air fence up
bemerkbar machen, sich draw attention to
bemerken notice
Bemerkung remark
benagen chew on (or up)
benutzen use
beobachten observe
Beobachter(in) observer
Beobachtung observation
Berater(in) counsellor
bereitstehen be ready
Bergafghane Mountain Afghan (Hound)
Bergamasker Bergamasco Herder, Bergamese Shepherd
Berger de Picard Picardy Sheepdog
Berger du Languedoc Cevennes Shepherd
Berghund Mountain Dog
Berner Laufhund Bernese Hound
Berner Niederlaufhund Small Bernese Hound
Berner Sennenhund Bernese Mountain Dog
Bernhardiner Saint Bernard
bernsteinfarbig amber
Berufsvorführer(in) professional handler
berühren touch
berühren (eines Zieles, z.B. mit Nase) targeting
Berührungsängste haben be scared at the idea of contact
berußt (Fellfärbung) blackened, sabled (coat)
Besamung insemination
Besamung, künstliche artificial insemination
besänftigen calm down
Beschäftigung, sinnvolle ingenious occupation
Bescheinigung certification
beschildern (z.B. Straßen) signpost
Beschilderung signposting
beschimpfen call someone names
beschnuppern sniff
beschreiben describe
beschützen (vor) protect (from)

Beschwichtigungssignal calming signal
beseitigen eliminate
Beseitigung elimination
Bestätigung reinforcement
Bestätigung, konditionierte conditioned reinforcement
Bestätigung, kontinuierliche continuous reinforcement
Bestätigung nach festem Schema ratio of reinforcement
Bestätigung nach Zufallsprinzip random reinforcement
Bestätigung, negative negative reinforcement
Bestätigung, positive positive reinforcement
Bestätigung, primäre primary reinforcement
Bestätigung, unkonditionierte primary reinforcement
Bestätigung, variable variable reinforcement
bestaunen marvel at
bestehen auf insist on
besteigen mount
bestrafen punish
bestrafende Person punisher
Bestrafung punishment
betteln beg
Beugemuskel flexor (muscle)
beurteilen, bewerten judge, evaluate
Beurteilung judging, process of judging
Beute prey, quarry, booty
Beutefangverhalten prey chasing behaviour
Beutegreifer predator
beutemotiviert(er Hund) prey motivated (dog)
Beutetier prey (animal)
Beutetrieb prey drive, predatory instinct
bevorzugen prefer (favourite)
bewachen guard
bewachen (des Schutzdiensthelfers) guard (the decoy)
bewältigen (einer Situation) cope (a situation)
beweglich mobile
Bewegung motion
Bewegung, verlangsamte slow movement, moving slowly
Bewegungsapparat musculo-skeletal system
Bewegungsfreudigkeit love of exercise
Bewegungsstereotypie stereotyped movement (and behaviour)
Beweis proof
Beweis erbringen prove something
beweisbar provable
bewerten judge, evaluate
Bewertungsblatt score sheet

Beziehung relationship
Bezugsperson parent person
Bhotia Bhotia, Himalayan Sheepdog
biberfarben beaver, dark beige
Bichon Frisé Bichon Frise
Bichon Havanais Havana Silk Dog
biegsam supple
billigend approving
Billigung approval
Bindehaut conjunctiva
Bindehautentzündung conjunctivitis
Biotonus vitality
Biotonustest test for evaluation a puppy's vitality
Bisben Bisben (Himalayan Bisben)
Biss bite, bite wound
Bissen (Happen) bite, snack
bissig snappish, vicious
Bissiger Hund! Beware of the dog!
Bissigkeit viciousness
Bizeps biceps
Black and Tan Toy Terrier English Toy Terrier
Black and Tan Coonhound Black and Tan Coonhound
blaffen give a short bark, yelp
Blase bladder
blau blue
blau fleckig blue-speckled
blau gestichelt blue roan
blau mit loh blue/ tan, blue and tan
blau scheckig blue-mottled
Blauer langhaariger Vorstehhund Picardie Blue Picardy Spaniel
blecken (Zähne) bare the teeth
Bleib! (Hörzeichen) Stay! (verbal command)
bleiben stay
bleibendes Gebiss permanent teeth
Bleistiftmarken penciling
Bleivergiftung lead poisoning
Blende (Schutzdienst/ Ringsport) blind (protection work, mondioring)
Blender dazzler
Blesse blaze, flare
Blicke, verständnislose blank looks
Blickkontakt eye contact
Blinddarm appendix
Blinden(führ)hund seeing eye dog, guide dog (for the blind)
Blinkhalsband safety light collar
Blinzhaut third eyelid
blond red fawn, blond
blue merle blue merle
Bluetick Coonhound Bluetick Coonhound

Blut blood
Blutarmut anaemia
Blutauffrischung infusion of new blood, outcrossing
Blutbild blood count
Blutdruck blood pressure
bluten bleed
Bluterguss blood blister
Bluthund Bloodhound, St. Hubert Hound
Blutlinie blood line
Blutplättchen platelet
Blutsturz haemorrhage
blutsverwandt related by blood
Blutsverwandtschaft consanguinity
Blutung (der läufigen Hündin) spotting
blutunterlaufen bloodshot
Blutvergiftung sepsis
Bobtail Old English Sheepdog
bockig sulky
Bodenbelag, Antirutsch- rubber floor matting
Bodenhaken spiral stake
bodennah cloddy
bodenweit basewide
Bogen arch
bogenförmig arched
Bogengang semicircular canal
Bogengehen (bei der Annäherung) arcing (while approaching)
Böhmischer Berghund Czech Mountain Dog
Böhmischer Raubart Bohemian Griffon
Bologneser Bichon Bolognese
Bordeaux Dogge Bordeaux Mastiff
Border Collie Border Collie
Border Terrier Border Terrier
Borreliose borrelia infection
bösartig vicious
Bosnische Rauhaarbracke Bosnian Rough-Coated Hound
Boston Terrier Boston Terrier
Boulet Griffon Boulet Griffon
Bourbonnais Vorstehhund Bourbonnais Pointer
Bouvier des Ardennes Ardennes Cattle Dog
Bouvier des Flandres Bouvier, Belgian Cattle Dog
Box kennel
Boxer Boxer
Boykin Spaniel Boykin Spaniel
Bracke scenthound
Bracke von Ariege Ariege Pointer
brackieren hunt fox or hare with scenthounds
Brand red (or tan) markings
Brandlbracke Austrian Black-and-Tan-Hound

Brasilianische Dogge
Fila Brasileiro
Brasilianischer Laufhund
Brazilian Tracker
Brasilianischer Terrier
Brazilian Terrier
Brasilianischer Windhund
Brazilian Greyhound
braun brown, bronze
braungelb brownish yellow
braunrot rust
braunschimmel liver roan, chestnut roan
Brav! (als Lob)
Good dog! (for praising)
Braver Hund! Good boy/ girl!
Brechdurchfall diarrhoea with vomiting
Brechmittel emetic
breit zwischen den Ohren broad in skull
Bretonischer Vorstehhund
Brittany (Spaniel)
Briard Briard
Brille spectacles
Bring! (Hörzeichen) Retrieve!, Fetch! (verbal command)
bringen retrieve, bring
Bringen auf ebener Erde
retrieve on flat
Bringen über die Hürde
retrieve over jump
Bringen über die Meter-Hürde (Schutzdienst)
retrieve over one meter jump (protection work)
Bringen über die Schrägwand (Schutzdienst) retrieve over the six feet wall (protection work)
Bringfreude joy of retrieving, willingness to retrieve
Bringholz dumbbell
Bringsel retrieving buck, bringsel
Bringselverweiser hunting dog that indicates ... by means of a bringsel
Bringtreue steadiness in retrieving
Briquet Griffon Vendéen
Medium Vendeen Griffon
Britische Hütehunde
British Sheepdogs
Broholmer Danish Broholmer
Bronchitis bronchitis
bronzefarben bronze coloured
Bronzehund Bronze Age Dog
Brunftzeit rutting season
Brunst heat, season oestrus
Brüsseler Griffon
Brussels Griffon
Brust chest, breast
Brustbein breastbone
Brustdrüse breast, mammary gland

Brustdrüsenentzündung mastitis
Brustgeschirr harness
Brustkorb rib cage
Brusttiefe depth of chest
Brustwarze nipple, teat
Brustwirbel thoracic vertebra
Brutalität brutality
Brutverhalten brood-tending behaviour
Buchung reservation
buddeln dig
Buddeln digging
Buenos Aires Nackthund Buenos Aires Hairless Dog
Büffelhaut rawhide
Büffelhautknochen rawhide bone
Buhund Norwegian Buhund
Bulgarische Bracke Bulgarian Hound
Bulldogge Bulldog
Bullenbeißer Bulldog, Drover
Bullmastiff Bullmastiff
Bullterrier Bull Terrier
Bully French Bulldog
Bundesjagdgesetz federal hunting law
Bundessieger(in), deutsche(r) German national winner
bunt gefleckt variegated
bunt gescheckt variegated
Bürste, bürsten brush
Bürstenrute brush tail
Büschel pencil (of hair), tuft
buschieren hunt game (or birds) in heavy cover
buschig bushy, plume like

C

Cairn Terrier Cairn Terrier
campieren camp
Canaan Hund Canaan Dog
Cane Corso Cane Corso
Canide canid
Carlin Pug
Carolina Hund Carolina Dog
Carpatin Carpathian Sheepdog
Cavalier King Charles Spaniel Cavalier King Charles Spaniel
Cesky Fousek Bohemian Griffon
Championat championship
Championklasse champion class, specials class
Charakteristika characteristics, hallmarks, traits
Chesapeake Bay Retriever Chesapeake Bay Retriever
Chihuahua Chihuahua
Chin Japan Chin, Japanese Spaniel
Chinesischer Faltenhund Shar Pei
Chinesischer Meutehund Chinese Hound
Chinesischer Nackthund Chinese Crested Dog
Chinesischer Schopfhund Chinese Crested Dog
Chinesischer Tempelhund Chinese Temple Chin
Chinesischer Windhund Chinese Greyhound, Chika
Chinook Chinook
Chip-Kennzeichnung microchip identification
Chow Chow Chow Chow
Click und Belohnung click and treat
Clicker clicker
Clicker benutzen use a clicker
Clickertraining clicker training
Clumber Spaniel Clumber Spaniel

Cocker Spaniel Cocker Spaniel
Collie, Kurzhaar- Smooth Collie
Collie, Langhaar- Rough Collie
Collieaugenanomalie collie eye anomaly, CEA
Coonhund Coonhound
Corgi Corgi
Coton de Tuléar Tulear Bichon
Coursing lure coursing
Couteulx Basset Hound Couteulxtype Basset Hound
creme(farben) cream
Cumberland Schäferhund Cumberland Sheep Dog
Curly Coated Retriever Curly Coated Retriever
Cynodrom dog (race)track
Czesky Terrier Bohemian Terrier

dachsfarben beaver, badger
Dachshund Dachshund
Dachverband parent umbrella organization
Dackel Dachshund
Dackellähme herniated disc syndrome
dagegen against (it)
Dalmatiner Dalmatian
Damm perineum
Dammbruch (medizinisch) peritoneal hernia (medical)
Damwild fallow deer
Dandie Dinmont Terrier Dandie Dinmont Terrier
danebenbenehmen, sich behave badly
Dänische Dachsbracke Danish Dachsbracke
Darmentzündung enteritis
dauerhaft durable
Daumen thumb
Daumenzehe dewclaw
davonlaufen run away
dazugehören belong to
dazwischendrängen, splitten split
dazwischentreten intervene
Deckakt copulation
Deckbereitschaft receptiveness (in bitch)
Decke blanket, coat
decken (im Sinne von befruchten, züchten) cover, serve (as in breeding)
Deckgebühr stud fee
Deckhaar top coat
Deckmeldung breeding notification
Deckrüde stud dog, sire
Decktaxe stud fee
Deckungswilligkeit receptiveness (in bitch)
Deckvereinbarung stud agreement
Deerhound Scottish Deerhound

Definition definition
Demodex-Räude follicular mange, red mange
demütig, unterwürfig submissive
Demutshaltung submissive posture
Denkaufgabe brain teaser
denkbar thinkable
denken think
Denkfehler flaw in one's reasoning
Denkpause pause for reflection
Denkprozess thought process
derb sturdy
derbknochig of heavy bone
desensibilisieren desensitize
Desinformation disinformation
Desinteresse indifference
Deutsch Drahthaar German Wirehaired Pointer
Deutsch Kurzhaar German Short-Haired Pointer
Deutsch Langhaar German Long-Haired Pointer
Deutsch Stichelhaar German Broken-Coated Pointer
Deutsche Bracke German Hound
Deutsche Dogge Great Dane
deutsche Kommandos German commands
Deutscher Champion (VDH) VDH German Champion
Deutscher Großspitz Giant German Spitz
Deutscher Jagdterrier German Hunt Terrier
Deutscher Kleinspitz Small German Spitz
Deutscher Kurzhaariger Vorstehhund German Short-haired Pointer
Deutscher Langhaariger Vorstehhund German Longhaired Pointer
Deutscher Mittelspitz Standard German Spitz
Deutscher Pinscher German Pinscher
Deutscher Schäferhund German Shepherd Dog
Deutscher Spitz German Spitz
Deutscher Wachtelhund German Spaniel
Deutscher Zwergspitz German Toy Spitz
Deutung interpretation
dicht (z.B. Fell) dense, thick (e.g. coat)
dick thick, fat
Dickdarm large intestine
dickköpfig obstinate
dickwanstig pot-gutted
Diensthund police dog

Dingo Australian Native Dog, Australian Dingo
Disc-Scheiben discs
disharmonisch discordant
Disqualifikation disqualification, dismissal
disqualifiziert dismissed (coursing), disqualified (agility, obedience)
Distanz distance
Distanz erweitern extending distance
distanziert aloof
Distanzkontrolle distance control
Disziplin discipline
Dobermann Dobermann
Dogdancing (Sport) dog dancing (sport)
Dogge Mastiff
doggenartig molossoid
Dogo Argentino Dogo Argentino
Do Khyi Tibetan Mastiff, Do Khyi
Dokumentation documentation
dokumentieren document
dolmetschen interpret
domestizieren domesticate
Dominanz dominance
dominieren dominate
dopen dope
Doping doping
Dornfortsatz spinal process
Dosenfutter canned food, tinned food
Drahtbürste pin brush
Drahthaar wire coat, wirehair, bristle coat
Drahthaar-Foxterrier Wire Fox Terrier
drahthaarig wire-coated, wire-haired, bristle-coated
Drahthaariger Ungarischer Vorstehhund Wirehaired Hungarian Pointer
Drehmuskel rotator muscle
Drehpunkt pivot
Drehung torsion
Drehung nach innen/ nach außen turn inside/ outside
dreifarbig tricolour
dreifarbig gescheckt pied tricolour
Dreifarbiger Jugoslawischer Laufhund Yugoslavian Tricolour Hound
Dressurhalsband training collar
Drogenspürhund drug (sniffer) dog
drohen threaten
drohend threatening
Drohstellung intimidating (or threatening) posture
Druck ausüben (auf jemanden) put someone under pressure

Drückjagd battue, drive
druckschmerzhafter Punkt trigger point
Drüse gland
ducken, sich crouch (down), cower, cringe
Duftfahne scent
Duftmarke scent mark
Duftstoff scent
dulden tolerate
Dummy dummy
dunkel gestromt fawn brindle
dunkelbraun dark brown
dunkel gestichelt dark stippled
dunkelhirschrot dark red
dunkelsemmelfarben russet gold
Dunker Norwegian Hound
Dünndarm small intestine
Dupuy Vorstehhund Dupuy Pointer
Durchbruch (der Zähne) eruption (of the teeth)
durchdacht reasoned
Durchfall diarrhoea
Durchfallquote failure rate
durchführbar practicable
durchhängend sagging
Durchschnitt average
Durchschnitt, über dem... liegen be above the average
Durchschnitt, unter dem... liegen be below the average
durchsetzen get something through
Durst thirst
durstig thirsty
Dysplasie dysplasia

E

Ecke corner
Ecken schneiden/ nicht ausgehen (Fußarbeit) corner-cutting (heelwork)
eckig angular
Eckzahn canine (tooth)
Ecuador Waldhund Ecuador Bush Dog
edel distinguished, refined
Edelstein precious stone
Edelsteintherapie precious stone therapy
effilieren (Fell, Haare) thin (coat, hair)
Effilierschere thinning shears
Ehrenpreis prize, trophy, award
Ehrgeiz ambition
ehrgeizig ambitious
Eichel (anatomisch) glans, penis glans
Eichelknollen, Schwellkörper bulb of the glans
Eierstock ovary
Eifer (im Sinne von Arbeitswille/ Begierde) eagerness
eiförmig egg-shaped
eifrig eager
Eigenart peculiarity
Eigenfährte own track, handler's track
Eigenwille self-will
Eihäute foetal membranes
Eileiter oviduct
einfach simple
Einfall (Gedanke) idea
einfallslos unimaginative
einfallsreich imaginative
einfarbig solid, self-coloured, wholecoloured
einfühlen, sich empathize with
einfühlsam sensitive
Einfühlungsvermögen empathy
Einführung introduction
Eingang entrance
eingattern (Vieh) gathering (live-stock)

eingedellt dished
eingeklemmter (Schwanz) clamped (tail)
eingerollt curling inward
eingesattelt saddle-backed
eingesenkt concave
eingesetzt sein als be served as
Eingeweide intestine
eingewöhnen, sich settle in
eingezogen (z.B. Rute) clamped between (e.g. tail)
eingliedern, sich integrate
Eingliederung integration
eingreifen intervene
einheitlich uniform
Einkreuzung outcrossing
Einlingswelpe only puppy, litter of one
Einmannhund one-man dog
einsam lonely
Einsamkeit loneliness
einsaugen absorb
einschläfern put to sleep, euthanize, put down, destroy
einschüchtern intimidate
Einschüchterung intimidation
Einsicht realization
einsperren lock up
Einspruch objection
Einspruch erheben/ einlegen put a veto (up) on
einstecken können can take a lot
einstellen, zur Zucht place at stud
Einstreu substrate
Eintagesprüfung one-day trial
eintönig monotonous
eintragen register
Eintrittsgebühr admission fee
Eintrittskarte admission ticket
einüben practise something
einwärts gedreht toeing-in, turned-in
einwirken auf have an effect on
Einwirkung/ Korrektur correction
Einwirkung, aversive aversive correction
Einwirkung, körperliche physical force
Einwirkung, tätige physical correction
Einwirkung, verbale verbal correction
einzäunen fence in
Einzäunung fence
Eiseskälte icy cold
eisig icy
Eisprung ovulation
Eiter pus
eitrig purulent, pussy
Eiweiß albumen, white of egg
Eizelle egg cell
Ejakulat ejaculate
Ejakulation ejaculation

Eklampsie eclampsia, milk fever
Ektoparasit ectoparasite
Ektropium ectropion
Ekzem eczema
elastisch pliant
Elastizität bounce
Elchhund Elkhound
elegant stylish, elegant
Elend misery
elfenbeinfarbig ivory
Ell(en)bogen elbow
Ellbogenbeule elbow cyst
Ellbogendysplasie elbow dysplasia
Ellbogengelenk elbow joint
Elle ulna
elterlich parental
Eltern parents
Elternschaft parenthood
Elterntier parent (animal), progenitor
Embryo embryo
embryonal embryonic
empfinden feel
empfindlich, heikel sensitive, touchy
Empfindlichkeit sensitivity
Endergebnis final result
Endhirn endbrain
Endlauf final run, final course
Endoparasit endoparasite
Endphase final stage
Energie energy
Energiebedarf energy demand
Energieblockade energy blockade
Energiefluss energy flow
energiegeladen bursted with energy
energielos lack of energy
energisch energetic
eng anliegend close
eng gestellt close together
Enge, in die ... treiben drive somebody into a corner
enghessig having close hocks
Englische Bulldogge English Bulldog
englische Schur English saddle clip
Englischer Cocker Spaniel English Cocker Spaniel
Englischer Fuchshund English Foxhound
Englischer Schäferhund Old English Sheepdog, Bobtail
Englischer Setter English Setter
Englischer Springer Spaniel English Springer Spaniel
English Coonhound English Coonhound
English Shepherd English Shepherd
English Toy Terrier English Toy Terrier

Engzucht mating of related individuals
entdecken discover
Entfilzungskamm dematting comb
entgegenwirken work against
Enthusiasmus enthusiasm
entkommen escape
entlassen release
Entlassungswort (im Sinne von Übung beendet) release word
entlaufen run away (from)
entlausen delouse
Entlebucher Sennenhund Entlebuch Mountain Dog
entleeren, sich... eliminate
entreißen snatch something from
Entropium entropion
entscheiden decide
Entscheidung decision
Entscheidungslauf run-off
entspannen relax
entspannt relaxed
Entspannung relaxation
Entspannungsübung relaxation exercise
enttäuschen disappoint
Enttäuschung disappointment
entwickeln develop
Entwicklung development
entwicklungsfähig capable of development
Entwicklungsphase period of development
Entwicklungsphase, vegetative neonatal period
Entwicklungsprozess process of development
Entwicklungsstufe stage of development
entwöhnen wean
entwurmen worm
Entwurmung worming
entziehen, etwas withdraw something
Entzündung inflammation
Épagneul Bleu de Picardie Blue Picardy Spaniel
Épagneul Breton Brittany Spaniel
Épagneul du Pont-Audemer Pont-Audemer Spaniel
Épagneul Français French Spaniel
Épagneul Larzac Larzac Spaniel
Épagneul Nain Continental Continental Toy Spaniel
Épagneul Picard Picardy Spaniel
Épagneul St. Usuge Saint Usuge Spaniel
Epilepsie epilepsy
erarbeiten, sich work for
Erbanlage heredity, genetic disposition

erbarmenswert pitiful
erbarmungslos merciless
erben inherit
erbeuten capture
Erbfehler hereditary defect
Erbfehlerermittlung screening for genetic defects
Erbfeind sworn enemy
erbgesund sound
Erbgesundheit soundness
Erbgut genotype
erbgutschädigend genetically damaging
Erbkrankheit hereditary disease
erblich hereditary
Erbmangel inherited defect
Erbmasse hereditary (or genetic) make up
erbrechen, kotzen vomit
Erdarbeit burrowing, burrow work
Erdélyi kopó Hungarian Hound
Erdhund burrow dog, earth dog
erdulden endure
ereifern, sich get excited (about)
ererbt inherited
Erfahrung experience
erfinderisch inventive
Erfolg success
erfolglos unsuccessful
erfolgreich successful
Erfolgschance chance of success
Erfolgserlebnis success experience
Erfolgsquote success rate
erfolgversprechend promising
Erfolgszwang, unter ... stehen be under pressure to succeed
erforderlich necessary
Erfordernis requirement
erforschen investigate
erfragen ask for
erfreulich pleasant
erfreulicherweise fortunately
erfrischen refresh
Ergänzungsfutter supplementary food
Ergebenheit devotion
Ergebnis result
ergebnislos without result
ergehen, über sich ... lassen endure something
ergrauen grey, grizzle
ergreifen (z.B. Beute) catch, take (e.g. prey)
ergründen get to the bottom of
erhalten/ erringen obtain
erholen, sich recover from
Erholung recovery
erinnern remind
Erinnerung memory
erkennbar recognizable
erkennen recognize
Erkenntnis knowledge

Erkenntnisstand, nach dem neuesten according to the latest findings
erklären explain
Erklärung, Erläuterung explanation
erkranken fall ill
erkunden explore
erkundigen, sich ... über inquire about
erlangen (Ausbildungskennzeichen) earn (title)
erlauben permit
Erlaubnis permission
erläutern explain
erleben experience
erlebnisreich eventful
erleiden suffer
erlernbar learnable
erlösen von release from
ermahnen admonish
ermöglichen make something possible
ermüden tire
Ermüdung tiredness
Ermüdungserscheinung sign of fatigue
ermuntern encourage
Ermunterung encouragement
Ernährung nutrition
erproben try out
erraten guess
Ersatz replacement, substitute
Ersatzhandlung restructured behaviour, act of compensation
Ersatzhandlung/ Übersprungshandlung displacement activity
Ersatzleistungsheft replacement scorebook
ersatzweise alternatively
erscheinen appear
Erscheinung, Erscheinungsbild appearance
Erscheinungsbild, allgemeines general appearance
erschöpft exhausted
erschrecken frighten
erschweren make something (more) difficult
ersetzbar replaceable
erstarren (in einer Haltung) freeze (in a position)
erstarren vor Schreck be paralysed with fear
erstaunen astonish
Erste-Hilfe-Ausrüstung für Tiere pet first aid kit
erstklassig first-class
Erstklassigkeit quality
Erstmilch colostrum
erstrahlen shine
erwägen consider
erwarten expect, await
Erwartung expectation
Erwartung/ Vorwegnahme/ Voraussicht anticipation

Erwartungshaltung expectancy
Erwartungsunsicherheit not to know what to expect
erwartungsvoll expectant
erwiesenermaßen as has been proved
erwünscht desired, wanted
Erzfeind archenemy
Erzgebirgsdachsbracke Alpine Hound
erziehbar trainable
Erziehung obedience training, schooling
Erziehungshalsband training collar
erzielen (Erfolg) obtain
erzogen, gut well trained
erzogen, schlecht bad trained
erzwingen force
Eskalation escalation
eskalieren escalate
essen eat
Estländische Bracke Estonian Hound
Estrela Berghund Estrela Mountain Dog
etablieren establish
Ethik ethics
ethisch ethical
Eurasier Eurasian
Eustachische Röhre Eustachian tube
Euthanasie euthanasia
Evolution evolution
exakt precise, exact
Existenzkampf struggle for existence
Exkremente excrements

F

Fachgebiet special field
Fachkreise(n), in among the experts
fachkundig competent
Fachliteratur specialized literature
Fachsimpelei shoptalk
fachsimpeln talk shop
Fachwörterbuch specialized dictionary
Fadenwurm nematode, roundworm
fähig sein to be able
Fähigkeit ability
fahl(gelb) fallow, pale-yellow, light brown
fahlrot tawny, yellow-orange
Fahlroter Bretagner Niederlaufhund Basset Fauve de Bretagne, Tawny Brittany Basset
Fahne(nrute) flag, pennant, plume
Fahnenmastrute flagpole tail
Fahrrad bicycle
Fährte track, trail, scent
Fährte, erkaltete stale track (or line)
fährten track, trail
Fährtenabgangsschild tracking sign
Fährtenarbeit tracking
Fährtengegenstand piece/ article for tracking
Fährtengeschirr/ Suchgeschirr harness for tracking
Fährtenhund tracking dog, scent dog, trailer
Fährtenlaut giving tongue to a scent
Fährtenleger(in) track-layer, person who lays the scent
Fährtenleine/ Suchleine tracking leash
Fährtenprüfung tracking test
fährtensicher accurate in trailing
falb tan, fawn, tawny

Falbfarbiger Rauhaariger Bretonischer Laufhund Brittany Fawn Griffon
falsch wrong
falsch verstehen misunderstand
falsch verweisen (Fährtenarbeit) wrong drop (tracking)
fälschlicherweise wrongly
faltbar collapsible
Falte fold
faltenlos creaseless
faltig wrinkly
Familie family
Familienanschluss haben live as one of the family
Familienhund pet (dog), family dog
Familienmitglied member of the family
Familienverhältnisse family background
Fang, Schnauze mouth
Fang, stumpfer blunt muzzle
fangen catch
Fangpartie muzzle area
Fangwinkel corner of the mouth
Fangzahn canine tooth
Farbe colour, us: color
Farbe, intensive rich colour
färben dye
Farbschlag colour variety
Farbtherapie colour therapy
Farbton shade, hue, cast
Färbung colouring, pigmentation
faseln (auf der Fährte) make an unsteady search
Fass! (Hörzeichen beim Schutzdienst) Get him! (verbal command at protection work)
fassbeinig bandy-legged
Fassrippen barrel ribs
Fastentag day of fasting
fauchen snarl
Faulheit laziness
Faust fist
favorisieren favour
Feder feather
Federwild wild fowl
Fehldeckung mismating
Fehldiagnose wrong diagnosis
Fehleinschätzung misjudgement
fehlen be absent
Fehlentscheidung wrong decision
Fehlentwicklung undesirable development
Fehler mistake
Fehler, disqualifizierender disqualifying fault
Fehler (Sport, Ausstellung) fault (sport, show)
Fehler (Training) mistake (training)
Fehler des Hundeführers owners' failure

fehlerfrei (Sport) faultless (sport)
fehlerhaft faulty
Fehlfarbe foul colour, off-colour
fehlfarbig mismarked
Fehlgeburt abortion, miscarriage
fehlschlagen go wrong
Feinabstimmung fine-tuning
Feind(in) enemy
Feindlichkeit hostility
feindselig (gegen) hostile (to)
feinnasig keen of scent
Feld field
Feldjagdsuche field trial
Feldleine, lange check cord
Feldweg country lane
Fell coat, hide, skin
Fell, stumpfes lustreless hair (or coat)
Fellfärbung coat colouring
Fellpflege grooming, coat care
Fellwechsel fur change
Fellzeichnung points
felsig rocky
Ferien holidays
Ferienkurs vacation course
Ferienwohnung holiday flat
Ferne, aus der from a distance
Fernglas binoculars
Fernziel long-term objective
Ferse heel
Fertigkeit, Fähigkeit skill
Fertignahrung commercial food
Fessel (anatomisch) pastern, fetlock (anatomic)
Fesselgelenke, vorgebogene overshot pasterns
Fesseln, weiße socks, white socks
Festakt ceremony
festbinden tie down
Festrede ceremonial address
Festredner official speaker
Festsaal banqueting hall
Festschrift commemorative publication
Festzelt marquee
fett(reich) fatty, adipose
fettarm low-fat
fettleibig obese
Feuchtfutter (oder -nahrung) wet (dog) food
Feuer fire
Feuerwehrhund firehouse dog
Feuerwerk fireworks
Feuerwerkskörper firework
Fieber fever, temperature
Field Spaniel Field Spaniel
fiepen mewl
Figurant(in) (Schutzdienst) helper, agitator (protection work)
Fila Brasileiro Fila Brasileiro
filzfrei free of matting
filzig matted, felted
Filzkamm dematting comb

Fingerzahnbürste finger toothbrush
Finnenbracke Finnish Hound
Finnenspitz Finnish Spitz
Finnischer Lapphund Finnish Lapphund
Finnischer Laufhund Finnish Hound
Finnischer Vallhund Lapponian Herder
Fischauge fish eye
Fistel fistula
Fitness, körperliche physical fitness
flach bladed
flach bemuskelt flat-muscled
flach getragen (Rute) carried flat (tail)
flachbrüstig flat-chested
Flämischer Treibhund Belgian Cattle Dog
Flanke flank, side
Flasche bottle
Flaschenaufzucht hand-raising, bottle-raising
Flat Coated Retriever Flat-Coated Retriever
Flatterlippen fluttering lips
Flausen im Kopf haben having silly ideas
flechten, etwas braid something
Flechtseil (Spielzeug) braided tug toy
Fleck dot, spot, splash, freckle
Flecken, fleischfarbene (Nasenschwamm) flesh marks
Fleisch meat
Fleischbrühe consommé
Fleischextrakt beef extract
Fleischfresser carnivore
fleischig fleshy, beefy, thick, stuffy
Fleischnase cherry nose
Fleischwurst pork sausage
Fleiß diligence
fleißig diligent
Flexi-Leine flexi-leash
fliehen vor flee from
flink quick
Flocke flake
Floh flea
Flohallergie flea allergy
Flohhalsband flea collar
Flucht escape
Flucht, die... nach vorn antreten seek refuge in attack
Flucht, in die... schlagen put to flight
fluchtartig hasty
Fluchtdistanz flight distance
Flüchtigkeitsfehler slip
Fluchtreflex flight reflex (or response)
Fluchtversuch attempt to escape
Fluchtweg escape route
Flugball flyball

flüstern whisper
Flutlicht floodlights
Flyball (Sportart) flyball (sport)
Flyball-Apparat flyball box
Flyball-Hürden (aus Holz) wooden flyball hurdles
Flyball-Wettbewerb flyball racing
fokussieren, etwas focus on something
folgen follow
folgenschwer grave
folgerichtig logical
folgern aus conclude from
folglich therefore
folgsam obedient
Folgsamkeit obedience, tractability
förderlich useful
fördern, förderlich sein promote, be good for
fordern demanding
Forderung nach demand for
Form einer 8, in ... (z.B. beim bei Fuß gehen) figure eight (e.g. heelwork)
Formation drill team
formen (eines Verhaltens) shaping
Formen eines Verhaltens shape
Formwert show-assessed merit
Formwertband show ribbon
Formwertnote conformation score
Formwertrichter(in) show judge, conformation judge
Forschung research
Förster(in) forester
Fortbestand existence
fortbestehen continue
Fortschritt (im Training) progression (in training)
Fortschritte, schnell ... machen make rapid progress
Fötus foetus, embryo
Fousek Bohemian Griffon
Fox Terrier Fox Terrier
Foxcollie Fox Collie
Foxhound Foxhound
Franse tassel
Französisch Langhaar French Spaniel
Französische Bracke French Pointer
Französische Bulldogge French Bulldog
Französischer Dreifarbiger Laufhund French Tricolour Hound
Französischer Langhaariger Vorstehhund Pointing Longcoated Griffon
Französischer Orange-Weißer Laufhund French Orange and White Hound

Französischer Rauhaariger Vorstehhund, Korthals Griffon Wirehaired Pointing Griffon, Korthals Griffon
Französischer Schwarz-Weißer Laufhund French Black and White Hound
Französischer Spaniel French Spaniel
französischer Stand French front, Chippendale front
Französischer Vorstehhund French Pointer
Frauchen (eines Hundes) mummy, mistress (of the dog)
frei beweglich freely moving
Freifolge heeling off-lead
freilaufend off-lead
Freisprung leap into freedom
freisuchend tracking off-lead
freiwillig voluntary
Freiwilligkeit voluntariness
fremd strange
Fremdangriff attack on stranger
Fremde(r) stranger
Fremdfährte stranger's scent (or track)
Fremdpaarung outcrossing
Fremdwort foreign word
fressen eat, take food
Fressnapf dog bowl, food dish
Freude (über) joy (at)
Freude, Genuss enjoyment
freudig joyful
freudlos cheerless
freuen, sich be happy
Freund(in) friend
freundlich friendly, outgoing
Freundschaft friendship
friedfertig peaceable
friedlich gentle
Friesischer Wasserhund Dutch Water Spaniel
Frisbeescheibe aus Softmaterial soft bite floppy disc
fröhlich cheerful
Front, schmale narrow front
Front, schmale (fehlerhaft) pinched front
frontal frontal
Frostwetter frosty weather
frottieren rub down
fruchtbar fertile
Fruchtbarkeit fertility
Fruchtblase amniotic sac
Fruchtwasser amniotic fluid
Frühgeburt premature birth
Frust(ration) frustration
frustrieren frustrate
fuchsähnlich, fuchsartig foxy
Fuchsbau fox's den
fuchsfarben mit schwarzem Sattel black and tan saddled
fuchsrot foxy-red
fügsam obedient
Führer(in) handler

Führerfährte handler's track
führerlos without a leader
führig obedient, tractable
Führigkeit obedience, tractability
Führtechnik (Agility) style of leadership, superintendent (agility)
Führung leadership
füllen fill
Furcht (vor) fear (of)
furchtbar terrible
furchtlos fearless
Fuß (Pfote) paw
Fuß! (Hörzeichen) Heel! (verbal command)
Fußabdruck footprint
Fußgehen heelwork
Futter food
Futter, festes solid food
Futterallergie food allergy
Futterbelohnung abbauen get rid of the food
Futterbelohnung, bevorzugte favourite treats
füttern feed
Futternapf food bowl, food dish
Futterneid envy (at food)
Futtertrieb food drive
Futterumstellung change of food
Fütterung feeding
Futterunverträglichkeit indigestibility of food
Futterversorgung food supply
Futterverweigerung inappetence, food refusal
Futterzusatz food additive, food supplement

gähnen yawn
Galgo Español Spanish Greyhound
Galopp, galoppieren gallop
Galopp, leichter canter
Gammel Dansk Honsehund Old Danish Pointer
Gang, bodenenger close moving gait
Gang, Gangart, Gangwerk gait
Gang, federnder springy gait
Gang, schaukelnder rolling gait
Gang, schwebender floating gait
Gang, stelzender stiff-legged movement
Gang, steppender hackney gait
Gang, wiegender rolling gait
Gangart, fehlerhafte gaiting fault
Gangart, langsame slow pace
Gangart, normale normal gait
Gangart, schnelle quick gait, fast pace
Gangart, Wechsel der change of pace
Gangwerk, freies free gait
Gangwerk, gebundenes (oder unfreies) constricted gait
Gangwerk, ungehemmtes free gait
Ganzkörperhetzanzug (Ringsport) full body suit (mondioring)
Gartenzaun garden fence
Gassi gehen take (a dog) for a walk, exercise (a dog)
Gatter fence
Gaumen palate
geartet disposed
gebändert banded
gebären give birth (to), bear
Gebärmutter uterus
Gebärmutterentzündung metritis
Gebärmutterhorn horn of the uterus

Gebärmuttervereiterung pyometra
Gebäude body, building
Gebiss teeth, dentition
Gebissbescheinigung certificate of correct bite
Gebissfehler faulty bite
Gebissüberprüfung tooth (or bite) check
geblockt blocky
geborgen safe
Geborgenheit safety
gebrauchen use
Gebrauchshund working dog, utility dog
Gebrauchshundausbildung utility training
Gebrauchshundprüfungsnachweis working certificate
Gebrauchshundrassen working breeds
Gebrauchshundwettbewerb field trial
Geburtsfarbe colour at birth
Geburtsprotokoll whelping record
Geburtsweg birth canal
Gedächtnis memory
gedankenlos thoughtless
Gedankenlosigkeit thoughtlessness
Gedankenübertragung telepathy
gedrungen cobby, compact, stocky
Geduld patience
geduldig patient, tolerant
Gefahr danger
gefährlich dangerous
Gefährte/ Gefährtin fellow, companion
gefleckt spotted, patched
Geflügel poultry
geflügelfromm gentle to poultry
gefräßig greedy
Gefräßigkeit greediness
Gefühl emotion
Gefühlsausbruch emotional outburst
Gefühlsleben emotional life
Gegebenheit circumstances
gegen den Strich against the hair
Gegenargument counter-argument
Gegenbeispiel counter-example
Gegenprobe (machen) crosscheck
Gegenstand (Fährtensuche) article (tracking)
gegenseitig mutual
Gegenwehr defence, opposition
Gehege enclosure
gehemmt inhibited
gehen walk
Geheul howling

Gehirn brain
Gehirnerschütterung concussion (of the brain)
Gehirnschädel skull
Gehör sense of hearing
gehorchen obey, listen
Gehörgang auditory canal
Gehörlosenhund hearing ear dog
Gehorsam obedience
Gehorsam für den Hausgebrauch household obedience
gehorsam obedient
Gehorsam verweigern disobey an order, deny obedience
Gehorsamsarbeit obedience work
Gehörsinn sense of hearing
Geifer foam
geistesverwandt congenial to
gekräuselt crisp, curly
gekrümmt arched
Gelände ground
gelangweilt bored
gelassen composed
Gelassenheit calmness, coolness
Geläuf surface of track
Geläufigkeit (z.B. in Übungen) fluency (e.g. exercises)
Geläufigkeitsübungen fluencies
gelaunt sein, gut (schlecht) be in a good (bad) mood
Geläut (Jagdlaut) baying of hounds at work
Gelbbackler Bernese Mountain Dog
gelbbraun fawn
Gelegenheit opportunity
gelegentlich occasionally
gelehrig easy to train, quick to learn
Gelenk joint
Gelenkentzündung arthritis
Gelenkpfanne joint socket
Gelenksteifigkeit ankylosis
gelockt curly, curled, crisp
Geltungsbedürfnis craving for admiration
gemeinsam mit combined with
gemeißelt chiselled, modelled
Gemüse vegetable
Gen gene
Genealogie genealogy
Genehmigung licence, us: license
Generalisierung generalization
Generation generation
Genetik genetics
Genick neck, nape
Genickschütteln scruff-shake
Genitalien genitals
gepflegt well-groomed
gepolstert cushioned
gequält pained
gerade straight, level

geradlinig straight (in a straight line)
Gerät (für Wettkampf/ Parcours) obstacle, equipment
Gerät/ Hindernis obstacle
Geräte, zu überkletternde step obstacles
Geräusch sound
Geräuschangst being afraid of (loud) noises
Geräusch-Kassette mit Prüfungslärm dog show racket audiotape
geräuschlos silent
geräuschvoll loud
Gerechtigkeit fairness
gerollt ringed
Geruch scent, smell
Geruchsnerv olfactory nerve
Geruchsorgan olfactory organ
Geruchssinn sense of smell
Geruchsspur finden make a find
Geruchsunterscheidung scent discrimination
Geruchsvermögen olfactory capacity
Gesamterscheinung general appearance
Gesäß buttocks
gesättigt full, replete
Gesäuge breasts, teats, dugs
gescheckt patched, dappled
gescheckt dreifarbig pied tricolour
geschimmelt mottled, speckled, ticked
Geschirr, Brust ... harness
Geschlechts-, geschlechts-, gender, genital, sexual
Geschlechtsteile genitals
Geschöpf creature
Geschwindigkeit speed
Geschwister littermate, sibling
Geschwulst tumour
Geschwür boil, ulcer
Gesellschaftshund companion dog
Gesetz des geringsten Aufwandes law of least effort
Gesichtsausdruck facial expression
Gesichtsausdruck, freundlicher gentle facial expression
Gesichtsmaske facial mask
Gesichtsschädel foreface
Gesichtssinn sense of sight
Gespann team
gespreizt splayed out
gesprenkelt speckled
Gestank stench
Geste gesture
gestichelt roan, ticked
gestromt brindled
gesund healthy

Gesundfährte scent trail of unwounded game
Gesundheit health
Gesundheitszeugnis health certificate
Getreide cereals
getüpfelt, getupft speckled, ticked, spotted
gewachsen sein (einer Situation) be able to cope (a situation)
Gewalt violence
Gewalt anwenden use force
Gewalt, mit by force
gewaltfrei non-violent
Gewaltherrschaft tyranny
gewaltlos non-violent
Gewaltlosigkeit non-violence
gewalttätig violent
Gewandtheit agility
Gewehr gun
Geweih branch
gewellt wavy
Gewicht weight
gewinkelt angulated
Gewitter thunderstorm
gewittrig thundery
gewöhnen, sich daran get used to
Gewohnheit habit
Gewohnheit, schlechte bad habit
Gewöhnung habituation
gewölbt arched
gewolkt sabled, overlaid, shaded
Gier nach greediness for
gierig greedy for
Gift poison, toxin
gift(halt)ig poisonous, toxic
Giftköder poisoned bait
Gipsverband plaster cast
Gitter-Transportbox wire crate
Glanz gloss, shine
glänzend glossy, shining
glanzlos without lustre, lustreless
Glasauge glass eye, china eye
glasäugig having a china eye
glatthaarig smooth-coated, smooth-haired
Glaukom glaucoma
Glen of Imaal Terrier Glen of Imaal Terrier
Glied (anatomisch) limb (anatomic)
Gliederhalsband chain link collar
Gliedmaße extremity
Gold gold
goldbraun golden yellow
Golden Retriever Golden Retriever
gold gestromt gold brindle
goldrot golden
Gordon Setter Gordon Setter

Gos d'Atura Catalan Catalan Sheepdog
Gotland Stövare Gotland Hound
Grabmilbenräude sarcoptic mange
Grand Anglo Français Great Anglo-French Hound
Granne top coat
Grannenhaar top coat
Granulom granuloma
Gras grass
Gras fressend graminivorous
Gräte spine of scapula
Gratwanderung tightrope walk
grau grey
grau marmoriert blue merle
Grauer St. Louis Hund St. Louis Gray Dog
Grauer Walisischer Hütehund Welsh Gray Herder
grau gefleckt harlequin (Beauceron)
grau gewolkt wolf sable
grau-kupferrot grey and fawn
grau meliert grizzle
grausam cruel
Grausamkeit cruelty
grausilber grey-silver
Grautiger (Farbe) grey tiger
Greifversuch attempted take (of the...)
Greifwille, Beutetrieb desire to take
Grenzbereich border area
Grenzen setzen set limits to
Grenzfall borderline case
Greyhound Greyhound
Griechische Bracke Greek Hare Hound
Griechischer Laufhund Greek Hare Hound
Griechischer Schäferhund Greek Sheepdog
Griff (Schutzdienst) grip (protection work)
Griff halten (Schutzdienst) hold the grip (protection work)
Griffon Griffon
Griffon à Poil Laineux Woolly-Haired Griffon
Griffon Belge Belgian Griffon
Griffon Bleu de Gascogne Blue Gascony Griffon
Griffon Boulet Pointing Longcoated Griffon
Griffon Bruxellois Brussels Griffon
Griffon Fauve de Bretagne Tawny Brittany Griffon
Griffon Nivernais Griffon Nivernais
Griffon Vendéen Vendeen Griffon
grob rough, coarse

Groenendael Belgian Groenendael
Grönlandhund Greenland Dog
großartig great
Großeltern grandparents
Größenklasse oversize class (for whippets at racing events)
Großer Anglo-Französischer Laufhund Great Anglo-French Hound
Großer Blauer Laufhund der Gascogne Large Blue Gascony Hound
Großer Gascon Saintongeois Large Gascon Saintongeois
Großer Münsterländer Large Munsterlander
Großer Schwedischer Elchhund Jamthund
Großer Schweizer Sennenhund Great Swiss Mountain Dog
Großhirn cerebrum
Großmutter grandmother
Großpudel Standard Poodle
Großspitz Giant Spitz
Großvater grandfather
Grunderziehung basic education
Grundfarbe ground colour
Grundgeräte ground obstacles
grundlegend rudimentary
Grundstellung heel position
Gruppe group, class
Gruppensieger(in) best in group
Gruppenübung group exercise, group training
Guatemalischer Nackthund Guatemalan Hairless Dog
Gummibürste rubber brush
Gürtel belt
gut aufgerippt well ribbed-up
gut aufgezogen well tucked-up
gut ausgeglichen well proportioned
gut bemuskelt well muscled
gut erzogen well trained, well educated
gut gelagert well laid back
gut getrennt well split up
gut gewinkelt well angulated
gut sozialisiert well socialised
gutherzig kind-hearted

Haar hair, coat
Haar/ Fell, gesträubtes staring hair, raised hackles
Haarausfall shedding, coat loss
Haarbalgmilbenausschlag follicular mange, demodectic mange
haaren shed (hair)
Haarkleid coat
Haarkleid, abstehendes standoff hair (or coat)
Haarkleid, offenes open coat
haarloser Hund hairless dog
Haarungsperiode molting period
Haarwechsel coat change, molt, shedding
Haarwirbel whirl, whorl, swirl of hair
Haarwurzel hair root
Habitus build, conformation
hackeneng having close hocks
Hackfleisch minced meat
Haftpflicht liability (legal liability)
Haftpflichtversicherung third party (liability) insurance
Hakenrute crook tail
Hakenwurm hookworm
halb gekippt (Ohr) semi-drop (ear)
halbe Drehung (Winkel bei Fußarbeit) half-turn (angle in heelwork)
Halbfeuchtfutter (-oder Nahrung) semi-moist dog food
Halbgeschwister half-brother, half-sister
halbherzig half-hearted
halblang longish, of medium length
Halbwahrheit half-truth
Haldenstover Halden Hound
Hallenwettbewerb indoor-competition

Hallstromhund Hallstrom Dog
Hals neck
Hals in guter Länge reachy neck
Hals, kurzer cloddy neck
Halsband collar
Halsband, reflektierendes signal collar
Halskrause neck ruff
Halsung collar
Halswirbel cervical vertebrae
Halti® (Kopfhalfter) head collar
Haltung (des Körpers) posture
Haltung, ablehnende disapproving posture
Hamiltonstövare Hamilton Hound
Hand, in die ... geben delivery to hand
Handbewegung gesture
Handeln, schnelles prompt action
handhaben, umgehen handle
Handhaltung (bei Vorführung) hand position (performance)
Handlung act
Handlungsbedarf, es besteht this calls for action
Handlungsfreiheit freedom of action
Handlungsweise way of acting
handscheu hand shy
Handschuhe gloves
Handsignal hand signal
Hängelefzen pendulous lips
Hängelid ectropion
hängen (beim Deckakt) tie (in mating)
Hängeohr hanging ear
Hängerute dropped tail
Hannoverscher Schweißhund Hannoverian Hound
harlekin harlequin
harmlos harmless
Harmlosigkeit harmlessness
Harmonie/ Symmetrie harmony, balance, symmetry
harmonieren harmonize
harmonisch balanced, harmonious
Harn urine
Harnabsatz urination
Harnblase bladder
harnen urinate
Harnröhre urethra
Harnträufeln urinary incontinence
Harnvergiftung uraemia
Harnverhaltung urinary retention
harsch coarse, harsh (coat)
hart (z.B. im Charakter) hard, tough, unyielding (character)
Hartballenkrankheit hard pad syndrome
Härte hardness

Hartholz-Bringsel
hardwood dumbbell
Hartkäse hard cheese
hartnäckig tenacious
Hartnäckigkeit tenacity
Hase hare
Hase, künstlicher lure, bunny
haselnussbraun hazel
Hasenattrappe lure, bunny
Hasenhetze coursing on hare
Hasenhund Hare-Hound
Hasenmaschine lure machine
hasenrein broken from hare
Hasentechnik lure system
hätscheln cosset, pet
Hauptanforderung (der Übung)
principal feature (of exercise)
Hauptmahlzeit main meal
Haushund domesticated dog, house dog
Haut skin
Haut, hängende, lose, die Falten an den Lefzen und am Kiefer bildet chops
Hautkrankheit skin disease
Havaneser Havana Silk Dog
Hebemuskel levator muscle
hecheln pant
Heckbelüfter trunk ventilator
hegen (Wild) preserve
Heidewachtel
Small Munsterlander
Heilkraft medicinal power
Heimbereich home territory
Heimtier pet
heiß werden (im Sinne von läufig) come in heat (or season)
helfen help
helfen/ unterstützen aid
Helfer (Ringsport)
decoy (mondioring)
Helfer(in) (Schutzdienst)
helper, agitator (protection work)
Helferanreiz stimulation from the helper
HD (Hüftgelenksdysplasie)
hip dysplasia
hellbraun fawn, light brown
hellbraun mit schwarzen Haarspitzen wolf sable
hellgelb light yellow
hellhirschrot light red
Hellinikos Ichnilatis
Greek Hare Hound
hellweizenfarben light wheaten
Hepatitis hepatitis
herabspringen von (z.B. Agility-Tisch) spring from (e.g. the pause table)
herankommen come
heranrufen call (come), recall
heranwagen, sich dare to approach
herausfordern challenge
Herausforderung challenge

herausgezüchtet (aus der Blutlinie) bred out (from their bloodline)
heraushängen (z.B. der Zunge) loll (e.g. tongue)
herausnehmen aus take out of
herbeibringen bring
herbstlaubfarben dead leaf
Herdenschutzhund live-stock guarding dog
hergeben, etwas give something back
Herkunftsland country of origin
Herrchen (eines Hundes) master, owner (of a dog)
herrenlos homeless
herrenloses (Tier) stray (animal)
Herrschsucht domineeringness
herrschsüchtig domineering
Hertha Pointer Hertha Pointer
herumkommandieren, jemanden order someone around
herumschnüffeln snoop around
herumstoßen, jemanden push someone around
hervorragend distinguished
hervorstehend bulging
hervortretend protruding, bulging
hervorwürgen regurgitate
herwagen, sich dare to come
Herz heart
herzeigen show
Herzkammer heart ventricle
Hetzärmel (Schutzdienst) protective sleeve (protection work)
Hetzarmüberzug mit Schlaufe (Schutzdienst) protection sleeve cover with handle (protection work)
Hetzattrappe (Schutzdienst) lure, bunny (protection work)
hetzen chase, course, hunt, pursue, run down
hetzen (auf) set (a dog) on someone, hound at
hetzen, nach- hunt
Hetzgeschirr (Schutzdienst) agitation harness (protection work)
Hetzhund sighthound, staghound
Hetzkette mit Feder (Schutzdienst) agitation chain with spring (protection work)
Hetzlaut bay, cry
Hetzschürze (Schutzdienst) long apron (protection work)
Hetztrieb chase instinct
heulen howl
Hiebe bekommen get a thrashing
Hier! (Hörzeichen) Come! (verbal command)
Hierarchie hierarchy
Hilfe, zu ... nehmen make use of

Hilfestellung support
hilfesuchend seeking for help
hilflos helpless
Hilflosigkeit helplessness
hilfreich helpful
Hilfsleistung assistance
Hilfsmittel aid
hin- und herlaufen run to and from
hinarbeiten auf work towards
Hinauf! (Hörzeichen) Up! (verbal command)
hinausziehen, jemanden pull someone out
Hindernis/ Gerät obstacle
hineingehen go in(to)
hineinsteigern, sich get worked up about
hinhocken, sich squat, cower
hinken be lame, carry a leg
Hinsetzen mit Sitzen-bleiben sit-stay
hinter posterior
Hinterbiss overshot mouth, overbite
Hintergrundinformation background information
Hinterhand rear, hindquarters
Hinterhandwinkelung rear angulation
Hinterhaupt occiput
hinterherlaufen run behind
Hinterlauf hind (or rear) leg
Hinterläufe, bodeneng closed behind legs
Hintermittelfuß metatarsus
Hinterpfote rear (or hind) paw
hinterrücks from behind
Hinterteil bottom
Hinweis auf indication of
Hinweis auf Stress stress indicator
Hirnhautentzündung meningitis
Hirsch deer, stag
Hirtenhund shepherd dog
Hitze heat
Hitze (im Sinne von Läufigkeit) heat, season
Hitzschlag heat stroke
hoch angesetzt set (on) high
hochbeinig high legged
Hochbrunst standing heat
Hochform peak condition
hoch gebaut high off the ground
Hochgefühl feeling of elation
hoch gezüchtet selectively bred
hochläufig high on leg, leggy
hochnehmen, jemanden pick someone up
Hochsitz raised hide
Hochspannung (Erwartungs-haltung) great suspense
Hochsprung high jump
Höchstpunktzahl maximum number of points

Hochwild big game
Hochzuchtrasse selectively bred breed
hocken squat
Höcker point
Hode testicle
Hodenentzündung orchitis
Hodensack scrotum
Hof yard
Hofhund farm dog
Höhe (im Sinne von Größe) height (at shoulders)
Hol's! (Hörzeichen) Fetch! (verbal command)
Holländische Steinbracke Dutch Steenbrak
Holländischer Kurzhaar-Schäferhund Dutch Short-Haired-Shepherd
Holländischer Langhaar-Schäferhund Dutch Long-Haired-Shepherd
Holländischer Rauhaar-Schäferhund Dutch Rough-Coated-Shepherd
Holländischer Schäferhund Dutch Shepherd
Holsteiner Bracke Holstein Hound
Holz wood
Holzbock tick
Holzbracke German Sauerland Hound
Homöopathie homoeopathy
Hopp! (Hörzeichen) Over!, Up!, Hup! (verbal command)
Hopp-Bring! (Hörzeichen) Jump-Fetch! (verbal command)
hören hear
Hormon hormone
Hörnerv auditory nerve
Hornhaut cornea
Hörweite hearing range
Hörweite, in (außer) within (out of) hearing
Hörzeichen (verbal) command
Hörzeichen ausschleichen/ abschwächen fading cue
Hörzeichen zum Aufhören cue to stop
Hovawart Hovawart
hubertoid bloodhound like
Hüfte hip, haunch
Hüftgelenksdysplasie hip dysplasia
Hüftgelenkspfanne acetabulum
Hüfthöcker haunch bone, hip bone
Hüftknochen bones of the hip
Hühnerhund bird dog
Humor sense of humour
humorlos humourless
humorvoll humorous
Hund dog
Hund, außer Konkurrenz vorgeführt green dog

Hund, scharfer savage dog
Hunde-, hunde- canine
Hunde, die bellen, beißen nicht barking dogs seldom bite
Hundeanhänger (Auto) dog trailer
Hundeausbildung dog training
Hundebandwurm tapeworm
Hundebedarfsartikel dog supplies
Hundebesitzer(in) dog owner
Hundebetreuung dog-sitting
Hundebox kennel
Hundedecke blanket for the dog
Hundefänger dog catcher
Hundeflocken cereals
Hundefreund(in) dog-fancier
Hundeführer(in) dog-handler, handler
Hundeführer-Fehler owners' failure
Hundefutter dogfood
Hundehalsband dog collar
Hundehalter(in) dog owner
Hundehändler(in) dog dealer
Hundehütte dog-house
Hundekampf dog fight
Hundekarren dog cart
Hundekorb basket, dog bed
Hundekotplatz exercise area
Hundekuchen dog biscuit
Hundekunde cynology
Hundeleine dogs' leash; lead
Hundeliebhaber(in) dog person, dog lover, cynophile
Hundemarke dog licence disc, dog tag, id tag
Hundepension boarding kennel
Hundepfeife (dog) whistle
Hundepolster dog cushion
Hundepsychologe(-in) dog psychologist, dog behaviourist
Hunderennen dog racing
Hundesalon grooming shop
Hundeschau dog show
Hundeschere grooming shears
Hundeschlitten dog sled(ge)
Hundeschlittenfahren mushing
Hundeschutzgitter, Auto- car safety fence, wagon barrier
Hundeschutznetz, Auto- car safety net, wagon barrier
Hundeshampoo dog shampoo
Hundesicherheitsgurt, Auto- safety belt
Hundesicht, aus der from the dogs' point of view
Hundesport dog sport(s), activities with dogs
Hundestaupe canine distemper
Hundesteuermarke dog tag, dog licence
Hundestreitigkeit, Rauferei dog fight, argument
Hundetransportbox kennel, dog box, crate

Hundeübungsplatz dog training site, training court for dogs
Hundeverein dog club
Hundewagen dog cart
Hundewelt dogery, dogdom
Hundezucht dogs breeding
Hündin bitch, female (dog)
hündinnenhaft bitchy
Hündinnentyp bitchiness
Hundler(in), (Hundesportler/ -aussteller) dog person
Hundswut rabies
Hunger hunger
hungern go hungry
Hürde hurdle, jump
Hürde (Schutzdienst/ Agility) jump (protection work/ agility)
Hürde, einfache (Agility) single-bar jump (agility)
Hürde, doppelte (Agility) double-bar jump (agility)
Hürde, dreifache (Agility) spread-bar jump (agility)
Husky Siberian Husky
Hütearbeit herding work
Hütehund herder
Hütehundrassen herding breeds
Hütehundwettbewerb herding trial, sheepdog trial
hüten herd, tend
Hüten (Vieh) herding (live-stock)
Hütespitz Shepherd Spitz
Hütestab (Hakenstock) crook
Hyänenhund African Hunting Dog
Hybride hybrid
Hygenhund Hygenhund
Hysterie hysteria

Identifikationsgegenstand personal item left by the tracklayer at the start point
ignorieren ignore
Illyrischer Schäferhund Sarplaninac
immun immune
Immunisierung immunization
Immunität immunity
Immunserum antiserum
Impfbescheinigung vaccination certificate
impfen vaccinate
Impfpass vaccination record (card)
Impfstoff vaccine, serum
Impfung vaccination, immunization
imponieren impress
imponieren (z.B. ein Rüde dem anderen) posture
Imponiergehabe posturing, intimidation display
in hohem Maße, überaus eminently
inaktiv inactive
inakzeptabel unacceptable
Inca Orchid Moonflower Dog Peruvian Hairless Dog
Individualdistanz individual distance
Indiz indication
Infektion infection
Infektionskrankheit infectious disease
infektiös infectious
infizieren infect
infiziert infected
informieren über inform of/ about
Inhalationsnarkose inhalation narcosis
Injektion injection, shot
injizieren inject
inkompetent incompetent
inkonsequent inconsistent

Inkonsequenz inconsistency
Inkubationszeit incubation period (or time)
Instinkt instinct
Instinkt-Drift instinctive drift
instinktiv instinctive
Instinktverhalten instinctive behaviour
instruieren, jemanden give someone instructions
Instruktion instruction
Interesse an interest in
Inzestzucht inbreeding
IPO/ Internationale Prüfungsordnung international trial regulations
irische Zeichnung Irish pattern
Irischer Rot-Weißer Setter Irish Red and White Setter
Irischer Terrier Irish Terrier
Irischer Wasserspaniel Irish Water Spaniel
Irischer Wolfshund Irish Wolfhound
Irish Setter Irish Setter (Irish Red Setter)
Irish Blue Terrier Kerry Blue Terrier
isabellfarben isabella, blond
Islandhund Iceland Dog
Islandspitz Iceland Dog
Istrische Drahthaarige Bracke Istrian Wirehaired Hound
Istrische Kurzhaar Bracke Istrian Short-Haired Hound
Istrischer Schäferhund Istrian Sheepdog
Italienische Bracke Bracco Italiano, Italian Pointer
Italienischer (kurzhaariger) Vorstehhund Italian Pointer
Italienischer Laufhund Italian Hound
Italienischer Rauhaariger Vorstehhund Italian Rough-Coated Pointer
Italienischer Spitz Italian Spitz
Italienisches Windspiel Italian Greyhound

J

Jackpot (besondere Belohnung) jackpot (extra dose of primary reinforcer)
Jack Russell Terrier Jack Russell Terrier
Jagd hunting
Jagdbeute bag
Jagd(gebrauchs)hund hunting dog, gun dog, hound
Jagdhundprüfung hunting test
Jagdhundrassen hunting breeds
Jagdrevier hunting ground
Jagdschein hunting licence, shooting licence
Jagdterrier German Hunt Terrier
Jagdtraining hunting training
Jagdtreffen meet
Jagdtrieb hunting instinct, chase instinct
Jagdzeit hunting season
jagen hunt, chase, run down
jagen, die eigene Rute ... chase one's tail
Jagen, gemeinsames hunting together
Jagen, spurlautes open trailing
Jäger hunter
Jägerhof hunting kennel
Jägerin huntress
Jahr year
Jahreshauptversammlung annual general meeting
Jahreszeit season
Jähzorn violent temper
jähzornig hot tempered
jammern whimper, whine
Jämthund Swedish Elkhound
Japan Chin Japan Chin, Japanese Spaniel
Japanischer Kampfhund Japanese Fighting Dog, Tosa Inu
Japanischer Spitz Japanese Spitz
Japanischer Terrier Japanese Terrier

jaulen howl, whine, yowl
Jochbein cheek bone
Joggen jogging
Joggen mit Hund dogging
Jogginganzug track suit
jucken itch
Jugendklasse puppy class, junior class
jugendlich youthful
jugendliche Schur puppy clip, working clip
Jugendmannschaft youth team
Jugendmeister(in) youth champion
Jugoslawische dreifarbige Bracke Yugoslavian Mountain Hound
Jugoslawische Gebirgsbracke Yugoslavian Mountain Hound
Jugoslawischer Gebirgslaufhund Yugoslavian Mountain Dog
Jugoslawischer Schäferhund Yugoslavian Sheepdog
jung young
Junges (im Sinne von Welpe) puppy
jungfräulich maiden
Junghund junior, juvenile
Junghundarm (Schutzdienst) puppy sleeve, young dog sleeve (protection work)
Junghundstadium juvenile period
Jüngstenklasse puppy class
Jura Laufhund Jura Hound
Jura Niederlaufhund Smaller Jura Hound

K

Kabylenhund Aidi
Kadavergehorsam blind obedience
Kai Kai-Inu
Kaikadi Kaikadi
Kaiserschnitt caesarean, section
Kalagh Kalagh
Kamerunhund Cameroons Dog
Kamm comb
Kämmhilfe-Spray detangling spray
Kampf einstellen (Schutzdienst) stop the fight, discontinue the fight (protection work)
kampfbereit ready to fight
kämpfen fight, argue
kämpfen um fight for
kämpfend, kämpferisch fighting
Kampfgeist (Sport) fighting spirit (sport)
Kampfhund fighting dog, pit dog
Kampftrieb fighting drive
Kanaanhund Canaan Dog
Kanadischer Eskimohund Canadian Eskimo Dog
Kanarische Dogge Canary Dog
Kangal Kangal Dog
Kanide canid
Kaninchen rabbit
Kaninchendachshund Miniature Dachshund
Kaninchenteckel Miniature Dachshund
Karabash Anatolian Karabash
Karabinerhaken spring hook
karamellfarben caramel
Karelischer Bärenhund Karelian Bear dog
Karelisch-Finnische Laika Karelo-Finnish Laika
Karpalballen carpal pad
Karpalgelenk carpal joint
Karpfenrücken carp back

kastanienbraun brown, chestnut, dark reddish brown
kastanienrot ruby
Kastration castration
kastrieren castrate
Katalog catalogue
Katalonischer Schäferhund Catalan Sheepdog
Katze cat
kaudal caudal
kauen chew
kauern crouch, cower
kaufen buy, purchase
Käufer(in) buyer
Kaufpreis price
Kaufvertrag contract of sale, sales contract
Kaukasischer Owtscharka Caucasian Owtcharka
Kaumuskel masseter muscle
Kaurolle chewing stick
Kavalettis (Agility) cavalettis (agility)
Keeshond Keeshond
Kegel (Markierungs-) cone
Kehle throat
Kehlhaut dewlap
Kehlkopf larynx
Kehlkopfentzündung laryngitis
Kehlwamme dewlap
Kehrt! (Hörzeichen) About turn! (verbal command)
Kehrtwendung about-face
keifen yelp
Keine-Belohnung-Signal no-reward-marker
Kelb tal Fenek Pharaoh Hound
Kelpie Australian Kelpie
Keltenbracke Celtic Hound
Kenndecke (Hund) signature cover
kennen know
kennen, vertraut sein mit be acquainted with
Kennzeichen characteristic
Kennzeichnung, dauerhafte permanent identification
Kentucky Muschelhaufenhund Kentucky Shell Heap Dog
Kerry Beagle Kerry Beagle
Kerry Blue Terrier Kerry Blue Terrier
Kette chain
Kettenhalsband chain collar, steel collar
Kettenhund chained guard dog, chained watchdog
Keule haunch, buttock
Kiefer jaw
Kieferklemme lock jaw
Kippohr, hohes tipped ear
Kindspech puppys' first stool
King Charles Spaniel English Toy Spaniel, King Charles Spaniel

Kinn chin
Kinnbart mandarins beard
Kinnlade lower jawbone
Kippohr semi-pricked ear
Kipp-Punkt der Wippe (Agility) pivot point of the seesaw (agility)
Kirgisischer Windhund Kirghiz Greyhound
Kishu Inu Kishu Inu
Kladde scribbling pad
kläffen babble, bark, yap
Kläffer babbler
klaglos without complaining
Klapperstock (Ringsport) stick of split bamboo (mondioring)
klarstellen state something clearly
Klasse class
Klasse, offene open class
klassifizieren classify
Klassifizierung classification
Klaue claw, toe nail
Kleiderordnung dress code
Kleidungsstück article of clothing
klein small
Kleiner Afrikanischer Windhund Small African Greyhound
Kleiner Anglo-Französischer Laufhund Small Anglo-French Hound
Kleiner Blauer Griffon der Gascogne Small Blue Gascony Griffon
Kleiner Blauer Laufhund der Gascogne Small Blue Gascony Hound
Kleiner Brabanter Belgian Griffon
Kleiner Französischer Vorstehhund Small French Pointer
Kleiner Gascon Saintongeois Small Gascon Saintongeois
Kleiner Münsterländer Vorstehhund Small Munsterlander
Kleiner Ogar Polski Small Polish Hound
Kleiner Rauhaariger Laufhund der Vendée Medium Vendeen Griffon
Kleinhirn cerebellum
Kleinhund toy, miniature dog
Kleinpudel Miniature Poodle
Kleinspitz Small (German) Spitz
Kleinvieh small domestic animals
Klemmbrett clipboard
klemmen (im Sinne von quetschen) pinch
klettern (über) climb (over)
Klettersprung (Schrägwand) climbing jump (over scaling wall)

Kletterwand (Schutzdienst, Agility) scaling wall (protection work, agility)
klobig bulky
Klugheit intelligence
Knackpunkt crunch point
Knacks crack
Knacks, er hat einen ... weg (geistig) he's slightly cracked
Knall bang
Knall (Schuss) crack
knallen (mit Peitsche) crack
knallen (mit Pistole) shot
Knallfrosch jumping cracker
knapp bestehen (Prüfung) scrape through
Knappheit (im Sinne von Mangel) shortage
knautschen (z.B. Apportierholz) mouthing (e.g. dumbbell)
kneifen pinch
Knick fold, break
Knie(gelenk) knee (joint)
Kniekehle hollow of the knee
knien, sich hin... kneel down
Kniescheibe patella, kneecap
knistern crackling
Knoblauchkapsel garlic pill
Knoblauchzehe clove of garlic
Knöchel knuckle
Knochen bone
knochenförmig bone-shaped
Knochenkot stool with bone chips
Knochenmehl bone meal
Knochensubstanz substance of the bone
Knopfohr button ear
Knorpel cartilage
knurren growl, snarl
Koerung koerung
Kohchi Ken Shikoku
Kohlehydrat carbohydrate
Kohshu Tora Kai-Inu
Kojote coyote
Kolostralmilch colostrum
Kombination combination
kombinieren (mit) combine (with)
Kombiwagen station wagon
Kommando command
Kommando geben give a command
Kommando, nächstes ... abwarten await the next command
Kommandos, ähnlich klingende similar sounding commands
kommentarlos without comment
kommentieren comment on
Kommunikation communication
Kommunikationsmittel means of communication

Kommunikationsschwierigkeiten lack of communication
Kommunikationssystem communication system
kommunizieren communicate
Komondor Komondor
kompakt cobby, compact, stocky
Kompensation compensation
kompetent competent
Kompetenz competence
Komplettfutter complete and balanced diet
Kondition condition, shape
Konditionierung (von Verhalten) conditioning (of behaviour)
Konditionierung, instrumentelle operant conditioning
Konditionierung, klassische respondent conditioning
Konditionierung, operante operant conditioning
Konditionsschwäche lack of stamina
Konditionstraining fitness training
Konflikt conflict
Konflikt, in ... geraten mit come into conflict with
Konfliktstoff matter for conflict
Konfrontation confrontation
konfrontieren mit confront somebody with
Kong® (Spielzeug) Kong® (toy)
Königspudel Standard Poodle
konisch cone-shaped
Konkurrent(in) competitor
Konkurrenz competition, entry
Konkurrenz, außer ... not for competition
Konsequenz consequence, persistance
Kontaktdermatitis contact dermatitis
Kontaktzone (Agility) contact zone (agility)
Konter (Sport) counter-attack (sport)
kontern (Sport) counter (sport)
Kontext context
Kontinentaler Zwergspaniel Continental Toy Spaniel
kontinuierlich continuously
Kontinuität continuity
Kontrolle auf Distanz control from the distance
Kontrolle über (im Sinne von Beherrschung) control of
Konzentration concentration
Konzentrationsfähigkeit power of concentration
Konzentrationspunkt focus point

Konzentrationsschwäche lack of concentration
konzentrieren, sich (auf) focus on, concentrate (on)
konzentriert arbeiten work with concentration
Kooichi Kooichi Dog
Kooikerhondje Kooiker Dog
Kooperation cooperation
kooperativ cooperative
kooperieren cooperate
Kopf head
Kopf ohne Adel coarse head
Kopf wegdrehen turning head away
Kopf, wohlproportionierter well-proportioned head
Kopfhaltung head position
Kopfhaut skin on head, scalp
Kopfhund (im Sinne von Alphatier) top dog
Kopflinien head planes
Kopfräude notoedric mange
Korallenhalsband pinch collar, pronged collar, spike collar
Körbchen basket
Koreanischer Gindo Korean Gindo dog
kören/ ankören evaluate a dog for his stud potential
Korkenzieherrute corkscrew tail
Körmaß measuring device
Körmaß (Gerät) calliper (equipment)
Körper wegdrehen turning away
Körperbandage body wrap
Körperhaltung posture
Körpersprache body language
Körperumfang girth
Korrektur/ Einwirkung correction
Korrektur, verbale verbal correction
Korthals Korthals Griffon
Körung determination of stud value, koerung
Kostromá-Bracke Russian Hound
Kot excrement, stool, faeces
Kotabsatz defecation
koten defecate, have a stool
Köter mongrel, mutt, mixed breed
Kotfressen stool eating, coprophagy
Krach noise
kraftvoll powerful
Kragen neck ruff
Kralle toe nail, claw
Krallenfeile nail file
Krallenzange nail clipper
Krampf cramp
krankgeschossen wounded
Krasky Ovcar Istrian Sheepdog

kratzen scratch
kraulen rub, scratch, stroke
Kraushaariger Retriever Curly-Coated Retriever
Krebs (medizinisch) cancer (medical)
Kreis nach links/ rechts circle left/ right
Kreuzband cruciate (ligament)
Kreuzbandriss torn cruciate
kreuzbar capable of being interbred
Kreuzbein sacrum
Kreuzbeinwirbel sacral vertebra
Kreuzbiss cross bite
kreuzen (im Sinne von züchten) cross, crossbreed, interbreed
Kreuzung interbreeding
kriechen cringe
Krimwindhund Crimean Hound
Kriterien, Anforderungen criteria
Kritik criticism
kritisieren criticize
Kroatischer Schäferhund Croatian Sheepdog
Kromfohrländer Kromfohrlander
Krone crown
Kropf goitre
krummbeinig crooked legged
Kruppe croup, rump
Kruppe, abfallende drooping croup
Kruppe, waagerechte flat croup
Kryptorchismus cryptorchidism
Kugelschreiber ballpoint pen
kuhhessig cow-hocked
Kühltasche cold bag (or box)
Kümmerling weakling
kümmern, sich (um) look after
kupferfarben tan
Kupfervergiftung copper toxicosis
kupieren (Körperteil) dock
kupieren (Rute) clip (tail)
kupieren (Ohren) crop (ears)
Kurdischer Windhund Kurdish Greyhound
Kuri Kuri dog
Kurländische Bracke Kurland Hound
Kurs besuchen (über) attend a course (in)
Kurzführer short lead (or leash), pull tab
kurzhaarig short-haired
Kurzhaar Zwergdachshund Shorthaired Miniature Dachshund
Kurzkopf short muzzle
kurzköpfig short-faced
kurzläufig short-legged
kurzlendig close-coupled

Kurznarkose short-acting narcosis
kurznasig short-nosed
kurzrückig short-backed
kurzschnauzig short-faced, short-muzzled
Kuvasz Kuvasz
Kyi Leo Tibetan Bearded Dog
Kynologie cynology

L

Labrador Retriever Labrador Retriever
Lachs salmon
Laekenaar Laekenois
Laekenois Belgian Laekenois
Lagerbildung nesting
Lagotto Italian Truffle dog
lahm lame
Laie layman, laywoman
Laie, da bin ich absoluter ... I don't know the first thing about it
laienhaft amateurish
Laika Laika
Lakeland Terrier Lakeland Terrier
Lakonier Laconian Greyhound
Lamm lamb
Lampenfieber stage fright
Lancashire Heeler Lancashire Heeler
Landesmeister(in) national champion
Landessprache national language
Landrasse, Landschlag country breed
Landschaftsschutzgebiet natural preserve
Landseer Landseer
Landstraße country road
Langhaardackel Longhaired Dachshund
langhaarig longhaired, roughcoated
Langhaariger Deutscher Vorstehhund German Longhaired Pointer
Langhaariger Moskauer Zwergterrier Moscow Longhaired Toy Terrier
Langhaariger Vorstehhund der Picardie Picardie Spaniel
langköpfig long-nosed
langohrig lave-eared
langsam slow

Langsam! (Hörzeichen) Slowly! (verbal command)
Langsamkeit slowness
Languedoc Schäferhund Cevennes Shepherd
langwierig lengthy
Lappenspitz, Lapphund Swedish Lapp Spitz
Lärm noise
lärmempfindlich sensitive to noise
Larzac Vorstehhund Larzac Spaniel
latent, verborgen latent
Latenz, Verborgenheit latency
Laterne street lamp
Laternenpfahl lamppost
Lauf (im Sinne von Bein) leg
Lauf (im Sinne von Wettrennen) course, race
Laufbahn, hundesportliche dog sport career
Laufdraht overhead trolley cable, running line
Laufeinteilung (der Geräte bei Agility) course
läufig werden come in season (or heat)
Läufigkeit heat, season, oestrus
Läufigkeit, versteckte silent heat
Laufschritt running gait, trot
Laufsteg (Agility) dog walk (agility)
Laus louse (plural: lice)
Lausbefall lice infestation, pediculosis
Laut geben (im Sinne von bellen) give tongue, bark, bay
Laut! (Hörzeichen) Bark!, Speak! (verbal command)
lautfreudig talkative
lautlos soundless
Lautsprecher loudspeaker
Lautsprecheranlage public-address system
lautstark loud
Laverack Setter English Setter
Lawine avalanche
Lawinenhund avalanche dog
Lebensangst existential anxiety
Lebensaufgabe life task
Lebensbedingungen living conditions
Lebensbedürfnisse necessaries of life
Lebensberechtigung right to live
Lebensdauer lifespan
lebensfähig viable
Lebensgemeinschaft partnership
Lebensgeschichte life story
lebenslang lifelong
Lebensqualität quality of life

Lebensraum living space
Lebenswerk lifework
Leber liver
Leberentzündung hepatitis
Leberentzündung, ansteckende canine infectious hepatitis
leberfarben liver, reddish-brown
Leberwurst liver sausage
Lebewesen creature
lebhaft lively, spirited, quick
Leckdermatitis lick granuloma
lecken lick
Leckerbissen, Leckerli bait, treat, snack
Leckerchenbeutel bait pouch
Leder leather
lederfarben buckskin, yellowish grey
Lederhalsband leather collar
Lederhaut corium
Lederleine leather leash
Lederohr smooth ear
leer empty
Leerdarm (oberster Teil des Dünndarms) jejunum
Lefze upper lip
Lefzen hochziehen show teeth, curl (up) the lips
Lefzenekzem lipfold dermatitis
Lefzenschluss way the lips meet
Lefzenschluss, guter lips meeting exactly
Lefzenschluss, offener loose lips
Legalität legality
Legalität, außerhalb der outside the law
Lehrgeld zahlen müssen learn it the hard way
lehrreich instructive
Leib body
leicht gebaut slightly built
leicht verdaulich easily digestible
leicht verständlich easy to understand
leicht verwundet lightly wounded
leichtführig tractable
Leichtgewicht lightweight
Leid sorrow
Leid, jemandem ... zufügen harm someone
leiden suffer
leidend suffering
Leidtragende(r) mourner
leihen, sich etwas (von) borrow something (from)
Leine leash, engl.: lead
Leine, den Hund an die ... nehmen (führen) put (keep) the dog on the leash
Leine, lange (Longe) long leash
leinenführig trained to heel on leash

Leinenführigkeit (als Eigenschaft des Hundes) willingness to heel on leash
Leinenführigkeit (als Übung im Hundesport) heeling on leash, on-leash heeling
Leinenruck jerk on the leash
Leinenzwang leash law, mandatory leashing of all dogs
leise quiet
leisten (im Sinne von Vollbringen/ Erfüllen) perform
leisten, Erstaunliches achieve (amazing things)
leisten, gute Arbeit do a good job
Leistenbruch inguinal hernia
Leistengegend inguinal area
Leistenwirbel lumbar vertebra
Leistung performance
leistungsbezogen performance-oriented
Leistungsdenken performance-oriented outlook
Leistungsdruck pressure to perform
Leistungsfähigkeit efficiency
Leistungsfutter performance diet
leistungsgerecht according to performance
Leistungsheft work record book
Leistungsheft/-buch/-urkunde, Original- original scorebook
Leistungskontrolle achievement control
Leistungsniveau standard of performance
leistungsorientiert achievement-oriented
Leistungsprinzip performance principle
Leistungsprüfung, -wettbewerb trial
Leistungsrichter(in) trial judge
leistungsschwach low-performance
Leistungssport competitive sport
Leistungsstand performance level
leistungsstark high-performance
leistungssteigernd performance-enhancing
Leistungssteigerung increase in performance
Leistungsträger(in) top performer
Leistungsurkunde certificate
Leistungswettbewerb efficiency contest
Leistungswille will to achieve
Leistungszeichen performance degree (or title)

Leistungszucht performance breeding
Leitbild model
Leiten auf Distanz commanding from a distance
Leitgedanke central thought, central theme
Leithund leader, lead dog
Lektüre reading matter
Lende loin, coupling
Lendenpartie, lange long-coupled
Lendenwirbel lumbar vertebra
lenkbar tracktable, manoeuvrable
Leonberger Leonberger
Leopard Cur Leopard Cur, Leopard Tree Dog
Leptospirose leptospirosis
lernbegierig eager to learn
Lerneifer eagerness to learn
lernen learn
lernen, aus Fehlern learn from ones' mistakes
lernfähig able to learn
Lernplateau learning plateau
Lernprinzipien learning principles
Lernprozess learning process
Lernpsychologie psychology of learning
lesen read
lesenswert worth reading
Lettische Bracke Latvian Hound
leugnen deny
Levesque Laufhund Levesque
Levrier Espanol Spanish Greyhound
Lexikon encyclopaedia, us: encyclopedia
Lhasa Apso Tibetan Apso
lichtscheu photophobia
Lichtung clearing
Lid eyelid
Lidmuskel muscle of the eyelid
Lidrand eyerim
Lidrandentzündung inflammation of the eyelids
Lidspalte palpebral fissure
liebebedürftig need a lot of love and affection
liebenswert lovable
liebevoll pflegen take loving care of
Liebhaberzüchter hobby breeder
lieblos loveless, unkind
Lieblosigkeit unkindness
Liegebeule elbow cyst
liegen lie
Liegeplatz dogs' place
Liegeschwiele callus
lindern (Not) relieve
lindern (Schmerz) soothe

Linderung verschaffen, jemandem bring somebody relief
Linie line
Linie, untere bottom line
Linienführung general outline
Linienführung, saubere clean outline
Linienzucht line breeding
links left
Links um! (Hörzeichen) Left turn! (verbal command)
Linse lens
Linsentrübung cloudiness of the eyelens
Lipom lipoma
Lippe lip
Litauische Bracke Lithuanian Hound
Literatur literature
Lizenzkarte racing licence
Lob, loben praise
locken (mit Futter) lure (with food)
locker loose
Lockhund tolling dog
lockig curly
Lockmittel (Futter) bait, lure (food)
Lockruf mating call
Lockvogel decoy
loh tan markings
lohnen, sich be worth
lohnend rewarding
lösbar (Aufgabe) solvable (lesson)
losbinden untie
löschen (Verhalten) extinguish (behaviour)
Löschung (eines Verhaltens) extinction
Löschungstrotz extinction burst
lose loose
lösen, sich (im Sinne von koten) defecate, have a stool
loslassen release
losreißen, sich (von) break away (from)
losrennen run off
Lösung solution
Losung (vom Wild) dung
Louisiana Catahoula Catahoula Leopard Dog
Löwchen Little Lion Dog
löwenartig leonine
löwenfarbig golden yellow, lion coloured
löwengelb lion coloured
Lucas Terrier Lucas Terrier
lückenhaft (z.B. Gebiss) full of gaps (e.g. teeth)
lückenlos without gaps
Luftröhre windpipe
Lumpenzerren tug-of-war
Lundehund Norwegian Puffin Dog
Lunge lung

Lungenarterie pulmonary artery
Lungenbläschen pulmonary alveolus
Lungendrehung lung torsion
Lungenentzündung pneumonia
Lustgewinn (psychisch) pleasure gain
lustlos listless, uninterested
lutschen suck
Luzerner Laufhund Lucerne Hound
Luzerner Niederlaufhund Lucerne Short-Legged Hound
Lyme-Krankheit Lymes disease
Lymphe lymph
Lymphosarkom lymphosarcoma

M

machbar practicable
machen make
Macht power
Macht der Gewohnheit force of habit
Machtkampf dominance fight
MacKenzie River Hund MacKenzie River Dog
Made maggot, mite
Magen stomach
Magen-Darm-Diät intestinal diet
Magen-Darm-Katarrh gastroenteritis
Magendrehung gastric torsion
mager lean, lank(y), thin
Magermilch skimmed milk
Magerquark low-fat curd cheese
Magyar Agar Hungarian Greyhound
Magyar Vizsla Hungarian Pointer
mahagonirot rich chestnut red
mähen paddle
Mahlzahn molar
Mähne mane
Mais maize
Maisflocken cornflakes
makellos (Ausstellung) flawless (show)
Malinois (Belgian) Malinois
Mallorca Dogge Mallorquin Bulldog
Mallorca Schäferhund Mallorquin Sheepdog
Malteser Maltese
Mammatumor mammary gland tumour
Manchester Terrier Manchester Terrier
Mandel (medizinisch) tonsil (medical)
mandelförmig almond-shaped
Mangel deficiency, lack of ...
Mangelerscheinung deficiency symptom

Manipulation manipulation
manipulieren manipulate
Mannarbeit protection work
Männchen machen sit up (and beg)
Mannschaft team
Mannschaftsführer(in) team captain
Mannschaftswertung team classification
Mannschaftswettbewerb team event
Mannschärfe aggressiveness towards people
Mantel saddle, mantle
manuell manual
Marathen Windhund Mahratta Greyhound
Marderhund raccoon dog
Maremma Abruzzenhund Maremma Sheepdog
Mark (medizinisch) marrow (medical)
markerschütternd bloodcurdling
markieren mark
Markierung marking
Markknochen marrow-bone
Marotte quirk
Maschendraht wire netting
Maske mask
Maske, dunkle dark mask
Maske in der Fellfarbe self-masked
Massentierhaltung battery farming
massiv massive, blocky
Maßnahme measure
Mastdarm rectum
Mastiff Mastiff
mastiffartig mastiff-type, molossoid
Mastin d'Aragon Pyrenean Mastiff
Mastin de los Pirineos Pyrenean Mastiff
Mastin Espanol Spanish Mastiff
Mastin Leones Spanish Mastiff
Mastin Machego Spanish Mastiff
Mastino Neapoletano Neapolitan Mastiff
Matsch mush
matschig muddy
Mauer (Agility) wall hurdle (agility)
Maul mouth, muzzle
Maulkorb muzzle
Maus mouse (plural: mice)
Mausefalle mousetrap
Mausefänger mouser
Mauseloch mouse hole
mausgrau mouse-grey, light grey
Mechelaar Malinois
Medelan Russian Bear Dog

mehrfarbig parti-coloured
mehrfarbig gescheckt dappled, variegated
meiden avoid
Meideverhalten avoidance behaviour
Meinung opinion
Meisterschaft championship
Meldefrist close of entry
Meldegebühr (oder -geld) entry fee, registration fee
Meldehund messenger dog
melden alert
Meldepflicht obligatory registration
Meldeschein entry form
Meldezahl size of entry
Meniskus meniscus
Menschenmenge crowd of people
Mentaltraining mental training
Merkmal characteristic
merle merle
Metall metal
Metallgegenstand (Geruchs-unterscheidung) metal article (scent discrimination)
Methode method
Methoden zur Verhaltensänderung behaviour modification methods
Meute (Hunde-) pack (of hounds)
Meuteführer(in) leader of the pack, top dog
Meutehund pack hound
Meutejagd hunting with a pack of hounds
Mexikanischer Nackthund Mexican Hairless Dog
Mexikanischer Zwergnackthund Toy Mexican Hairless Dog
Miethündin leased bitch
Mikawa Inu Mikawa Inu
Mikrochip microchip
Mikrophon microphone
Milbe mite
Milbenbefall mite infestation
Milch milk
Milchdrüse mammary gland
Milchdrüsentumor mammary gland tumour
Milchfieber milk fever
Milchflasche feeding bottle
Milchgebiss milk teeth
Milchmangel agalactia, absence of milk
Milchtritt kneading
Milchzahn milk (or temporary or deciduous) tooth
Milchzucker milk sugar
Militärhund military dog
Milz spleen
mindern reduce
Mindestalter minimum age requirement

Mine mine
Minensuchhund land mine dog, mine detection dog
Mineralsalze minerals
Miniatur Bullterrier Miniature Bull Terrier
Mioritic Hirtenhund Rumanian Shepherd Dog
Mischform hybrid
Mischling mixture, mixed breed, mongrel
Missachtung, missachten disregard
Missbildung malformation
missbilligen disapprove (of)
Missbilligung disapproval
Misserfolg failure
missfarben off-colour
missgebildet malformed
misshandeln maltreat
Misshandlung maltreatment
Missstand deplorable state of affairs
Missstände abschaffen remedy abuses
misstrauen distrust
Misstrauen (gegen) distrust (of)
misstrauisch distrustful
Missverständnis misunderstanding
missverstehen misunderstand
Mist (Tierkot) dung
Mitarbeit cooperation
miteinander with each other
Mitglied member
Mitgliederversammlung general meeting
Mitgliederzahl membership
Mitgliedsausweis membership card
Mitgliedsbeitrag membership fee
Mitgliedschaft membership
Mittelasiat Mid-Asiatic (Russian) Shepherd
Mittelasiatischer Owtscharka Middle Asian Owtcharka
Mittelfurche median line
Mittelfuß pastern
Mittelgewicht middleweight
mittelgroß medium, midsize
Mittelgroßer Anglo-Französischer Laufhund Middle-Sized Anglo-French Hound
Mittelhirn mid-brain
Mittelpudel Miniature Poodle
Mittelschnauzer Medium-Sized Schnauzer
Mittelspitz Standard German Spitz
mitverantwortlich responsible
Mitverantwortung joint responsibility
Möbel furniture
Modehund fashionable (dog) breed

Modifikation, Modifizierung modification
modifizieren modify
Möglichkeit possibility
Molosser Molossian Dog
molossoid mastiff like
Mongolischer Hund Mongolian Dog
Monorchide monorchid
Mops Pug
Moskauer Langhaariger Zwergterrier Moscow Longhaired Toy Terrier
Moskauer Wachhund Moscow Watchdog
Motivation motivation
Motivationsobjekt motivator
Motivationsumschwung shifting motivation
motivieren motivate
Mountain Cur Mountain Cur
Mücke midge
müde tired
Mudhol Windhund Mudhol Hound
Mudi Mudi
Müll rubbish, garbage, trash
Mülleimer rubbish bin, trash can
Mundfäule trench mouth
Mundwinkel corner of the mouth, labial commissure (anatomical)
Mundwinkellecken licking the corner of the mouth
Münsterländer Munsterlander
munter lively, spirited
Munterkeit alertness
Musher musher
Musiktherapie music therapy
Muskelkater stiffness
Muskeltonus muscle tone
Muskulatur muscular system, muscles
Muster pattern
Mut courage, heart, bravery
mutig brave, game, courageous
Mutprobe (Schutzdienst) test of courage, courage test (protection work)
Mutterinstinkt maternal instinct
Muttertier dam, mother
Mutzschwanz stump tail

N

Nabel navel
Nabelbruch umbilical hernia
Nabelschnur umbilical cord
nach außen drehend turning out
nach dem Rüden (Name) sired by (name)
nach innen drehend turning in
nachahmen imitate
Nachahmung imitation
Nachbar(in) neighbour
nachdecken repeated breeding
nachdenken think about
Nachdruck verleihen emphasize
Nachgeburt afterbirth
Nachgeburtsphase stage in labour
nachgehen follow
nachhängen (Fußarbeit) drop back (heelwork)
Nachholbedarf backlog demand
nachimpfen give (or administer) a booster shot
Nachimpfung booster (shot)
Nachkomme descendent, offspring
Nachsuche search for wounded game on blood trail
nachtrauern mourn someone/something
Nachweis certificate
nachweisbar detectable, proofable
Nachwirkung after-effect
Nachzucht breeding activity, progeny, offspring
Nachzuchtgruppe progeny group, studdog class, brood-bitch class
nachzuholen, er hat viel ... he has a lot to catch up on
Nacken neck
Nackenfell sträuben hackles up
Nackenfleck withers spot
Nackengriff take (a dog or an animal) by the scruff of the neck

Nackenhaare hackles
Nackthund Hairless Dog
Nadel needle
Nagel, Kralle nail, toe
nagen (an) gnaw (on)
Nager, Nagetier rodent
Nähe nearness
nahe bei near to
nahe beieinander close together
nähern, sich approach
Nahrungsmangel lack of food
Naht suture line
Nahtentfernung stitch removal
Nahziel immediate objective
Namensetikett tag
Namensschild name plate, tag
Narbe scar
Nase nose
Nase, rosa pink nose
Nase in der Farbe des Haarkleides self-coloured nose
Nase, mit tiefer with nose on the ground
Nase, zurückgesetzte pushed-in nose
Nasenarbeit scent work, scenting
Nasenband nose band
Nasenbein nasal bone
Nasenflügel wing of nose
Nasenhöhle nasal cavity
Nasenkatarrh runny nose
Nasenloch nostril
Nasenrücken bridge of the nose
Nasenscheidewand nasal septum
Nasenschwamm nose leather
Nasenspiegel nasal plane
Nasenspitze tip of the nose
Nässe wetness
nässen, urinieren urinate
nasskalt damp and cold
Nationalflagge national flag
Nationalmannschaft national team
Natur nature
Naturell disposition
naturgemäß natural
Naturgesetz law of nature
Naturheilkunde naturopathy
natürlich natural
natürlichen Todes sterben die a natural death
naturwissenschaftlich scientific
Navarro Vorstehhund Navarro Pointer
Neapolitaner Dogge Neapolitan Mastiff
Nebenhode epididymis
Nebenwirkungen side effects
Neigung slope
Nein! (Hörzeichen) No! (verbal command)
Nematode roundworm
Nenzen Rentierhütehund Nenets Herding Laika

Nerv nerve
Nervenentzündung neuritis
nervenstark of sound temperament
Nervensystem nervous system
Nervensystem, vegetatives autonomous nervous system
nervös nervous
Nervosität nervousness
nervtötend nerve-racking
Nerzöl mink oil
Nestbau nesting
Netzhaut retina
Neufundländer Newfoundland Dog
Neugier curiosity
neugierig auf curious about
Neuguinea Dingo New Guinea Singing Dog
Neuirland Eingeborenenhund New Ireland Dog
Neuling novice
Neuseeländer Eingeborenenhund New Zealand Native Dog
Neuseeländer Schäferhund New Zealand Sheepdog
neutral, sich ... verhalten remain neutral
Neutralität neutrality
nicht bellend barkless
nicht kastriert entire
nicht registrierter Hund non-registered dog, unregistered dog
nicht sozialisiert non-socialized
nicht sterilisiert entire
Nickhaut third eyelid
Nidation nidation
niederbrüllen, jemanden shout someone down
niederdrücken press down
Niederlaufhund short-legged hound
niederläufig short-legged
Niederwild small game
niederziehen pull down
niedlich sweet, cute
Niere kidney
Nierenentzündung nephritis
Nierenpartie loin region
Nierenversagen kidney failure
Nihon Supittsu Japanese Spitz
Nihon Teria Japanese Terrier
Niveau level
Nootka Schäferhund Nootka Dog
Norbottenspitz Nordic Spitz
nordisch nordic
Nordische Rassen arctic breeds
Nordkaukasischer Steppenschäferhund North Caucasian Steppe Ovtcharka
Norfolk Retriever Norfolk Retriever
Norfolk Terrier Norfolk Terrier
normalerweise normally
normalisieren normalize

normalisieren, sich return to normal
Norwegischer Buhund Norwegian Buhund
Norwegischer Elchhund Norwegian Elkhound
Norwegischer Laufhund Norwegian Hound
Norwegischer Vogelhund Norwegian Puffin Dog
Norwich Terrier Norwich Terrier
Notizblock notepad
Notlösung temporary solution
Notmaßnahme emergency measure
Nova Scotia Duck Tolling Retriever Nova Scotia Duck Tolling Retriever (Toller)
Nubischer Nackthund Nubian Dog
Nudel noodle
Nummer (im Ring) ring card
Nuss (medizinisch) vulva (medical)
Nutzen utility
nutzlos useless
Nutzlosigkeit uselessness
Nylon nylon
Nylonhalsband nylon collar
Nylonleine nylon leash

Oberarm upper arm
Oberarmbein humerus
Oberarmknochen humerus
Oberbegriff generic term
Oberfläche surface
Oberhaar, Oberfell top coat
Oberkiefer upper jaw, maxilla
Oberkopf occiput
Oberlinie topline
Oberlinie, abfallende high in withers
Oberlinie, ansteigende low in withers
Oberlippenspalt philtrum
Oberschenkel thigh
Oberschenkelknochen upper thighbone
Oberschenkelschlagader femoral artery
Oberzuchtwart chief breed warden
Obmann(-frau) für Ausbildung und Sport/ OFS national training director
Ochsenziemer beef dog chew, rawhide
Ödem oedema
öffentlich bekannt machen make public
Öffentlichkeit general public
Östrus, stiller silent heat
Ogar Polski Polish Hound
Ohr ear
Ohr, kupiertes cropped ear
Ohr, schweres ear too large and/ or heavy
Ohren, tief angesetzte low set ears
Ohrenansatz set-on of ear(s)
Ohrenentzündung ear infection
Ohrenzwang ear ache
Ohrkneifen ear pinch
Ohrlappen ear flap, leather

Ohrmilbe ear mite, otodectes mite
Ohrmuschel ear leather
Ohrräude ear mite infestation
Ohrschlitz ear opening
Ohr-Trimm-Messer pet ear and nose trimmer
Öl oil
Olper Bracke German Hound
optimieren optimize
orangeschimmel orange roan
Ordner steward
Organismus organism
orientieren orientate
Orientierung orientation
Ort place
Ortssinn sense of location (or direction)
Ortung locating
Osteoporose osteoporosis
Österreichische Bracke Austrian Hound
Österreichische Glatthaarbracke Tyrolean Mountain Hound
Österreichischer Jagdgriffon Austrian Hunting Griffon
Österreichischer Kurzhaarpinscher Austrian Short-Haired Pinscher
Östrus heat
Ostsibirische Laika East Siberian Laika
Otitis ear inflammation
Otodectes (Ohrmilbe) otodectes mite
Otterhund Otterhound
Otterrute otter tail
oval oval
Overall overalls
Ovulation ovulation
Owczarek Podhalanski Tatra Mountain Sheepdog
Owtscharka Russian Sheepdog

Paar brace
Paarjäger hound hunting in pairs
Paarung mating, copulation
paarungsbereit receptive (bitch)
Paarungszeit mating season
Packerhund boar hound
Palisade (Ringsport) scaling wall (mondioring)
Panik panic
Panikhaken quick release hook
Pannonischer Spürhund Hungarian Foxhound
Pansen tripe
Papiere papers
Papiere, Ahnentafel pedigree
Papillon Papillon, Continental Toy Spaniel
Papuahund Papuan Dog
Paradebeispiel classic example
paradox paradoxical
Parainfluenza-Virus canine parainfluenza virus
parallel zum Körper in line with the body
Parasit parasite
Parasitenhalsband flea (and tick) collar
Parasitenpulver antiparasite powder
Parcours (Agility) course (agility)
Parforcejagd coursing
Pariahund Pariah Dog
Park park
Parson Jack Russell Terrier Parson Jack Russell Terrier
Parvovirose parvo infection
Passgang pace
Passierschein pass
patschnass soaking wet
Patterdale Terrier Patterdale Terrier, Black Fell Terrier
Patti Tamil-Nomad Shepherd Dog
Pause break

pausenlos non-stop
pausieren take a break
Pech pitch
Peintinger Bracke Styrian Rough-Coated Alpine Hound
Peitsche (Schutzdienst) whip (protection work)
Peitschenhieb whiplash
Peitschenrute whiptail
Peitschenwurm whipworm
Pekinese Pekingese
Penis penis
Penisknochen baculum
Perdigueiro Navarro Old Spanish Pointer
Perdigueiro Portugues Portugese Pointer
Perdigueiro Burgales Spanish Pointer
Perfektion perfection
perfektionieren make perfect
perlweiß pearl white
Perro de Agua Español Spanish Water Dog
Perro de Pastor Mallorquin Perro de Pastor Mallorquin
Perro de Pelea Cordobés Old Fighting Dog of Cordoba
Perro de Presa Canario Canary Dog
Perro de Presa Mallorquin Mallorquin Bulldog
Perro sin Pelo del Perú Peruvian Hairless Dog
Person person
Personengruppe, gehen durch die walking through a group of people
Peruanischer Nackthund Peruvian Hairless Dog
Pfannengelenk ball-and-socket joint
pfeffer und salz(farben) black and silver, salt and pepper
pfefferfarben pepper
Pfeife whistle
pfeifen (dem Hund) whistle (for the dog)
Pfeil arrow
Pferd horse
Pferdeäpfel horse droppings
Pferdekoppel paddock
Pfiff whistle
Pflege grooming
pflegen groom, attend to
Pfosten post
Pfötchen geben shake hands
Pfote paw, foot
Pfote heben lifting paw
pföteln pawing
pfoteneng pigeon-toed
Pfui! (Hörzeichen) Phooey! No! (verbal command)
Pfütze puddle

Pharaonenhund Pharaoh Hound
Phase phase
Philippinenhund Philippine Islands Dog
Philippinen Spaniel Manila Spaniel
Phobie phobia
Phu-Quoc Hund Phu-Quoc Dog
physisch physical
Picard Picardy Sheepdog
Piepser beeper
Pigment pigment
Pigmentmangel lack of pigmentation
Pigmentverlust off-colour
Pillenween Terrier Pillenween Terrier
Pilzbefall fungus infection, mycosis
Pinscher Pinscher
Pinzette tweezers (pair of)
Pirsch, pirschen stalk
Pirsch, auf die ... gehen go deerstalking
Pistole pistol
plädieren (für) plead (for)
Plagegeist nuisance
plagen trouble
Plakat placard
Plan schedule
planen plan
planlos without plan
Planlosigkeit lack of plan
plantschen splash
Plastik plastic
Plastikbeutel polythene bag
Plastikfolie polythene sheet
Plastiktüte plastic bag
Platte patch
Plattfuß flat foot
Platz (Raum) space
Platz machen für make room for
Platz! (Hörzeichen) Down! (verbal command)
Platz-Bleib! (Hörzeichen) Down-Stay! (verbal command)
Platz-Bleib-Übung resting (down)
Platz-Bleib-Übung (Obedience) long down (obedience)
platzieren place
Platzierung placement
Platzmangel lack of space
Platzpatrone blank cartridge
Platzregen cloudburst
Platztierarzt veterinarian on site
Platzverweis erhalten be sent off
Plauderei chat
Plazenta placenta
Plotthund Plott Hound
plötzlich sudden

plötzlich auftauchen crop up
plump without refinement
Pluspunkt credit point
Podenco Andaluz Andalusian Hound
Podenco Canario Canarian Warren Hound
Podenco Ibicenco Ibizan Hound
Podengo Portugues Portuguese Hound
Podest platform
Podhalaner Polish Mountain Dog
Podiumsdiskussion panel discussion
Pointer Pointer (English Pointer)
Poitevin Poitevin
Pokal cup
Pokalsieger(in) cup winner
Poligar Windhund Poligar Sighthound
Polizeihund police dog
Polnische Bracke Polish Hound
Polnischer Niederungs-Hütehund, PON Polish Lowland Sheepdog, PON
Polnischer Windhund Polish Greyhound
Polski Owczarek Nizinny, PON Polish Lowland Sheepdog, PON
Polynesischer Eingeborenenhund Hawaiian Poi Dog
Pommernspitz Pomeranian
Pommerscher Hütehund Pomeranian Sheepdog
Pont-Audemer Spaniel Pont-Audemer Spaniel
Porcelaine Porcelaine
Portugiesischer Berghund der Serra da Estrela Estrela Mountain Dog
Portugiesischer Niederläufiger Laufhund Small Portuguese Hound
Portugiesischer Pointer Portuguese Pointer
Portugiesischer Schäferhund Portuguese Sheepdog
Portugiesischer Treibhund Portuguese Cattle Dog
Portugiesischer Vorstehhund Portuguese Pointer
Portugiesischer Wasserhund Portuguese Water Dog
Porzellanscheckung grey, yellow, or brindled spots
Prachtkerl splendid fellow
Prädikat mark, title, grade, score
prägen (Hund, Verhalten) imprint (dog, behaviour)
Prager Rattler Czech Miniature Pinscher

Prägung (Junghund, Welpe) imprinting
Prägungsphase period of imprinting
Prämierungsliste premium list
Prämolar premolar
Preis price, award
Preisträger(in) prizewinner
Prellung bruise, contusion
Premack-Prinzip Premack-Principle
Presswehen bearing-down pains
primär primary
Prince Charles Spaniel Tricolour English Toy Spaniel
Probehund (Ringsport) dog in white (mondioring)
Problem problem
Problem herausarbeiten/ isolieren isolating the problem
Problem(stellung) formulation of a problem
Problemhund problem dog
Problemkreis complex of problems
problemlos unproblematic
Problemlösung problem solving
Problemverhalten problem behaviour
Produkt product
Profil profile
Promenadenmischung mongrel
Prostata prostate gland
Protein (Eiweiß) protein
Protest protest
Protest einlegen gegen enter a protest against
protestieren gegen protest against
Provokateur(in) troublemaker
provozieren provoke
Prüfung trial, test, examination
Prüfungsabteilungen trial phases
Prüfungsangst exam nerves
Prüfungsdisziplin/-sparte/ -abteilung distinct phase
Prüfungsgebühr examination fee
Prüfungsleiter(in) trial chairman (chairwomen)
Prüfungsnachweis certificate
Prüfungsnervosität exam nerves
Prüfungsordnung regulations, trial rules and regulations
Prüfungspapiere trial paperwork
Prüfungsregelwerk trial regulations
Prüfungsstufe level
Prüfungsstufen (Schutzdienst) levels of schutzhund titles (protection work)
Prüfungsteilnehmer(in) participants

Prügel beziehen get a (sound) thrashing
prügeln thrash
Pseudowut pseudo-rabies
Psyche psyche
psychisch psychic(al)
Psychogramm psychograph
psychologisch psychological
Psychoterror psychological intimidation
Pubertät(sphase) puberty
pubertieren go through puberty
Publikum public
Pudel Poodle
Pudelpointer Pudelpointer
Puder powder
Puli Puli
Pulka Pulka
Puls pulse
Puls(schlag) pulsation
Pulsschlag, erhöhter high pulse rate
Pulsschlag, normaler normal pulse rate
Pulsschlag, verlangsamter low pulse rate
Pulszahl pulse rate
Pulver powder
Pumi Hungarian Cattle Dog
Punkt, druckschmerzhafter trigger point
Punkt, bis zu einem gewissen up to a point
Punktabzug penalty
Punktesystem point system, scoring system
Pupille pupil
purzeln tumble
putzen clean
Putzhandschuh hound glove
Pylone (Markierungs-) cone
Pyrenäenberghund Great Pyrenees
Pyrenäenschäferhund Pyrenean Sheepdog

Qual agony
Qual (seelische) anguish
quälen torment
Qualifikation qualification
Qualifikationsrunde qualifying round
Qualifikationswettkampf/ -prüfung qualifying scores
qualifizieren, sich qualify for
qualifiziert qualified
Qualität quality
Qualzucht inhumane breeding practice(s)
Quarantäne quarantine
Quaste pompon
quetschen squeeze
Quetschung contusion
quietschen squeak
Quietschventil (im Spielzeug) squeaker (toy)

R

Rachen pharynx
Rachitis rickets
Radfahrer(in) cyclist
Radfahrweg cycle track, bicycle path
Rafeiro do Alentejo Alentejo Herder
Rallye-Obedience rally (obedience)
Rampur Windhund Northwest Indian Greyhound
Ramsnase aquiline, ram's nose
ramsnasig down-faced
Ramsung ram's head
Rang rank
Rang streitig machen compete with somebody
rangeln scuffle
ranghöher higher-ranking
rangniedriger subordinate
Rangordnung hierarchy, rankorder, order
Rangordnungsfolge hierarchy, rankings
rannehmen, jemanden ride someone hard
Rasen (Gras) grass
Rasenmäher lawn mower
Rasenplatz lawn
Rasse breed
Rasse, bevorzugte favourite breed
Rasse, riesenwüchsige giant breed
Rasse, seltene rare breed
Rassenbeste(r) best of breed
Rassehund pedigree dog
Rassehundezuchtschau, allgemeine all-breed dog show
Rassekennzeichen breed characteristic(s)
Rassekommission breed council
Rassering show ring
Rassestandard breed standard

rassetypisch characteristic of the breed
Rassezuchtklub, -verein breed club, breed society
ratlos helpless
Ratlosigkeit helplessness
ratsam advisable
Ratschlag piece of advice
Ratte rat
Rattenschwanz rat tail
Ratten Terrier Rat Terrier
Raubtier carnivore, beast of prey, predator
Raubvogel bird of prey
Raubwild predatory game
raubzeugscharf vermin hunting
Rauch smoke
Rauchmeldehund smoke detection dog
Räude mange
räudig mangy, scabious
Raufbold rowdy
raufen fight
raufen, sich brawl for
Rauferei (dog) fight
Rauhaardackel Wirehaired Dachshund
Rauhaar Foxterrier Wire Fox Terrier
rauhaarig rough-coated, wirehaired
Raumgriff extension
Rauschgiftsuchhund drug detection dog
rautenförmig diamond-shaped
reagieren react
Reaktion reaction
Reaktion/ Antwort response
realisieren realize/ carry out
Realität reality
Rebhuhn partridge
rechteckig rectangular
rechts on the right hand side
Rechts um! (Hörzeichen) Right Turn! (verbal command)
recken, sich stretch
Red Deer Dingo Red Deer Dingo
Redbone Coonhound Redbone Coonhound
reden talk
Redeschwall flood of words
reduzieren reduce
Reflex reflex
Reflex, bedingter conditioned reflex
Reflexbewegung reflex action
regelwidrig against the rules
Regen rain
Regeneration regeneration
Regenerationsfähigkeit regenerative power
regenerieren regenerate
Regenmantel raincoat

Regenschauer shower
Regenschirm umbrella
registriert registered
Reglement regulation(s)
reglos motionless
Regung (Anwandlung) impulse
Regung (Bewegung) movement
Regung (Gefühl) emotion
Reh deer
Rehbock roebuck
rehbraun fawn-coloured
rehfarben fawn-coloured
Rehkitz fawn
Rehpinscher Miniature Pinscher
rehrein broken from deer
rehrot fawn-red
Rehwild deer
Reibegebiss tight scissors bite
reichlich profuse
Reichweite, in (außer) reach, within (out of)
Reifen tire
Reifen-Sprung (Agility) tire jump (agility)
Reihenfolge order
Reihenfolge, umgekehrte in reverse order
Reihung placement
Reiki-Behandlung reiki-treatment
Reinlichkeit cleanliness
reinrassig purebred
reinweiß solid white
Reise journey
Reiseführer für Hundehalter travel guide for dog owners
Reisekrankheit travel sickness, car sickness
Reisemobil camper
reisen travel
Reißaus nehmen take to one's heels, clear off
reißen tear
reißen (töten) kill, worry
reißen, in Stücke tear pieces
Reißzahn shearing tooth
Reithalle riding hall
Reiz stimulus
Reiz (Verlockung) lure
Reiz abschwächen, ausschleichen fading stimuli
Reiz, konditionierter conditioned stimulus
Reiz, unangenehmer aversive stimulus
Reizbarkeit irritability
reizen (im Sinne von provozieren) provoke, agitate
Reizschwelle threshold
Reizüberflutung fludding with stimuli
reklamieren object, lodge a protest
rekonstruieren reconstruct
Rekordzeit record time
rektal rectal

Rektum rectum
rempeln bump, jostle
Rennbahn race course
Renndecke racing blanket
Rennen race, run
Rennhund racing dog
Rennhundzwinger racing kennel
Rennleiter(in) field trial director (or chairman/ -woman)
Rennmaulkorb racing muzzle
Rennpiste track
Rennstrecke trail
rentieren, sich be profitable
Repertoire (an Verhaltensweisen) repertoire (package of behaviours)
resozialisieren rehabilitate
Respekt, respektieren respect
respektlos irreverent, disrespectful
respektvoll respectful
Restrisiko residual risk
Retriever retriever
retten save
Rettung rescue
Rettungshund search and rescue dog
Revier territory
Revier! (Hörzeichen) Search!, Find! (verbal command)
revieren seek, quarter
Revieren (Schutzdienst) search of hiding places or blinds (protection work)
Revierkontrolle, -behauptung control of territory
Reviermarkierung marking the territory
Revierverteidigung defence of the territory
Rezept (medizinisch) prescription (medical)
Rhodesian Ridgeback Rhodesian Ridgeback, African Lion Hound
richten (bewerten) judge
Richter(in) judge
Richter-Anwärter(in) apprentice judge
Richteranweisung judge's orders
Richterbericht judge's commentary, judge's sheet
Richtertisch judge's table
Richtung direction
Ricke doe
Ridge (Rassekennzeichen) ridge
riechen smell, scent
Riemen (Jagd) hunting leash
Riemenarbeit (Jagd) tracking on the leash (hunting)
Riesenschnauzer Giant Schnauzer
Riesenwuchs (Rasse) giant breed

Rindfleisch beef
Ring ring
Ring-Bedingungen (Wettkampf) ring conditions
Ringbegrenzungszaun (z.B. Obedience) ring gates (e.g. obedience)
Ringbegrenzungszaun, faltbar (z.B. Obedience) folding ring gates (e.g. obedience)
Ringdressur show training
Ringelrute curled-up tail, ring tail
ringerfahrener Hund (routinierter Hund) ring wise dog
Ringmitte centre of ring
Ringsekretär(in) ring steward
Ringwart(in) ring steward
Rippe rib
Rippe, echte true rib
Rippe, falsche false rib, asternal rib
Rippenbogen costal arch
Rippenwölbung spring of ribs
Risiko risk
Risikoaversion risk aversion
Rist back
Risthöhe height at shoulders
Ritual, rituell ritual
Rivale, Rivalin rival
Rivalität rivalry
robust sturdy
roh raw
Rohheit roughness
Rohkost raw vegetables
Röhrenknochen long bone
Rohrstock reed stick
Roll-Lid entropion
röntgen x-ray
Röntgenbild x-ray, radiograph
Roseneath Terrier Roseneath Terrier
Rosenohr rose ear
Rosette rosette
rostbraun tawny
rostfarben tan
rostfarbener Schimmer rustiness
rot red
rot merle red merle
rotbeige russet
Roter Walisischer Hütehund Welsh Red Herder
rotfalb red fawn
rot fleckig red speckled
Rotfuchs red fox
rotgelb reddish yellow
rot gestichelt red roan
rot gestromt red brindle
Rothbury Terrier Rothbury Terrier
rötlich reddish
rötlich grau reddish grey
rot meliert red grizzle
rot scheckig red-mottled
Rotte horde

Rottweiler Rottweiler
Rotweißer Irish Setter Red and White Irish Setter
rotweizenfarben red wheaten
Rotwild red deer
Rotwildfährte deer track (or trail)
Routine routine
Routineübungen fluencies
routiniert experienced
Routiniertheit routinization
Rowdy rowdy
rubinrot ruby
Ruck (z.B. mit Leine) jerk (e.g. at the leash)
ruckartig jerky
Rückbiss overbite
Rücken back
Rücken, überlanger long back
Rücken, weicher soft back
Rückendeckung support, backing
Rückenhaar hair on back
Rückenlinie backline
Rückenlinie, ansteigende rising topline
Rückfall relapse
rückfällig relapsing
rückfällig werden have a relapse
Rückgrat backbone
Rückkehr return
Rückkreuzung backcross(ing)
Rucksack rucksack
Rüde male dog
Rüde, nicht kastrierter entire male dog
Rudel pack
Rudelführer(in) leader of the pack
Rudelmitglied, ranghöheres higher-ranking member of the pack
Rudelmitglied, rangniedrigeres subordinate member of the pack, lower-ranking member of the pack
Rudelordnungsphase period of development of group organization
Rudeltier pack animal
rüdenhaft doggy
Rufweite calling distance
ruhebedürftig in need of a rest
ruhelos restless
ruhen rest
Ruhepause break
Ruheplatz resting place
Ruhestellung rest position
ruhig calm, steady, quiet
Ruhig! (Hörzeichen) Quiet! (verbal command)
ruhig bleiben keep calm, keep quiet
ruhig werden quieten down
Rumänischer Hirtenhund Rumanian Sheepdog

Rumpf trunk
Runzel wrinkle
Rüpel lout
rüpelhaft rude
ruppig shaggy
Ruß (Fellfarbe) black overlay (colour of fur)
Russisch Europäischer Laika Russo-European Laika
Russische Bracke Russian Hound
Russische Gescheckte Bracke Russian Parti-coloured Hound
Russischer Harlekin Hund Russian Harlequin Hound
Russischer Hirtenhund Russian Sheepdog
Russischer Jagdspaniel Russian Spaniel
Russischer Terrier Black Russian Terrier
Russischer Windhund Borzoi
Rute tail
Rute, fröhlich bewegte merry tail
Rute, geringelte curled-up tail, ring tail
Rute, schwingende lashing tail
Rute, tief angesetzte low set tail
Rutenansatz tail set
Rutenspitze tip of the tail
Rutenwurzel base of the tail
Rutsche, rutschen slide
rutschig slippery

S

Saarloos Wolfshund Saarloos Wolfhound
sabbern salivate, slaver, drool
Säbelrute sabre tail
Sabueso Espanol Spanish Hound
Sabueso Espanol de Monte Large Spanish Hound
Sabueso Espanol Lebrero Small Spanish Hound
Sache object
Sache des Vertrauens a matter of trust
sachgerecht appropriate
Sachkundenachweis certificate of proficiency
Sachschaden material damage
sachte softly, calmly
Sachverhalt facts of the case
sachverständig competent
Sachverständigengutachten expert opinion
Sachverständige(r) expert
Sacktunnel (Agility) closed tunnel (agility)
Sägemehl sawdust
Sagen, das ... haben be the boss
Saint Germain Vorstehhund Saint Germain Pointer
Saison season
Salbe ointment, salve
Saluki Saluki
Samenbank sperm bank
Samenleiter seminal duct
Sammelbegriff generic term
sammeln collect
Samojede Samoyed
Samojedenlächeln samoyed smile
sandfarben sandy-coloured
Sandfloh sand flea
sandig sandy
Sandplatz clay court
Sandsack (Agility) sandbag (agility)
sandweiß light fawn

sanft gentle
Sanftheit softness
Sanftmut gentleness
sanftmütig placid
Sanitäter(in) first-aid man (woman)
Sanitätshund ambulance dog
Sanktion, sanktionieren sanction
Sanshu Inu Sanshu Dog
Sansibar Jagdhund Zanzibar Dog
Sarcoptesmilbe itch mite
Sarcoptesräude sarcoptic mange
Sarplaninac Illyrian Sheepdog
satt satisfied
Sattel saddle
Satteldecke mantle
Satzung, Vereins- statutes and articles
satzungsgemäß statutory
sauber clean
Sauerländer Bracke German Hound
saufen drink
saugen suck
säugen nurse, suckle
Säugetier mammal
Saupacker, Saurüde boar hound
Savetal Bracke Posavac Hound, Yugoslav Hound of the Save Valley
Schädel cranium, skull
Schädeldach topskull
Schaden, schaden damage
Schaden nehmen be damaged
Schadstoff harmful substance
Schaf sheep
Schafbock ram
Schäfchenschur lamb clip
Schäfer shepherd
Schäferhund shepherd (dog), sheepdog
Schäferhund der Beauce French Short-Haired Sheepdog
Schafherde flock of sheep
Schafpudel German Sheeppoodle
Schafrüde Sheepdog
Schambein pubic bone
schämen, sich be ashamed
Schapendoes Dutch Sheepdog
scharf (aggressiv) sharp (aggressive)
Schärfe sharpness
scharren dig, scratch
Schatten shadow
Schattenmaske shading on the face
schattiert shaded
schattig shady
Schatzmeister(in) treasurer
Schaum foam, froth
schäumen foaming
scheckig piebald
Scheibe disc

Scheibenbelüftungsgitter air fence up
Scheide vagina
Scheidenentzündung inflammation of the vagina
Scheinangriff mock attack
Scheinkampf mock fight
scheinschwanger in false pregnancy
Scheinschwangerschaft false pregnancy
Scheintäter suspect, agitator
Scheinwerfer spotlight, floodlight
scheitern fail
Schema, variables variable schedule
schematisch schematic
schematisieren schematize
Schenkel thigh
scheppern rattle
Scherapparat clippers
Scherbe broken piece
scheren clip
Scherengebiss scissors bite
Scherengebiss, knappes tight scissors bite
Scherengebiss, umgekehrtes reverse scissors bite
Scherenkarabiner scissors hook
Schermaschine clippers
scheu shy, timid
scheuchen shoo away
Scheuheit shyness, timidity
Scheune barn
Schicksal fate
Schiedsgericht field committee
Schiedsrichter(in) arbitrator, judge, plural: jury
schieferblau slate
schiefergrau silver-fawn
Schienbein tibia
Schikari Shikari dog
Schilddrüse thyroid gland
schildern describe
Schilderung description
Schilf reed
Schiller-Stövare Schiller Hound
Schimmel roan
schimmeln go mouldy
Schimmelpilz mould
schimpfen scold someone
schinden (quälen) maltreat
Schipperke Schipperke
Schirmmütze peaked cap
schlabbern (laut) drink (noisily)
schlafen sleep
schlaff flabby
Schlaffheit flabbiness
schläfrig sleepy
Schlag (Faust) punch
Schlag (Zuchtrichtung) variety
Schlagader artery
schlagen strike
Schlagstock (Schutzdienst) stick (protection work)

Schlagstock, Softstock padded stick
Schlamm mud
schlammig muddy
schlank slim
schlapp (lustlos) listless
Schlappohr hanging ear
schlau clever
schlecht beraten sein be ill-advised
schlecht erzogen bad trained
Schlechtwetterfront bad weather front
Schlechtwetterperiode spell of bad weather
schlecken, (auf-) lick (up)
schleichen sneak
Schleimhaut mucous membrane
Schleppe drag
Schleppjagd drag hunt
schlicht straight and flat (hair)
Schlichthaar straight and flat coat
schlichthaarig flatcoated
Schließmuskel constrictor muscle
Schlingel scallywag
Schlitten sledge
Schlittenfahren (mit Hinterteil über den Boden) scooting (with back on the floor)
Schlittenführer musher
Schlittenhund sled dog
Schlittenhund, unmittelbar hinter dem Leittier wing dog
Schlittenhund, unmittelbar vor dem Schlitten wheel dog
Schlittenhund, Leittier lead dog
Schlittenhunderennen sled dog race
schlucken swallow
Schlund fauces
Schlüsselbein collar bone
Schlüsselerlebnis formative experience, crucial experience
schmalbrüstig narrowchested
Schmarotzer parasite
schmecken taste
Schmelzflocken pablum
Schmerz pain
Schmerzgrenze pain threshold
schmerzhaft painful
Schmerzschrei yelp (of pain), distress yelp
Schmerzunempfindlichkeit high pain threshold
Schmetterlingsnase butterfly nose, spotted nose
Schmetterlingsohren butterfly ears
schmusen cuddle
Schmutz dirt
schmutzig dirty
schmutzig, sich ... machen get dirty

schnallen release (a hunting dog from leash)
schnalzen mit der Zunge click one's tongue
schnappen (nach) snap (at)
Schnapphalterung (für den Clicker) snap (for the clicker)
schnarchen snore
schnauben, vor Wut foam with rage
schnaufen breathe hard
Schnauzbart moustache
Schnauze, Fang mouth, muzzle, snout, foreface
Schnauzenband muzzle band
Schnauzer Standard Schnauzer
Schnee snow
Schneegestöber snow flurry
Schneematsch slush
Schneeregen sleet
Schneeverhältnisse snow conditions
Schneidekamm dematting comb
Schneidezahn incisor
Schneidezähne, durcheinanderstehend scrambled mouth
Schnelligkeit speediness
Schnellverfahren summary procedure
Schnittpunkt point of intersection
Schnittwunde cut
schnüffeln sniff
Schnupfen runny nose
schnuppern sniff
Schnürenhaar corded hair
Schnürenpudel corded poodle
Schnurgang single-tracking (gait)
Schnurrbart moustache
Schnurrhaare whiskers
Schock shock
schokolade(nbraun) chocolate, liver
Schondecke, Auto- dogs' car blanket
schonend careful
schonend behandeln treat with care
Schönheitswettbewerb dog show
Schönheitszucht show-dog breeding
Schonkost light food
schonungslos merciless
Schonzeit close season
Schonzeit closed hunting season
Schopf crest, tuft, topknot
Schoßhund lap dog, sleeve dog
Schottischer Hirschhund Scottish Deerhound
Schottischer Schäferhund Collie
Schottischer Terrier Scottish Terrier

schräg slanting
Schrägwand (A-Wand) a-frame
Schrägwand (Schutzdienst, Ringsport) palisade (protection work, mondioring)
Schrägwand (Schutzdienst, Agility) scaling wall (protection work, agility)
Schreck shock
schreckhaft nervous
Schrei scream, yell
schreien shout
schreien, anbrüllen yell
Schritt step
Schritt (als Maß) pace
Schrittlänge reach
schrittweise step-by-step
Schub drive
Schuhwerk footwear
Schulter shoulder
Schulter, vorgeschobene set forward shoulder
Schulterblatt shoulder blade
Schultergelenk shoulder joint
Schulterhöhe height at shoulders
Schulterlage lay of shoulder
Schultern, zurückgelegte laidback shoulders
Schulung training, practice
Schulungskurs course of training
schummeln cheat
Schuppe (Haut) dendruff, scale (skin)
Schur clip
Schur, englische English saddle clip
Schur, jugendliche puppy clip, working clip
Schur, klassische classical clip, lion clip
Schursalon groomer's
Schuss shot
Schussangst being afraid of gun fire/ noises
Schüssel bowl
schussfest steady to gunshot
Schussfestigkeit indifference to gunshot
Schussfestigkeit, Überprüfung der gunfire test
schusshitzig unsteady to shot
schuss-scheu gun-shy
Schussunsicherheit gun shyness
schütteln shake
Schutz protection
Schutzanzug (Ringsport) protection suit (mondioring)
Schutzanzug (Schutzdienst) protective suit (protection work)
Schutzanzug, Hetzkleidung (Schutzdienst) protection clothes (protection work)
Schutzarm (Schutzdienst) sleeve (protection work)

Schutzdienst protection work
Schutzdiensthelfer(in) agitator, trial helper, helper
Schutzdiensthelfer(in) abführen to escort away
Schutzdiensthelfer(in), geprüfte(r) certified (or qualified) helper
Schutzdiensthelfer bewachen guard the trial helper
Schutzdiensthelfer-Arbeit bei Prüfung agitator's work at trial
Schutzdiensthelfer-Beurteilung helper evaluation
Schutzdiensthelfer-Beurteilungsbogen helper evaluation form
Schutzdiensthose (Leder) protective (leather) pants
Schutzdienst-Versteck blind
Schutzhund protection dog, schutzhund
Schutzhundprüfung schutzhund trial (or test)
Schutzhundsport sport of schutzhund
Schutzimpfung vaccination
Schutzjacke (Schutzdienst) protective vest (protection work)
Schutzkleidung (Schutzdienst) protection clothes (protection work)
schutzlos unprotected
Schutznetz, Auto- car safety net
Schutztrieb protectiveness
schwach weak
Schwäche weakness
Schwanz tail
Schwanz einziehen tucking of tail
Schwanzansatz set-on of tail
Schwanzdrüse tail gland
Schwanzjagen tail chasing
Schwanzwedeln tail wagging
Schwanzwirbel caudal vertebra
Schwanzwurzel root of the tail
schwarz black
schwarz gewolkt blackened
schwarz-beige black and tan
schwarz-blau black and blue
schwarze Wolkung blackening
Schwarzer Russischer Terrier Black Russian Terrier
schwarz-grau meliert grey-black mixed
schwarz-loh(farben) black and tan
schwarz-rot black and tan
Schwarz-Roter Waschbärenhund Black and Tan Coonhound
schwarz-schimmel blue roan
schwarz-silbern black and silver
Schwarzwild wild boars
Schwedische Dachsbracke Swedish Drever

Schwedischer Elchhund Swedish Elkhound
Schwedischer Lappenspitz Swedish Lapp Spitz
Schweineohr pigs' ear
Schweiß perspiration
Schweiß (Blut) blood
Schweißarbeit searching after wounded game on blood trail
Schweißfährte blood trail
Schweißhalsung tracking collar
Schweißhalsung (Jagd) hunting collar (hunting)
Schweißhund bloodhound
Schweißprüfung tracking test on a blood trail
Schweißriemen tracking leash
Schweizer Laufhund Swiss Hound
Schweizer Niederlaufhund Small Swiss Hound
Schwellkörper erectile tissue
Schwertrute scimitar tail
Schwiele callus
schwierig difficult
Schwierigkeit difficulty
schwimmen swim
Schwimmhaut webbing
Schwingklappe (an der Tür) flap (of dog door)
schwitzen perspire
schwül sultry
Schwüle sultriness
Scottish Terrier Scottish Terrier
Sealyham Terrier Sealyham Terrier
sedieren sedate
Seele soul
Seelenleben inner life
Seelenqual mental anguish
Seelenruhe peace of mind
Seelenzustand emotional state
Segugio Italiano Italian Segugio
Segusier Celtic Hound
Sehne sinew
Sehnerv optic nerve
sehnig sinewy
Sehvermögen eyesight
seidig silky
Seite/ Flanke flank
Seitenblick sidelong glance
Seitenwind crosswind
seitlich lateral
seitwärts sideways
sekundär secondary
Selbstbedienung self-service
Selbstbeherrschung self-control
Selbstbeherrschung verlieren lose one's temper
Selbstbeschädigung self-inflicted injury
Selbstbestätigung ego-boost
Selbstbetrug self-deception
selbstbewusst self-confident

Selbstbewusstsein self-confidence
Selbstdarstellung promotion of one's public image
Selbstdisziplin self-discipline
Selbsteinschätzung self-assessment
Selbsterhaltungstrieb survival instinct, defence drive
Selbsterkenntnis self-knowledge
selbstgefällig complacent
Selbstgefälligkeit complacency
selbstsicher self-confident
Selbstsicherheit self-confidence
selbstständig denken think for oneself
Selbstständigkeit independence
Selbstverteidigung self-defence
Selbstwertgefühl self-esteem
selektiv selective
seltsam strange
Seminar, Kurs seminar
semmelfarben wheaten
senffarben mustard
Seniorenklasse veterans class
Senkrücken swayback
Sennenhund Mountain Dog
sensibel sensitive
sensibilisieren sensitize
Sensibilität sensitiveness
septisch septic
Sequenz (Training, Vorführung) sequence
Setter Setter
Setz- und Brutzeit laying and brooding period
Shampoo shampoo
Shaping, sekundäres bridging stimulus („bridge“)
Shar Pei Shar Pei
Sheltie Shetland Sheepdog
Shetland Schäferhund Shetland Sheepdog
Shi Tzu Shi Tzu, Chrysanthemum Dog
Shiba Inu Shiba Inu
Shikoku Inu Shikoku (Inu)
Shilluk Windhund Shilluk Greyhound
Shiloh Schäferhund Shiloh Shepherd Dog
Shropshire Terrier Shropshire Terrier
Sibirischer Husky Siberian Husky
Sichelrute sickle tail
Sicherheit safety
Sicherheit, in ... sein be safe
Sicherheit, sich in ... bringen get out of danger
Sicherheitsabstand safe distance
Sicherheitsgefühl safety sensation
Sicherheitsgurt für Hund im Auto safety belt

sicherheitshalber be on the safe side
Sicherheitshalsband, blinkendes safety light collar
Sicherheitsmaßnahme safety measure
Sicherheitszone (Agility) contact zone (agility)
sicherstellen guarantee
Sicht sight
Sicht, in (außer) in (out of) sight
sichtbar visible
Sichthetze hunt by sight
Sichthund Sight Hound
Sichtlaut barking at sight of game
Sichtzeichen hand signal
Siebenbürger Bracke Hungarian Hound
Sieg win, victory
siegen win
Sieger(in) winner
Siegerehrung presentation ceremony
Siegertreppchen, -podest victory rostrum
Siegerurkunde winner's certificate
siegessicher confident of victory
siegreich victorious
Signal, signalisieren signal
Signal (Hör- oder Sichtzeichen) cue (verbal command or hand signal)
Signal, optisches optic signal
Signal, unbewusstes extraneous cue
Signalkontrolle stimulus control
silber(farben) silver
silbergrau light grey
silbrig silver
Silky Terrier Australian Silky Terrier
Sinnesschärfe acuity of senses
Situation situation
Situation retten save the situation
Situation, stressvolle stressful situation
Sitz beim Anhalten automatic sit
Sitz! (Hörzeichen) Sit! (verbal command)
Sitzbeinhöcker point of buttocks
Sitz-Bleib-Übung (Obedience) long sit (obedience)
Sitzung conference
Sizilianischer Windhund Sicilian Greyhound
Skateboardfahrer(in) skateboarder

Skrotum scrotum
Skrupel scruple
skrupellos unscrupulous
Skye-Terrier Skye Terrier
Slalom slalom
Slalom (Agility) weave (agility)
Slalom-Stangen (Agility) weave poles (agility)
Sloughi Arabian Greyhound, Sloughi
Slovensky Cuvac Slovac Cuvac
Slowakische Bracke Slovakian Hound, Black Forest Hound
Slowakische Schwarzwildbracke Slovakian Hound
Slowakischer Hirtenhund Slovakian Sheepdog
Slowakischer Raubart Slovakian Pointing Griffon
Slowakischer Rauhaariger Vorstehhund Slovakian Pointing Griffon
Smalandsstövare Smalands Hound
Smithfield Collie Smithfield Collie
Smoushond Dutch Smoushond
Snoopy (Hund aus Comic) Snoopy (comic dog)
Soft Coated Wheaten Terrier Soft-Coated Wheaten Terrier
Softstock (Schutzdienst) softstick (protection work)
Sohlenballen communal pad
solange as long as
Solling Leitbracke Solling Bloodhound
Somerset Harrier Somerset Harrier
Sonangi Indian Miniature Hairless Dog
Sonderfall special case
Sonderleiter(in) ring steward
Sonderrecht privilege
Sonderregelung special arrangement
Sonderschau specialty show
Sorgfalt care
sorgfältig careful
Southern Harrier Southern Harrier
souverän sovereign
Souveränität sovereignty
sozial social
Sozialdeprivation social deprivation
Sozialisation socialization
sozialisieren socialize
Sozialisierungsphase period of socialization
sozialverträglich socially acceptable
Spaltgebiss non-level bite
Spaltnase split nose

Spaltrachen cleft palate
Spaniel Spaniel
Spanischer Laufhund Spanish Hound
Spanischer Mastiff Spanish Mastiff
Spanischer Pyrenäenhund Pyrenean Mastiff
Spanischer Vorstehhund Spanish Pointer
Spanischer Wasserhund Spanish Water Dog
Spanischer Windhund Spanish Greyhound
spannend exciting
Sparte field
Spaß fun
Spätentwickler(in) late developer
Spätfolgen late squeal
spazieren walk
spazieren führen take out for a walk
spazieren gehen go for a walk
Spaziergang walk
Spaziergänger(in) walker
Speck bacon
Speiche (medizinisch) radius (medical)
Speichel saliva, spittle
speicheln salivate
Speiseröhre oesophagus
Spezialausbildung specialized training
Spezialgebiet special field
spezialisieren, sich ... auf specialize in
Spezialzuchtschau specialty show
Spiel play
Spielaufforderung invitation to play
spielend leicht easily
spielerisch playing
Spielkamerad(in) playmate
Spielregel rule
Spielsachen toys
Spieltrieb play instinct
Spielzeug toy
Spielzeug aus Kunstfell synthetic fur dog toy
Spinone Italiano Italian Coarsehaired Pointer, Italian Spinone
Spitz German Spitz
Spitze (Rute oder Ohr) tip (of tail or ear)
spitzen (Ohren) prick (ears)
Spitzenergebnis top score
Spitzenleistung top performance
Spitzensport high-performance sports
Spitzenvorführung peak performance

Spitzohr pointed ear
Splentring split ring
splitten splitting up
Spondylose spondylosis
Sport sport
Sporthund working dog
Sportplatz sports ground
Spott mockery
spötteln über mock at
spöttisch mocking
sprachlos speechless
sprechen speak
Spreizfuß (-pfote) flat foot, open foot
sprengen (z.B. Fuchs aus dem Bau) bolt (e.g. fox out of the dan)
Sprengstoffspürhund bomb detection dog
Sprenkel splash
springen jump
Springer Spaniel English Springer Spaniel
Spritze injection
Sprung jump
Sprunggelenk tarsal joint
Sprunggelenk, lockeres slipped hock
Sprunggelenke, durchgetretene weak hocks
Sprunggelenke, weiche weak hocks
Sprunghürde, zerlegbare portable jump
Spulwurm roundworm
Spur track
Spur halten keep track
spüren feel
spuren (sich fügen) toe the line
Spürhund tracking dog, scenthound
Spurlaut voice (of the hound on the scent)
Spurlaut geben giving tongue to a scent
Spurlautprüfung test of proper use of voice
Spursicherheit/ Spurtreue accuracy in trailing
Spürsinn good nose
Spurwille determination in trailing
St. Bernhardshund Saint Bernard
St. Hubertus Hund Saint Hubert Hound
St. Johns Hund St. Johns' Dog
St. Usuge Vorstehhund Saint Usuge Spaniel
Stabijhoun Stabijhoun
stabilisieren, sich become stabilized
Stabilität stability
Stachelhalsband pinch collar, spike collar, pronged collar

Stachelwürger (Halsband) pinch collar
Stadion stadium
Stadt town
Stadtgebiet municipal area
Stadthalle municipal hall
Stadtrand outskirts of the town
Staffordshire Bullterrier Staffordshire Bull Terrier
Stagnation stagnation
stagnieren stagnate
Stall stable
Stammbaum pedigree, family tree
Stammbuch studbook
Standard standard (breed)
Standardzeit (Agility) standard course time (agility)
Standpunkt vertreten take the view that
Stange pole
Stange (Geweih) branch
Stangenhürde (Agility) bar-jump (agility)
stark strong
Stärke power
stärken, sich fortify oneself
starkknochig of ample bone
Stärkungsmittel tonic, restorative
starren stare (at)
starrer Blick staring eye(s)
starrköpfig obstinate
Starrsinn obstinacy
Start start
startbereit ready to start
Startbox starting box
Startkasten starting box
Startlinie starting line
Startmannschaft starting team
Startpfahl (Fährtensuche) starting flag (tracking)
Statistik statistics
statistisch statistical
Statussymbol status symbol
staunen über be astonished at
Staupe canine distemper
Staupezähne distemper teeth
Stautasche stowage pocket
Steckenpferd hobbyhorse
Steg footpath
Steh! (Hörzeichen) Stand! (verbal command)
stehlen steal
Stehohr prickear
Stehvermögen endurance
steigern increase
steigern, sich increase
Steigerung increase
steil straight
Steilwand scaling wall
Steinbock ibex
steinig stony
Steirische Rauhaarige Hochgebirgsbracke Styrian Rough-Coated Alpine Hound

Steißgeburt breech delivery
Stellen und Verbellen (Schutzdienst) hold and bark (protection work)
Stellenwert rating
Stellung (Ansehen/ Rang) status
Stellung (des Körpers) position, stance (of the body)
Stellung und Anzahl der Zähne dentition
Stellung, soziale social rank
Steppenafghane Desert Afghan
Steppenowtscharka Caucasian Owtcharka
Steppenwindhund South Russian Steppen Hound
Sterbehilfe euthanasia
steril sterile
Sterilisation sterilization
sterilisieren sterilize
Steuermarke dog licence disc, revenue stamp
Stichelhaar bristle coat
stichelhaarig broken-coated
Stiefel boot
Stille silence
stillhalten keep still
stillstehen stand still
Stimmband vocal cord
Stimme voice
Stimme, mit lauter with loud voice
Stimme, mit leiser with soft voice
stinken stink
Stirn forehead
Stirnabsatz stop
Stirnbein frontal bone
Stirnfalte overnose wrinkle
Stirnfurche frontal groove
Stirnlocke forelock
Stirnstrich frontal line
Stöberhund springer
stöbern search for game
Stock stick
Stockhaar double coat
stockhaarig double-coated
Stockmaß height
Stofftunnel collapsed tunnel
stolpern (über) stumble (over)
stolz proud
Stoppelfeld stubble field
stoppelig stubbly
Stoppuhr stop watch
Stoppzone (Agility) pause area (agility)
stören disturb
Störenfried troublemaker
Störfaktor disruptive element
Störung disturbance
störungsfrei undisturbed
strafbar punishable
Strafe punishment
strafen punish
straffen tighten up

stramm firm
strangulieren strangle
Strapaze, strapazieren strain
strapazierfähig hardwearing
Straßenrand roadside
Straßenverkehr road traffic
Strategie strategy
sträuben (Fell) raise, bristle up
sträuben, sich rise up, resist
sträuben, sich ... gegen struggle against
streben zu move towards
strecken stretch
Streckmuskel extensor (muscle)
Streicheleinheiten love and attention
streicheln pet, stroke
streicheln, tätscheln petting
Streife nach dem Scheintäter (Schutzdienst) locating the agitator (protection work)
Streifen streak, stripe
streifen (Hürdensprung) touch (hurdle)
Streifschuss grazing shot
Streit argument
Streitfrage controversial issue
streitig contentious
streitlustig belligerent
streitsüchtig quarrelsome
Strenge strictness
Stress stress
stressen put someone under stress
stressfrei stress-free
stressgeplagt stressed-out
Stresshinweis stress indicator
stressig stressful
Stressoren stressors
streuen spread
streunen stray
Streuner stray dog
Strich, gegen den against the hair
Strich, mit dem with the hair
Strick cord
Striegel curry comb, slicker
striegeln curry
strikt strict
strikt, etwas ... ablehnen refuse something flatly
Stromung brindling
Struktur (des Haarkleides) texture (coat)
struppig (Fell) staring (hair or coat)
stubenrein house-trained, us: housebroken
stubenrein machen house-train
Stufe stage
stufenweise by degrees
Stuhl chair
Stuhlgang bowel movement, stool
stumm silent
Stummelrute docked tail
Stummelrutiger Cattle Dog Stumpy-Tail Cattle Dog

Stumpfnase pug nose
stumpfwinkelig obtuse
stupsen, anstupsen nudge
stur stubborn
stürmisch stormy
stürmt, es there's a gale blowing
stürzen fall
stürzen auf, sich fly (at), lunge (at)
Stuttgarter Hundeseuche canine leptospirosis
stutzen (Ohren) crop (ears)
stutzen (Rute) dock (tail)
subtil subtle
Such! (Hörzeichen) Find!, Search!, Seek! (verbal command)
Suche, suchen search
suchen (revieren, Schutzdienst) seek, quarter (protection work)
Suchgeschirr/ Fährtengeschirr tracking harness
Suchhund tracker, searching dog
Suchleine/ Fährtenleine tracking leash
Sudanwindhund Sudan Greyhound
Südrussischer Owtscharka South Russian Ovtcharka, South Russian Sheepdog
Sussex Spaniel Sussex Spaniel

Tablette pill
Tabu, tabuisieren taboo
Tabu setzen put under a taboo
tadeln blame
Tagebuch führen keep a diary
Tagesanbruch daybreak
Tagesbeste(r) best of day, best of show, best in field
täglich daily
tagsüber during the day
Tahltan Hund Tahltan Bear Dog
Tahl Tan Bärenhund Tahl Tan Bear Dog
Taille waist
Tal valley
Talbot Laufhund Talbot Hound
Talent talent
talentiert talented
talentlos untalented
Talgdrüse sebaceous gland
tänzeln prance
tänzelnd high-stepping, prancing
Tanzen mit dem Hund (Sportart) dog dancing (sport)
Tapferkeit bravery
Targetstick target stick
Targetstick, faltbarer folding target stick
Targetstickhalter(ung) target stick holder
tarnen camouflage
Tarsalgelenk tarsal joint
Tasche bag
Taschenmesser penknife
Tasthaar tactile hair
Tastsinn sense of touch
Tätowierung, tätowieren tattoo
Tatrahund Tatra Mountain Sheepdog
tätscheln pat
Tau(tropfen) dew(drop)
taub deaf
Taube pigeon

taubenblau pigeon blue
Taubheit deafness
tauchen dive
taugen für be suited for
Tauglichkeit suitability
Tausch, tauschen exchange
Tauschobjekt object of exchange
Täuschungsversuch attempt to deceive
Tauwetter thaw
Teamarbeit teamwork
Teckel Dachshund
Teich pond
Teigwaren pasta
teilen divide
Teilerfolg partial success
teilnahmeberechtigt eligible
Teilnahmslosigkeit apathy, listlessness, indifference
teilnehmen (im Sinne von wetteifern, konkurrieren) compete
teilnehmen an take part in
teilnehmen an einem Seminar attend a seminar
Teilnehmer(in) competitor
Teilnehmer(in), Prüfungs- participants
Teilnehmerzahl entry
Teilstück section
Teletakt-Gerät electronic collar (for training purposes)
Tellington Touch, TTouch Tellington Touch, TTouch
Temperament temperament
temperamentlos lifeless
Temperamentsveranlagung temper
temperamentvoll vivacious
Temperatur temperature
Tempo speed
Tempo, volles full speed
Tendenz tendency
Termitensuchhund termite detection dog
Terrain ground, terrain
Terrier Terrier
Terrierauge terrier-like eye
Terrierausdruck terrier appearance
Territorialverhalten territorial behaviour
Tervueren Belgian Tervueren
Tetanus lock jaw
Thai Ridgeback Thai Ridgeback Dog
Thema subject
Therapiehund therapy dog
Thermometer thermometer
These thesis
Thüringer Schäferhund Thuringian Shepherd Dog
Thymusdrüse thymus gland
Tibetanischer Löwenhund Shi Tzu, Chrysanthemum Dog
Tibet Spaniel Tibetan Spaniel
Tibet Terrier Tibetan Terrier

tief deep
tiefbrüstig deep chested
Tiefenschutz (Schutzdienst) underneath protection (protection work)
tiefrot deep red
tiefschwarz jet black
Tier animal
Tier, soziales social animal
Tierarzt veterinary surgeon, us: veterinarian, vet
Tierhalter(in) pet owner
Tierhandlung pet store
Tierheim animal shelter
Tierpfleger kennel help, animal care specialist
Tierquälerei cruelty to animals
Tierschutz animal welfare, protection of animals
Tierschutzgesetz animal welfare law
Tierschutzverein animal protection society
Tiervermehrer puppy mill operator, back yard breeder
Tigerung brindling
Tiroler Bracke Tyrolean Mountain Hound
Tisch (Agility) pause table (agility)
Titelverteidiger(in) titleholder
Todesangst fear of death
Todverbeller death howler
tolerant tolerant
Toleranz tolerance
tolerieren tolerate
Tollwut rabies, hydrophobia
Tollwutschutzimpfung rabies shot
Tonfall intonation
Tonne cask
tonnenförmig barrel shaped
Topographie topography
Torfhund Peat Bog Dog
Tosa Inu Japanese Fighting Dog (Tosa Inu)
tot beißen kill
tot geboren stillborn
Totgeburt stillbirth
Toy Foxterrier Toy Fox Terrier
Toy Pudel Toy Poodle
Toy Spaniel King Charles Spaniel
Trab, traben trot
Trab, verkürzter mincing trot
trächtig pregnant, gravid
Trächtigkeit pregnancy, gestation
Tragezeit (Schwangerschaft) gestation (period)
Trägheit sluggishness
Trainer(in) coach, trainer
Trainer, Übungsleiter instructor
Trainierbarkeit trainability
Training mit unangeleintem Hund off-lead training

Training, unter Wettkampfbedingungen practice dog-competition, practice matches
Training, konventionelles command-based training, traditional training
Training, mentales mental training
Training, schlechtes mistraining
Training, spielerisches play training
Training, über Zwang compulsory training
Trainingsanzug track suit
Trainingsassistenzhund training assistance dog
Trainingseinheit training session
Trainingsgerätschaften training tools
Trainingshilfsmittel training aids
Trainingsmethode training method
Trainingsmethode über positive Motivation positive motivational trainings method
Trainingsmethode, harte rough training method
Trainingsmethode, primitive primitive training method
Trainingsphase, -sequenz training sequence
Trainingstisch training table
Trainingszubehör training equipment
Tränendrüse lachrymal gland
Transponder-Kennzeichnung microchip identification
Transportbox crate, kennel
Transsylvanischer Spürhund Transsylvanian Hound
Trauer um mourning for
Trauma trauma
traumatisch traumatic
Trawler Spaniel Trawler Spaniel
Treeing Walker Coonhound Treeing Walker Coonhound
Treffen meeting
Treffpunkt meeting place
treiben (Vieh) drive (live-stock)
Treiber(in) auf der Jagd beater
Treibhund cattle dog
Treibjagd battue, drive
Treppe staircase
Tribüne (Stadion) terraces
Trieb instinct, drive
triebstark arbeiten high drive working
Triefauge watering eye
Trimmen stripping
trimmen trim
Trimmmesser stripping tool
Trimmschere grooming shears

Trimmtisch grooming table
trinken drink
Trockenergänzungsnahrung dry supplementary food
Trockenfutter dry dog food, kibble
Trockenheit dryness
tropfnass dripping wet
Trophäe trophy
trotten trot
Trotz defiance
Trubel bustle
Trüffel truffle
Trüffelsuchhund truffle dog
Trugschluss fallacy
Trümmerhaufen heap of rubble
Trümmersuchhund search and rescue dog
TSB (Trieb, Selbstsicherheit, Belastbarkeit) courage and hardness
Tschechischer Rauhaariger Vorstehhund Bohemian Griffon
Tschechischer Terrier Bohemian Terrier
Tschechoslowakischer Wolfshund Czechoslovakian Wolfhound
Tschika Chinese Greyhound
Tuareg Windhund Tuareg Greyhound
Tüpfelung, farbige belton
Tüpfelung, braune auf weiss liver belton
Tüpfelung, gelbe auf weiss lemon belton
Tüpfelung, orange auf weiss orange belton
Tüpfelung, schwarze auf weiss blue belton
Tulpenohr tulip ear
Tunnel tunnel
Tunnel aus Stoff collapsed tunnel
Tunnel, fester (Agility) pipe tunnel (agility)
Tunnel, flexibler (Agility) open tunnel (agility)
Tunneleingang (Agility) entrance of the tunnel (agility)
Tüpfel, Tupfen speckle
Tüpfelung speckling
Türkischer Nackthund Turkish Hairless Dog
Turkmenischer Windhund Turkmenian Greyhound
Tüte bag
Tweed Water Spaniel Tweed Water Spaniel
Typ type
typvoll typey
tyrannisieren tyrannize

üben practise
überängstlich overanxious
überbaut overbuilt
übereifrig overzealous
übereilen rush something
Übereinstimmung conformity
überempfindlich hypersensitive
Überfall attack
Überfall (Schutzdienst) surprise attack (protection work)
überfordern demanding too much
überfüttern overfeed
Übergangsphase transition(al) period
übergehen zu transition to
Übergröße outsize
überholen pass
überhören (Worte) ignore
überladen overloaded
überlegen sein dominant
Überlegenheit superiority
überreagieren overreact
überspielen (Fehler, Schwächen) cover something up
überspringen jump over
Übersprungshandlung displacement (or sparking-over) activity
Übersprungsverhalten redirected behaviour
übertragbar (medizinisch) infectious (medical)
übertrainiert over exercised, over trained
übertreten overreach
übertrieben excessive
überwachen check
überwinden (z.B. Angst) overcome (e.g. fear)
überwinkelt over angulated
Überwinkelung excessive angulation
überzeugen convince
überzüchtet hyper refined

Jberzüchtung excessive breeding
Jberzug cover
Jbung (Aufgabe) exercise
Jbungen aus der Bewegung motion exercises
Übungsleiter(in) training director
Jbungsleiter, Trainer instructor
Übungsplatz dog training site
Übungssache, reine it's just a matter of practice
Übungssprung (Hürde) practice jump
Übungsstunde training session, (dog) class
Uhrzeigersinn clockwise
umbenennen rename
umdenken change one's view
Umerziehung re-education
Umfang girth
Umfeld surrounding
Umfeld, familiäres family environment
Umgang mit Hunden handling with dogs
umgänglich sociable
Umgebung environment
umgehen, er kann mit Hunden ... he has a way with dogs
umgekehrt reverse
umkreisen circle round
umlernen relearn
umreißen (umstoßen) knock down
Umriss outline
umschalten switch
Umschlag, kalter cool pack
Umschlag, warmer warm pack
umschnallen buckle on
umschwenken wheel round
umsehen, sich look around
Umsicht circumspection
Umstehende bystanders
umwandeln change
Umwelt environment
Umwelteinfluss environmental impact
Umweltgeräusch-Kassette für Welpen puppy racket audiotape
Umweltgewöhnung habituation to the environment
Umweltsicherheit environmental safety
umwenden, sich turn round
unabsichtlich unintentional
unangemessen inadequate
unangenehm unpleasant
Unart bad habit
unartig naughty
Unartigkeit naughtiness
unaufgefordert unasked
unaufmerksam inattentive
Unaufmerksamkeit inattention
unausgeglichen unbalanced

Unausgeglichenheit imbalance
unausgewogen unbalanced
Unausgewogenheit imbalance
unbeachtet lassen disregard
unbegabt untalented
unbehaglich uncomfortable
unbeherrscht lacking self-control
unbekannt unknown
unbemerkt unnoticed
unbeobachtet unobserved
unberechenbar incalculable
unberücksichtigt unconsidered
unbeständig unsteady
unbestätigt unconfirmed
unbeweglich immobile
unbewusst unconscious
undiszipliniert undisciplined
unempfindlich insensitive
unerfahren inexperienced
unerfreulicherweise unfortunately
unerheblich insignificant
unerlaubt unauthorized
unerschrocken brave, game, dauntless, fearless
unerträglich unbearable
unerwartet unpredictable
unerwünscht undesirable
unfähig unqualified
unfair unfair
unfolgsam disobedient
unfreiwillig unintentional
unfreundlich unfriendly
unfruchtbar infertile
Unfruchtbarkeit infertility
Ungarischer Vorstehhund Hungarian Pointer
Ungarischer Windhund Hungarian Greyhound
ungeduldig impatient
ungefährlich harmless
ungehindert unhindered
Ungehorsam disobedience
ungehorsam disobedient
ungekämmt uncombed ungroomed
ungeladen (Waffe) unloaded
ungepflegt neglected
ungerecht unjust
ungeregelt(es Leben) irregular
ungern unwillingly, grudgingly
ungeschützt unprotected, exposed
ungesetzlich illegal, unlawful
ungestört undisturbed, uninterrupted
ungestraft unpunished
ungestüm vehement, impetuous
ungesund unhealthy
ungeübt untrained, unskilled
Ungeübtheit lack of training
ungewöhnlich unusual
ungewohnt strange
ungewollt unintentional

Ungeziefer vermin, external parasite(s)
Ungezieferpuder flea powder
Ungeziefershampoo flea shampoo
Ungezieferspray flea spray
ungezwungen relaxed
ungleichmäßig uneven
ungültig invalid
unharmonisch discordant
unhöflich impolite
uninteressant uninteresting
unklar unclear
unkompliziert uncomplicated
unkontrollierbar uncontrollable
unkontrolliert uncontrolled
unlösbar insoluble
unmittelbar, sofort immediately
unmotiviert unmotivated
unplatziert unplaced, out of the ribbons
unreif unripe
unruhig restless
unsachgemäß improper
unsicher insecure
Unsicherheit insecurity
Unsicherheitsfaktor element of uncertainty
unsozial antisocial
unsympathisch disagreeable
Unterarm forearm
Unterart subspecies
Unterbiss overbite
unterbrechen interrupt
unterbringen accommodate
unterdrücken repress, suppress
Unterdrückung repression
Unterdrückung von Verhaltensweisen suppression of behaviour
unterdurchschnittlich below average
Unterernährung malnutrition
untergeordnet subordinate
Unterholz undergrowth
Unterkiefer lower jaw
unterlegen inferior
Unterlegenheit inferiority
Unterleib belly
Unterlid lower eyelid
unterliegen be defeated
unterordnen subordinate
unterordnen, sich submit
Unterordnung subordination
Unterordnung (Gehorsam)/ Obedience obedience
Unterordnungsarbeit obedience training
Unterordnungsring obedience ring
Unterordnungsübung obedience exercise
Unterordnungswettbewerb obedience trial
unterscheiden distinguish
Unterschenkel shank
Unterschied difference

unterstützen assist
unterstützen/ helfen aid
untersuchen investigate
Untersuchung investigation
Unterwerfung submission, subjection, subjugation
Unterwolle undercoat
unterwürfig, demütig subservient, submissive
Unterwürfigkeitsverhalten submissive behaviour
Unterzieharm (Schutzdienst) hidden sleeve (protection work)
untypisch atypical, not typical
unverdaut undigested
unvereinbar incompatible
unverstanden misunderstood
Unverträglichkeit (Futter) intolerance (of food)
Unverträglichkeit mit Hunden incompatibility (with other dogs)
unvollkommen rudimentary
unvorbereitet unprepared
unvorhergesehen unforeseen, unexpected
unvorhersehbar unpredictable
unwirksam ineffective
unzeitgemäß old-fashioned
unzuverlässig unreliable
üppig profuse
Urin urine
urinieren urinate
Urinieren, unterwürfiges involuntary (or submissive) urination
Urkunde certificate, document
Ursache cause
Urtyp primitive type

Vaghari Vaghari Hound
Vallhund Swedish Vallhund
variabel variable
Variation variation
variieren vary
Vater(tier) father
Veadeiro Catarinense Brazilian Greyhound
Vene vein
verabreichen administer
verallgemeinern generalize
verängstigt frightened
Veranlagung disposition
Veranlagungsprüfung aptitude test
veranlassen induce
veranstalten organize
Veranstalter(in) organizer
Veranstalter, Ausrichter organizer, sponsor
Veranstaltungskalender calendar of events
verantworten take the responsibility for
verantwortlich, verantwortungsbewusst responsible
Verantwortlichkeit responsibility
verarbeiten (Eindrücke) digest
verbeißen, sich sink its teeth into
verbellen bark at
verbessern improve
Verbindung mating
verboten forbidden
verdauen digest
Verdaulichkeit digestibility
Verdauung digestion
verdeutlichen, jemandem etwas make something clear to someone
verdursten die of thirst
verdutzt nonplussed
vereinbar mit compatible with
vereinfachen simplify

Vereinfachung simplification
vereinsamen become isolated
Vereinsamung isolation
Vereinsheim/-haus clubhouse
Vereinskamerad(in) club mate
vereitert infected
Vererblichkeit heredity
verfeinern refine
verfilzen mat
Verfilzung matting
verflochten tangled
verfolgen chase
Verfolgen und Stellen (Schutzdienst) follow and hold (protection work)
verfüttern feed
Vergangenheitsbewältigung coming to terms with the past
vergeben award
vergessen forget
vergewissern, sich make sure
vergiften poison
Vergiftung poisoning
Vergleich, im ... zu compared to
Vergnügen, Freude enjoyment
Verhalten behaviour, us: behavior
verhalten, sich behave
Verhalten anbieten offer behaviours
Verhalten ändern changing behaviour
Verhalten, anhaltendes long-duration behaviour
Verhalten, antrainiertes trained behaviour
Verhalten, arttypisches specific behaviour
Verhalten, Aufmerksamkeit forderndes attention seeking behaviour
Verhalten, erlerntes learned behaviour
Verhalten, feindliches hostile behaviour
Verhalten, operantes operant behaviour
Verhalten, unerwünschtes undesired, unwanted behaviour
Verhalten, unvereinbares incompatible behaviour
Verhaltensänderung behaviour modification
Verhaltensauffälligkeit behavioural disorder
Verhaltensforscher(in) behavioural scientist
Verhaltensforschung behavioural science
verhaltensgestört maladjusted
Verhaltenskette behaviour chain
Verhaltenskette, rückwärts back chaining
Verhaltensketten bilden repertoire cuing

Verhaltensmuster behavioural pattern
Verhaltensstörung abnormal behaviour
Verhaltenstherapie behaviour therapy
Verhaltenstraining behaviour modification training
Verhältnis relation
verharmlosen play something down
verharren (in einer Haltung) freeze (in a position)
verhätscheln coddle
verhindern prevent
verhungern die of starvation
verinnerlichen internalize
verjagen chase away
verjüngen, sich taper
verkleben mat
verknöchern ossify
verkraften cope with
verkriechen, sich hide
verkrümmt crooked
verkümmern become stunted
verkümmert rudimentary
verlangen require
verlangsamen (Tempo) slacken
verlässlich reliable
Verleitungsfährte decoy track
Verletzung (an) injury (to)
Verlierer(in) loser
verlocken tempt
Verlockung temptation
Verlorenbringer (Jagd) a dog that can find and retrieve wounded game (hunting)
Verlorensuche search for (wounded game/ a lost object)
vermehren, sich breed
vermeiden avoid
vermenschlichen humanize
vermenschlichend anthropomorphism
vermuten suppose
Vernachlässigung, vernachlässigen neglect
verpaaren breed
Verpaarung mate
verprügeln thrash
Verrenkung dislocation
verringern reduce
Versagen failure
versagen refuse
versammeln assemble
Versäuberungsplatz, Abkotstelle exercise area
versäumen etwas zu tun fail to do something
verscharren bury
verschlechtern, sich deteriorate
Verschlechterung deterioration
verschleiert veiled
verschlimmern make worse
verschlingen devour, wolf down
verschlucken swallow

verschreiben prescribe
verschweigen conceal
verschwinden disappear
Versicherung insurance
Versicherungsgesellschaft insurance company
Versicherungsschutz insurance cover
verspannen stay
verspielt playful
Verständigung communication
Verständigungsprobleme communication problems
verständlich comprehensible
verständnislos uncomprehending
Verständnislosigkeit lack of understanding
verständnisvoll understanding
Verstauchung sprain
verstauen stow away
Versteck hiding place
Versteck (Schutzdienst) blind (protection work)
Versteck(en) spielen play hide-and-seek
verstecken, hinter etwas hide behind something
verstecken, sich ... vor hide from
versteckt hidden
verstehen comprehend
verstehen, sich get along with each other
versteifen stiffen
Verstopfung constipation
verstört badly upset
Verstörtheit confusion
Verstoß (gegen) offence (against)
verstoßen aus cast somebody out of
verstreuen scatter
verstümmeln mutilate
Verstümmelung mutilation
Versuch (Bemühung) effort
Versuch (Sport) attempt
Versuchsbedingung test condition
Versuchsreihe series of tests
Versuchstier experimental animal
versuchsweise by way of trial
verteidigen defend
verteidigen gegen defend against
Verteidigung defence
Verteidigungsbereitschaft preparedness for defence
Verteidigungsbiss defensive bite
verteilen distribute
Verteilung distribution
vertiefen (Lehrstoff) consolidate
Vertiefung (geistige) absorption

Vertiefung (im Gelände) depression
verträglich sein be easy to get along with
Vertrauen, vertrauen trust
Vertrauensbeweis mark of confidence
Vertrauensbruch breach of trust
Vertrauensperson reliable person
Vertrauenssache, das ist that's a matter of confidence
Vertrauensverlust loss of confidence
vertrauensvoll trustful, confident
vertrauenswürdig trustworthy
vertreiben, jemanden/ etwas drive somebody/ something away
vertretbar acceptable
verübeln, etwas take something amiss
verunsichern, jemanden make someone feel insecure
vervollkommnen perfect
Vervollkommnung perfection
vervollständigen complete
Vervollständigung completion
verwahrlosen be neglected
verwahrlosen lassen neglect
verwahrlost neglected
Verwahrlosung neglect
verwandeln, sich transform
verwandt (mit) related (to)
Verwandtschaftsgrad degree of relationship
Verwarnung warning
verwaschen washed out
verwechseln (mit) confuse (with)
Verwechslung confusion
verwehen (Spuren) cover up
verwehren refuse
verweichlichen, jemanden make someone soft
verweigern refuse
Verweigern eines Kommandos disobey an order
Verweigerung refusal
Verweildauer length of stay
verweilen stay
verweisen (Fährtengegenstand) identify, indicate (article)
verwendbar usable
Verwendungsbereich range of use
verwildern return the wild state
verwildert gone wild
verwirren confuse
verwirrt (Fell) tangled (coat)
verwöhnen spoil
verwundet wounded
Verwundung wound
verwüsten devastate
Verwüstung devastation
Verzagtheit despondency
verzärteln mollycoddle

Verzicht renunciation
verzichten auf do without
verzogen (verwöhnt) spoilt
verzögern (verlangsamen) slow down
Verzögerung, verzögern delay
verzweifeln despair
verzweifelt despairing
Verzweiflungstat act of desperation
verzwickt complicated
Veterinär(in) veterinary surgeon, veterinarian, vet
V-förmig (Ohr) v-shaped (ear)
Videokamera video camera
Vieh cattle
Vieh(bestand) live-stock
vielerorts in many places
vielfarbig multicoloured
vielschichtig complex
vielseitig many-sided
Vielseitigkeit versatility
Vielseitigkeitsprüfung versatility trial
vielversprechend promising
Vielzahl multitude
Vieraugenflecken melon pips
vierbeinig four-legged
Virus virus
visuell visual
vital fit
Vitalität vitality
Vitamin vitamin(e)
vitaminarm poor in vitamins
Vitamingehalt vitamin content
vitaminhaltig containing vitamins
Vitaminmangel vitamin deficiency
Vitaminpräparat vitamin preparation
vitaminreich rich in vitamins
Vitrine showcase
Vize-Vorsitzende(r) vice-president
Vizsla Drahthaar Wirehaired Vizsla
Vizsla Kurzhaar Shorthaired Vizsla
Vogelhund bird dog
Vollanzug (Ringsport) full body suit (mondioring)
vollbringen accomplish
vollentwickelt full-grown
Vollnahrung commercially prepared balanced dog food
Vollnarkose general narcosis
Vollversammlung plenary assembly
vollwertig of high value
Vollwertkost whole foods
Vollzahnigkeit full dentition
Volpino Italiano Italian Spitz, Florentine Spitz
Vor- und Nachteile abwägen consider the pros and cons

Voran! (Hörzeichen)
Forward! (verbal command)
Voran/ Voraus! (Hörzeichen)
Go (out)! (verbal command)
vorausdenken look ahead
vorausschauend foresighted
vorausschicken send-out, send-away
Voraussicht anticipation
vorbeifahren drive past
vorbeigehen pass by
vorbeilassen, jemanden let someone pass
Vorbeißer dog with undershot mouth
vorbelastet, erblich have a hereditary handicap
vorbereiten (eines Hundes)
prepare (a dog)
vorbereiten auf prepare for
Vorbereitung preparation
Vorbericht history, preliminary report
Vorbesprechung
preliminary talk
vorbeugen prevent
vorbildlich exemplary
Vorbiss undershot mouth (or jaw)
Vorbrunst proestrus
Vorbrust forechest
Vorder- anterior
Vorderfuß front paw
Vorderfußwurzelgelenk
carpal joint
Vorderhand forequarters
Vorderhandwinkelung
front angulation
Vorderlauf front leg
Vordermittelfuß pastern
Vordermittelfußknochen
metacarpal bones
Vorderpfote front paw
vordrängen, sich push forward
Vorfall incident
vorführen perform, present
Vorführer(in) handler
Vorführkunst showmanship
Vorführleine show leash
Vorführung performance
Vorführung (im Show-Ring)
handling (in show)
Vorführung der Spitzenklasse
peak performance
Vorführungswettbewerb
handling competition
Vorführungswettbewerb für Jugendliche junior handling competition
Vorgabe (Bedingung)
precondition
Vorgabezeit allowed time
vorgebogen knuckling over
Vorgeschichte prehistory
Vorgesicht foreface

vorgreifen (in einer Sache) anticipate something
Vorhaut, Vorhautschlauch foreskin
Vorhof vestibule
Vorkaufsrecht right of pre-emption
Vorkenntnisse previous knowledge
vorlassen, jemanden let someone go first
Vorlauf (im Wettkampf) preliminary course
vorläufig temporary
Vorliebe für preference for
Vorliebe, etwas mit ... tun love doing something
Vormilch colostrum
Vorplatz forecourt
Vorprüfung preliminary examination
Vorrangstellung pre-eminence
Vorrecht privilege
Vorschlag suggestion
vorschlagen suggest
vorschnell hasty
Vorschrift instruction
Vorsekret preliminary fraction (of the canine ejaculate)
Vorsicht – Bissiger Hund! Beware of the dog!
Vorsichtsmaßnahme precaution measure
Vorsichtsmaßnahmen treffen take precautions
Vorsitz front position
Vorsitzende(r), Vorstand president
Vorstandsmitglied member of the board
Vorstandssitzung board meeting
Vorstandsvorsitzende(r) chairman (chairwoman) of the board
Vorstandswahl board elections
Vorsteherdrüse prostate gland
Vorstehhund pointer
Vorstehhundrute beesting tail
Vorstufe preliminary stage
Vorteil advantage
Vortrag lecture
Vortragssaal lecture hall
Vorurteil prejudice
vorverdaut pre-digested
vorwiegend predominant
vorwürgen (Futter für Welpen) regurgitate (food for pups)
vorzeitig premature
Vulva vulva

wachen über watch over
Wachhund guard dog, watchdog
wachsam watchful, alert, vigilant, guarding
Wachsamkeit watchfulness, vigilance
Wachstum growth
Wachtelhund German Spaniel
wackeln wobble
Wadenbein fibula
wagen, sich trauen venture
Wahl(möglichkeit) choice
wahllos indiscriminate
wahlweise alternatively
wahrnehmbar perceptible
wahrnehmen perceive
Wahrnehmung perception
Wahrnehmung (Beobachtung) observation
Wahrnehmungsvermögen perceptive faculty
wahrscheinlich probably
Wahrscheinlichkeit probability
Waidlaut giving tongue, voice
Waidloch anal opening
Wald forest
Waldgebiet wooded area
Waldrand edge of the forest
wälzen (in Schmutz/ Kot/ Aas) wallow (in mud/ faeces/ carrion)
wälzen, hin- und her toss and turn
wälzen, sich roll
Wamme dewlap
Wanderer, Wanderin wanderer
wandern hike, walk
Wanderpokal challenge cup
Wanderung walking tour
Wanderweg footpath
Wange cheek
Wangenmuskel cheek muscle
Wärme warmth
wärmen warm up
warnen vor warn against
Warnschild warning sign
Warnung warning

warten wait
Waschbärenhund Coonhound
Wasser water
Wasser lassen urinate
wasserabstoßend water-repellent
Wasserarbeit water work
Wasserflasche water bottle
wasserfreudig taking readily to water
Wassergraben ditch
Wassergraben (Agility) water jump (agility)
Wasserhaushalt water supply
Wasserhund water dog
Wasserkopf hydrocephalus
Wassermangel water shortage
Wassernapf, faltbarer collapsible water bowl
wasserscheu afraid of water
Wasserscheue hydrophobia
Wasserspaniel Water Spaniel
Wassersuche sport of water trial
Wasservogel water bird
Wattierung padding
Wechsel, Wild- (Jagd) game trail (hunting)
Wechselbeziehung interrelation
Wechselgelände (z.B. Fährtenarbeit) mixed terrain (e.g. tracking)
wechselseitig mutual
Wechselwirkung interaction
wedeln wag
wedeln mit der Rute wag its tail
weder ... noch neither ... nor
Weg zum Erfolg road to success
Wegdrehbewegung turning manoeuvre
weggehen go away
wegjagen chase away
wegkommen, gut/ schlecht (Sport) come off well/ bad (sport)
weglaufen run away
wegnehmen, etwas take something away
wegschicken, jemanden send someone away
wegschleppen, etwas drag something off
wegschnappen, etwas snatch something away
wegsehen look away
wegziehen, etwas pull something away
Wehen contractions
Wehenspritze labour-inducing injection
wehren, den Anfängen nip things in the bud
wehren, sich (gegen) defend oneself (against)
wehrlos defenceless
Wehrlosigkeit defencelessness
Wehrtrieb instinct to protect

wehtun hurt
weich soft
Weiche flank
Weichteile soft parts
weidmännisch huntsman like
Weidmannsheil! Good sport!
weigern, sich refuse
Weimaraner Vorstehhund Weimaraner
Weisheit wisdom
weiß white
weiß bestrumpft with white stockings
Weißer Schäferhund American-Canadian White Shepherd
weißgelb fawn
Weisung instruction
weiterarbeiten go on working
weitergehen go on
weiterempfehlen recommend
weiterentwickeln develop further
weitererzählen tell others
weiterführen, fortführen continue
weiterhelfen, jemandem help someone on
weiterkämpfen continue fighting
Weitsprung (Agility) long jump (agility)
weizenfarben wheaten
Wellhaar hair with wavy undercoat
wellig wavy
Welpe puppy
Welpenaufzucht, künstliche hand raising
Welpenerziehung puppy training
Welpengitter puppy pen
Welpenhalsband puppy collar
Welpenkurs puppy class
Welpenmilch puppy formula
Welpennahrung puppy food
Welpenschule puppy kindergarten
Welpenschutz puppy licence
Welpensterben fading puppy syndrome
Welpentest puppy test
Welsh Corgi Cardigan Welsh Corgi Cardigan
Welsh Corgi Pembroke Welsh Corgi Pembroke
Welsh Springer Spaniel Welsh Springer Spaniel
Welsh Collie Welsh Collie
Welsh Gray Herder Welsh Gray Herder
Welsh Hound Welsh Hound
Welsh Red Herder Welsh Red Herder
Welsh Terrier Welsh-Terrier, Old English Terrier

Weltanschauung ideology
Welthundeausstellung world dog show
Weltmeister(in) world champion
Weltmeisterschaft world championship
Wendepunkt turning point
Wendigkeit agility
Wendung turn
Werdegang, hundesportlicher dog sport career
werfen throw
werfen (gebären) whelp
Wertschätzung esteem
Wertung, (Ergebnis) score
Wertungsaspekte scoring considerations
Wertungsergebnis scoring issue
Wertungssystem scoring systems
Werturteil value judgement
Wertvorstellungen values
Wesen, Wesensart character
wesensfest of steady character, of steady temperament
Wesensprüfung test of character
Wesensschwäche faulty character
West Country Harrier West Country Harrier
Westfälische Dachsbracke Westphalian Hound
Westgotenspitz Swedish Vallhund
West Highland White Terrier West Highland White Terrier
Westsibirische Laika West Siberian Laika
Wettbewerb competition, trial
Wettbewerb im Freien outdoor-competition
Wettbewerb in der Halle indoor-competition
Wettbewerbsgelände trial grounds
Wetter weather
Wetterbedingungen weather conditions
Wetterhound Dutch Water Spaniel
Wettkampfstart (als Training) practice matches (training)
Whippet Whippet
widerlegbar refutable
Widerrist shoulders
Widerristhöhe height at shoulders
widersetzen, sich put up resistance
widerspenstig obstinate
widerspiegeln reflect
widerstandsfähig sturdy
wiederbringen, etwas bring something back

Viedereingliederung/-einfügung eincorporating
viederholen repeat
Wiederholung repetition
Wiederholungsimpfung booster shot (or vaccination), evaccination
Wiese meadow
Wild game
Wilddieb poacher
wildern (durch Hunde) kill game
wildfarben agouti
Wildgehege game preserve
Wildhund feral dog
Wildpark game park
Wildruhe silence of game
Wildschwein wild boar
Willensfreiheit freedom of will
willfährig amenable
willig willing
Willkür, jemandes ... ausgeliefert sein be at someone's mercy
willkürlich arbitrary
wimmern whine
Wimper eyelash
Wimpernreihe, doppelte distichiasis
Windhund Sight Hound
Windhundhalsband sight hound collar, racing collar
Windhundjagd coursing
Windhundohr rose ear
Windhundrennbahn race course
Windrichtung direction of the wind
Windspiel Italian Greyhound
Windstärke wind force
Windstoß gust of wind
Winkel angle
Winkel (Fußarbeit) half-turn (heelwork)
Winkel verkürzen/ schneiden (Fährtenarbeit) corner-cutting (tracking)
Winkelkopf downfaced head
Winkelung angulation
winseln whine
Winterpause winter break
winzig tiny
Wippe (Agility) seesaw (agility)
Wirbel vertebra (plural: vertebrae)
Wirbelsäule vertebral column, spine
Wirbeltier vertebrate
wirksam effective
Wirksamkeit effectiveness
Wirkung effect
wirkungslos ineffective
wirkungsvoll effective
Wirkungsweise mode of operation
Wissen knowledge

Wissen, lückenhaftes sketchy knowledge
Witterung, wittern scent
Witterung aufnehmen take the scent
Witterungseinflüsse influence of the weather
witterungslos scentless
wohlerzogen well-behaved
Wohngebiet residential area
Wohnung flat
Wohnungshund house-dog
Wohnverhältnisse housing conditions
Wölbung arch
Wolf wolf
Wolfsmischling wolf hybrid
wolfsfarben wolf grey
wolfsgrau wolf grey
Wolfsklaue, Wolfskralle dewclaw
wolfsstreifig brindle
Wollhaar wooly hair
Wollhaariger Griffon Woolyhared Griffon
Working Sheepdog Border Collie
Working Terrier Working Terrier
Wucht force
Wucht, mit voller with full force
wuffen woof
Wunde wound
Wundfährte blood trail
wünschenswert desirable
Würde dignity
Wurf litter
Wurfgeschwister littermate
Wurfgröße litter size
Wurfkette throw chain
Wurfkiste whelping box
Wurfmeldung whelping report
Wurfspiele play fetch
Würgehalsband, Würger choke collar
Würgekette choke chain
würgen strangle
Wurm worm
Wurmbefall worm infestation
Wurmkur worming
Wurmmittel vermifuge, wormer
Wurst sausage
Württemberger Kurzhaariger Vorstehhund Wurttemberg Pointer
Wuschelhund mop dog
Wüstenafghane Desert-Type Afghanhound
Wut rage
Wutanfall outburst of rage

XY

Xarnelo Ibizan Hound
x-fach ever so often
Xoloitzcuintle
Mexican Hairless Dog

Yorkshire Terrier
Yorkshire Terrier

zaghaft timid
zäh tough
zahm domesticated
zähmen domesticate
Zahmheit tameness
Zahn tooth, (plural: teeth)
Zähne, vorstehende protrudering teeth
Zähne fletschen showing one's teeth, snarling
Zähneklappern teeth chattering
Zahnfleischentzündung peridontal disease
Zahnkontrolle bite and teeth inspection
zahnlos toothless
Zahnschluss occlusion
Zahnstein plaque
Zahnstellung dentition
Zahnwechsel second dentition, teething
Zangenbiss level bite, even bite
Zangengebiss pincer bite
zaudern hesitate
Zaun fence
Zecke tick
Zeckenband tick collar
Zeckenzange tick tweezers
Zeh(e) toe
Zehen, offene splay feet
Zehenballen toe pad
Zehengänger digitigrade animal
Zehenknochen phalanges
Zeichen sign
Zeigefinger forefinger
zeigen demonstrate
zeigen, seine Macht demonstrate someone's power
zeigen, von seiner besten Seite present oneselfs' best advantage
Zeigestock target stick
Zeitablauf timing
zeitaufwändig time-consuming
Zeitdruck time pressure
Zeitdruck, unter ... stehen be pressed for time

Zeitfaktor time factor
Zeitfenster limited hold
zeitgemäß current
Zeitgewinn time gained
Zeitmangel lack of time
Zeitnehmer(in) timer
zeitraubend time-consuming
Zeitraum space of time
zeitsparend time-saving
Zeitungsmeldung press item
zerfetzen, etwas tear something in pieces
zerfleddern tatter
zerfleischen mangle
zerkauen chew
zerkratzen scratch
zernagen gnaw
zerreißen, etwas tear something up
zerren drag, pull, strain, tug
zerren (an der Leine) pull (on leash)
Zerrspiel tug-of-war
Zerrspielzeug, -seil tug toy
zerstören destroy
Zerstörung destruction
Zerstörungstrieb destruction instinct
zerteilen divide
Zertifikat certificate
Zeugnis der Anwartschaft auf das internationale FCI-Arbeitschampionat CACIT certificate of aptitude for the international utility championship CACIT
Zeugnis der Anwartschaft auf das internationale FCI-Schönheitschampionat CACIB certificate of aptitude for the international beauty championship CACIB
Zeugnis der Anwartschaft auf das Schönheitschampionat challenge certificate CC (uk)
zeugungsfähig fertile
Zeugungsfähigkeit fertility
zeugungsunfähig infertile, steril
Zeugungsunfähigkeit infertility, sterility
Ziegenbart chin whiskers
Ziehhund cart dog
Ziel, End- goal, finish, objective
ziellos aimless
Zielpunkt target
Zielrichter(in) line judge
Zielsetzung objective
zielstrebig determined
Zielstrebigkeit determination
Zielverhalten, Zielübung goal behaviour
Zirkushund circus dog
ziseliert chiselled

Ziselierung chiselling
Zitat quotation
zitieren quote
zittern tremble
Zitze nipple
zobelfarben gold sable
Zögern, ohne without hesitation
zögernd hesitating
Zollhund customs dog
Zoonose zoonosis
Zorn anger
Zornausbruch fit of anger
zornig über angry at
Zottel braided tug toy
Zottelhaar corded coat
zottelhaarig corded
zuallererst first of all
zuallerletzt last of all
Zubehör accessories
zubeißen bite
zublinzeln, jemandem wink at someone
Zucht breeding
Zucht, einstellen zur place at stud
Zucht, wilde backyard breeding
Zuchtaltersbeschränkung age limitation for breeding
Zuchtbuch studbook
Zuchtdaten breeding particulars
züchten breed
Züchter(in) breeder
Zuchtgruppe breeder's group
Zuchtgruppenwettbewerb breeder's class
Zuchthündin brood bitch
Zuchtklasse bred-by class
Zuchtmaterial breeding stock
Zuchtprogramm breeding program
Zuchtrichter conformation judge
Zuchtrüde stud dog
Zuchtschau dog show
Zuchtschauordnung show regulations
Zuchtstamm strain
Zuchttauglichkeitsprüfung examination as to suitability for breeding
Zuchttier breeding animal
Zuchtverband breeders' association
Zuchtverein breed club
Zuchtverwendung utilization as breeding stock
Zuchtwahl selection for breeding
Zuchtwart(in) breed warden
Zuchtwertschätzung evaluation of breeding potential
Zuchtziel(e) breeding goal(s)
Zuchtzulassung permit to be bred with

Zuchtzulassungsprüfung examination as to suitability for breeding
Zuckerbrot und Peitsche, mit ... with a stick and a carrot
Zuckung convulsion
zudecken cover up
zudrehen, den Rücken turn one's back on someone
zudringlich obtrusive
zueinander each other
zuerkennen award
Zufall chance
zufällig accidental, random
Zufälligkeit coincidence
Zufallsbestärkung random reinforcement, contingencies of reinforcement
Zufallspaarung random mating
Zufallstreffer lucky hit
zufassen take hold of it
Zufriedenheit, innere contentment
zugänglich für accessible to
zugelassen admitted, licensed
zugestehen concede
zugestehen, erlauben (dem Hund) empowering (the dog)
Zughalsband choke collar
Zughalsband, gestopptes humane choke collar
Zughund cart dog
zukunftsweisend forward-looking
zulassen, etwas permit
zulässig permitted
Zulassung licence
Zulassungsalter minimum age requirement
zumuten, sich zuviel overdo things
Zunge tongue
züngeln licking
Zungenbein hyoid bone
Zungenblecken tongue lolling
zunicken, jemandem nod to someone
zunicken, jemandem freundlich give someone a friendly nod
Zurechtweisung, zurechtweisen rebuke
Zurück! (Hörzeichen) Back! (verbal command)
zurückgeben, den Ball pass the ball back
zurückhaltend reserved, aloof
Zurückhaltung reserve
zurückholen, etwas bring something back
zurückkehren return
zurücklaufen run back
zurückrufen, jemanden call someone back
zurückscheuen shrink back

zurückschicken, jemanden send someone back
zurückschrauben (Ansprüche) cut down
zurückschrecken vor recoil from
zurückspringen jump back
zurückweichen step back
zurückziehen (von Teilnahme) pull (a dog from competition)
Zusage promise word
Zusammenarbeit cooperation
Zusammenarbeit (Hund und Mensch) teamwork
zusammengehören belong together
Zusammenhang connection
Zusammenleben live together
zusammenstoßen clash
zusammentun putting together
Zuschauer(in) spectator
zuschnappen snap
zusehen look on
zusehen, untätig sit back and watch
zuspringen auf rush up at
Zustand state
zuständig competent
zustimmen, jemandem agree to somebody
Zustimmung agreement
zustürzen auf rush up
Zutaten ingredients
Zutrauen confidence
Zutrauen fassen begin to have confidence
zutraulich friendly, confiding
Zutraulichkeit friendliness, confidingness
zuverlässig reliable
Zuverlässigkeit reliability
Zuversicht confidence, trust
Zuwachs increment
zuwachsen (Wunde) heal up
zuwenden (das Gesicht) face somebody
zuwenden (den Rücken) turn one's back on someone
zuwenden, sich turn to
Zuwendung attention
Zwang, Druck pressure
Zwang, etwas ohne ... tun do something without being forced to
Zwang, Gewalt force
Zwang, psychischer compulsion
zwanglos (Verhalten) be free and easy
Zwanglosigkeit informality
Zwangsausbildung compulsory training
Zweck purpose
Zweck der Übung whole point of the exercise
zwecklos pointless
zweckmäßig functional

Zweierkoppel brace
zweifarbig bicolour
Zweifel, zweifeln doubt
Zweikampf duel
Zweitagesprüfung two-day trial
Zweitplatzierte(r) runner-up
Zwerchfell diaphragm
Zwergbullterrier Miniature Bull Terrier
Zwergdachshund Miniature Dachshund
Zwergfoxterrier Toy Fox Terrier
Zwerghund miniature dog
Zwergpinscher Miniature Pinscher
Zwergpudel Toy Poodle
Zwergschnauzer Miniature Schnauzer
Zwergspaniel English Toy Spaniel
Zwergspitz Toy German Spitz
Zwergteckel Toy Dachshund
Zwergwindhund Italian Greyhound
Zwergwuchs dwarfism
zwicken pinch
Zwinger kennel building, kennels
Zwingerhaltung kennelling
Zwingerhusten kennel cough
Zwingername kennel name
Zwingerwart kennel help
zwinkern blink
Zwischenbelohnung (in Verhaltenskette) selective reinforcement (behaviour chain)
Zwischenzehen interdigital
Zwischenzehenhaut webbing (between toes)
Zwischenzehenraum interdigital space
Zwittertum hermaphroditism
Zwölffingerdarm duodenum
zyklisch cyclic
Zylinderepithel cylindrical epithelion

ENGLISCH – DEUTSCH

paw → Pfote

abdomen Bauch
abdominal aorta Bauchschlagader
abdominal cavity Bauchhöhle
abductors (muscle) Abduktoren („Abziehmuskel“, Muskeln zur Bewegung eines Körperteils von der Medialachse weg)
abhorrence (of) Abscheu (vor)
ability Fähigkeit
ablactation absäugen
able to learn lernfähig
abolish abschaffen
abortion Fehlgeburt
About turn! (verbal command) Kehrt! (Hörzeichen)
about-face Kehrtwendung
absence of milk Agalaktie, Milchmangel
absorb absorbieren, einsaugen
absorption Vertiefung (geistige)
accept akzeptieren, anerkennen
accept as a breed als Rasse anerkennen
acceptable vertretbar
acceptance Akzeptanz, Anerkennung
accessible to zugänglich für
accessories Zubehör
accidental zufällig
accommodate unterbringen
accomplish vollbringen
according to performance leistungsgerecht
according to the latest findings nach dem neuesten Erkenntnisstand
accordion drop (fold-back-down) Platzübung, rückwärts einknickend bei Positionswechsel beim Obedience
accuracy in trailing Spursicherheit/ Spurtreue
accurate in trailing fährtensicher

acetabulum Hüftgelenkspfanne
achieve erreichen
achieve amazing things Erstaunliches leisten
achievement control Leistungskontrolle
achievement-oriented leistungsorientiert
achilles tendon Achillessehne
acral lick dermatitis akrale Leckdermatitis
acromegaly Akromegalie
act Handlung
act of desperation Verzweiflungstat
act of escorting away Abführung, Ausbildung
action Aktion
activate aktivieren
activities with dogs Hundesport
acuity of senses Sinnesschärfe
adapt, adjust sich anpassen
adaptability Anpassungsfähigkeit
adaptable to anpassungsfähig an
adaptation Anpassung
add (up) addieren
addison's disease Addisonsche Krankheit
addition Addition
adductors (muscle) Adduktoren („Anziehmuskel", Muskeln zur Bewegung eines Körperteils zur Medialachse)
adequate adäquat
adipose fett
administer verabreichen
admission fee Aufnahmegebühr, Eintrittsgebühr
admission ticket Eintrittskarte
admonish ermahnen
adopt adoptieren
adoption Adoption
adrenaline Adrenalin
advantage Vorteil
advisable ratsam
advocate befürworten
affectionate anhänglich
Affenpinscher Affenpinscher
Afghan (Hound) Afghane, Afghanischer Windhund
afraid of water wasserscheu
a-frame (agility) Schrägwand (A-Wand) (Agility)
African Elephant Dog Afrikanischer Elefantenhund
African Hairless Dog Afrikanischer Nackthund
African Hunting Dog Hyänenhund
African Sand Dog Afrikanischer Sandhund
afterbirth Nachgeburt

after-effect Nachwirkung
against the hair gegen den Strich
against the rules regelwidrig (Sport)
agalactia Agalaktie, Milchmangel
age (Lebens)Alter
age determination Altersbestimmung
age limitation for breeding Zuchtaltersbeschränkung
aggression Aggression
aggression drive Aggressionstrieb
aggression towards people Aggression gegenüber Personen
aggressive aggressiv
aggressiveness Aggressivität, Angriffslust
aggressiveness towards people Mannschärfe
agility Gewandtheit, Wendigkeit, Behändigkeit
agility (sport) Agility (Sport)
agility course Agility-Parcours
agility regulations Agility-Reglement
agility test Agility-Prüfung
agility trial Agility-Turnier
agitate reizen, provozieren
agitation chain with spring (protection work) Hetzkette mit Feder (Schutzdienst)
agitation harness (protection work) Hetzgeschirr (Schutzdienst)
agitation work Schutzdienst
agitator (protection work) Figurant(in), Helfer(in) (Schutzdienst)
agitators' work at trial Schutzdiensthelfer-Arbeit bei der Prüfung
agony Qual
agouti wildfarben
agree (to somebody) zustimmen (jemandem)
agreement Abmachung, Zustimmung
Aichi Aichi
aid helfen, unterstützen; Hilfsmittel
Aidi Aidi, Kabylenhund
aimless ziellos
Ainou Dog Ainou
Ainu Dog Ainu Hund
air fence up Autobelüftungsgitter, Scheibenbelüftungsgitter
Airedale Terrier Airedale-Terrier
Akbash Dog Akbash Inu
Akita Inu Akita
Alano Alano

Alapaha Blue Blood Bulldog Alapaha Blue Blood Bulldog
Alaskan Husky Alaskan Husky
Alaskan Malamute Alaskan Malamut
albinism Albinismus
albino Albino
albumen Eiweiß
Alentejo Herder Rafeiro do Alentejo
alert anzeigen (z.B. Rettungshundearbeit), melden
alert aufgeweckt
alert by barking anschlagen (bellen)
alertness Munterkeit
alien artfremd
alignment Ausrichtung
all rounder (judge) Allround-Richter
all-breed dog show Allgemeine Rassehundezuchtschau
allergy Allergie
allowed time Vorgabezeit
all-rounder Allroundsportler(in)
all-rounder judge Allgemeinrichter(in)
almond-shaped mandelförmig
aloof distanziert, zurückhaltend
alopecia Alopezie
alpha female Alpha-Hündin
alpha figure Alpha-Figur
alpha male Alpha-Hund
alpha roll Alpha-Position
Alpine Basset Hound Alpenländische Dachsbracke
Alpine Hound Alpenbracke, Erzgebirgsdachsbracke
alternatively ersatzweise, wahlweise
Alunk Alunk
amateurish laienhaft
amber bernsteinfarbig
ambition Ehrgeiz, Ambition
ambitious ehrgeizig
ambivalent ambivalent
ambulance dog Sanitätshund
amenable willfährig
American Blue Gascon Hound Amerikanischer Blauer Gascon Laufhund
American Bulldog Amerikanische Bulldogge
American Canadian White Shepherd Weißer Schäferhund
American Cocker Spaniel Amerikanischer Cockerspaniel
American Eskimo Amerikanischer Eskimo Hund
American Foxhound Amerikanischer Fuchshund
American Hairless Terrier Amerikanischer Nacktterrier
American Pit Bull Terrier Amerikanischer Pit Bull Terrier

American Staffordshire Terrier American Staffordshireterrier
American Water Spaniel Amerikanischer Wasserspaniel
American-Canadian White Shepherd Amerikanisch-Kanadischer Schäferhund, Weißer Schäferhund, Berger Blanc Suisse
amniotic fluid Fruchtwasser
amniotic sac Fruchtblase
among the experts Fachkreise(n), in
ample bone, of starkknochig
anaemia Blutarmut
anal greeting Analkontrolle
anal opening Waidloch
anal sac Analbeutel, Aftersack
Anatolian Karabash Karabash, Anatolischer Hirtenhund
anatomical anatomisch
anatomy Anatomie
Andalusian Hound Podenco Andaluz
anger Zorn, Ärger
angle Winkel
angry at zornig über
anguish Qual (seelische)
angular eckig
angulated gewinkelt
angulation Winkelung
animal Tier
animal assisted activity tierunterstützte Aktivität
animal care specialist Tierpfleger
animal humane association (AHA) Tierschutzverein
animal shelter Tierheim
animal welfare Tierschutz
animal welfare law Tierschutzgesetz
ankylosis Gelenksteifigkeit
announcement Bekanntgabe
annoyance Ärgernis
annual general meeting Jahreshauptversammlung
annually alljährlich
anoestrus Anöstrus
anterior Vorder-
anthropomorphism vermenschlichend
anticipate something vorgreifen (in einer Sache)
anticipation Erwartung/ Voraussicht
antiparasite powder Parasitenpulver
antiserum Immunserum
antisocial asozial, unsozial
anus After
anxiety Angstneurose
aorta Aorta, Körperschlagader
apart from abgesehen von
apathetic apathisch
apathy Apathie, Teilnahmslosigkeit

appear erscheinen
appearance Erscheinung, Erscheinungsbild, Aussehen
appendix Blinddarm
Appenzell Mountain Dog Appenzeller Sennenhund
applaud applaudieren, Beifall klatschen
applause Applaus, Beifall
applicable (to) anwendbar (auf)
apply anwenden
apprentice judge Anwärter(in) auf das Richteramt, Richter-Anwärter(in)
approach sich nähern
appropriate sachgerecht
approval Billigung
approved (by breed club) for breeding angekört
approving billigend
aptitude test Veranlagungsprüfung
aquiline Ramsnase
aquiline nose Adlernase
Arabian Greyhound Sloughi
arbitrariness Willkür
arbitrary willkürlich
arbitrator Schiedsrichter(in)
arch Bogen, Wölbung
arched bogenförmig, gekrümmt, gewölbt
archenemy Erzfeind
arcing (while approaching) Bogengehen (bei Annäherung, Begegnung)
arctic breeds Nordische Rassen
Ardennes Cattle Dog Ardenner Treibhund, Bouvier des Ardennes
area Areal
argue argumentieren, streiten
argument Argument; Streit, Rauferei
argumentation Argumentation
Ariege Pointer Bracke von Ariege
Ariegeois Ariege Laufhund
arm cuff (mondioring) Armmanschette (Ringsport)
Armant Ägyptischer Schäferhund, Armant
armpit Achselhöhle
arrive ankommen
arrow Pfeil
artery Schlagader
Artesien Normand Basset Basset Artésien-Normand
arthritis Arthritis, Gelenkentzündung
arthrosis Arthrose
article Artikel (Text)
article (e.g. in tracking) Gegenstand (z.B. Fährtensuche)
article bag Aufbewahrungstasche für Zubehör

article of clothing Kleidungsstück
articles (items used in scent discrimination exercise) Gegenstände (Geruchsunterscheidung)
artificial insemination künstliche Besamung, künstliche Samenübertragung
Artois Hound Artois Laufhund
Aryan Molossus Afghanische Bulldogge, Arischer Molosser
ask for erfragen
asphalt ground Asphaltplatz
assist unterstützen
assistance Hilfsleistung
assistance dog Behindertenbegleithund
associate assoziieren
association Assoziation
asternal rib Asternale Rippe, falsche Rippe
astonish erstaunen
at rest in Ruhestellung
Atlas Sheepdog Kabylenhund, Aidi, Atlasschäferhund
atmosphere Atmosphäre
atopy Atopie
atrophy Atrophie
attack Anfall, Angriff, Überfall, angreifen, attackieren, anfallen
attack on owner Eigenangriff
attack on stranger Fremdangriff
attempt Versuch (Sport)
attempt to deceive Täuschungsversuch
attempt to escape Fluchtversuch
attempted take (of the ...) Greifversuch
attend a course (in) Kurs besuchen (über)
attend a seminar teilnehmen an einem Seminar
attend to pflegen
attention Aufmerksamkeit, Zuwendung
attentive aufmerksam
attract attention Aufmerksamkeit erregen/ erheischen
atypical untypisch
auditory canal Gehörgang
auditory nerve Hörnerv
Aujeszkys' disease Aujeszkysche Krankheit
Australian Cattle Dog Australian Cattle Dog, Australischer Viehhund
Australian Dingo Dingo
Australian Greyhound Australischer Windhund
Australian Kelpie (Australischer) Kelpie
Australian Native Dog Dingo
Australian Shepherd Australian Shepherd, Australischer Hütehund

Australian Silky Terrier (Australischer) Silky Terrier
Australian Terrier Australischer Terrier
Austrian Black-and-Tan-Hound Brandlbracke
Austrian Hound Österreichische Bracke
Austrian Hunting Griffon Österreichischer Jagdgriffon
Austrian Short-Haired Pinscher Österreichischer Kurzhaarpinscher
author Autor(in)
authoritarian autoritär
authority Autorität
auto-immune disease Autoimmunkrankheit
automatic sit Sitz beim Anhalten
autonomous nervous system vegetatives Nervensystem
Auvergne Pointer Auvergne Vorstehhund
avalanche Lawine
avalanche dog Lawinenhund
average Durchschnitt
aversive (e.g. stimulus) aversiv, unangenehm (z.B. Reiz)
aversive correction aversive Einwirkung
avoid vermeiden
avoidance Meiden
avoidance behaviour Meideverhalten
await erwarten
await the next command nächstes Kommando abwarten
award Auszeichnung, Ehrenpreis
award vergeben (Preis), zuerkennen
awfully unheimlich
Azawakh Azawakh

B

babble kläffen
babbler Kläffer
Bach flowers Bachblüten
back Rist, Rücken
back, soft weicher Rücken
back, true eigentlicher Rücken
back chaining Verhaltenskette, rückwärts
back yard breeder Tiervermehrer, Hinterhofzüchter
Back! (verbal command) Zurück! (Hörzeichen)
backbone Rückgrat
backcross(ing) Rückkreuzung
background information Hintergrundinformation
backing Rückendeckung
backline Rückenlinie
backlog demand Nachholbedarf
backtrace Aalstrich
backyard breeding wilde Zucht
bacon Speck
baculum Penisknochen
bad habit schlechte Gewohnheit, Unart
bad weather front Schlechtwetterfront
badger dachsfarben
badly upset verstört
bag Jagdbeute
bag Tasche, Tüte
Baganda Hunting-Dog Baganda (Jagdhund)
Bagirmi Dog Bagirmi (Jagdhund)
bait Lockmittel, Leckerbissen, Leckerli, Belohnungshappen
balance Ausgewogenheit, Harmonie, Symmetrie
balanced ausgeglichen
balanced (body) harmonisch
Bali Mountain Dog Bali Berghund
Balkan Hound Balkanbracke
ball Ball
ball game Ballspiel

ball-and-socket joint Pfannengelenk
ballpoint pen Kugelschreiber
banded gebändert
bandy-legged fassbeinig
bang Knall
banqueting hall Festsaal
barbed wire Stacheldraht
Barbet Barbet
bare the teeth Zähne blecken, drohen
bar-jump (agility) Stangenhürde (Agility)
bark bellen
bark and hold (protection work) Stellen und Verbellen (Schutzdienst)
bark at verbellen, ankeifen
Bark! (verbal command) Gib Laut! (Hörzeichen)
barking bellen, anschlagen
barking at sight of game Sichtlaut
barking dogs seldom bite Hunde, die bellen, beißen nicht
barkless nicht bellend
barn Scheune
barrel ribs Fassrippen
barrel shaped tonnenförmig
base of the tail Rutenwurzel
Basenji Basenji
basewide bodenweit
basic control issues Basis-Kontroll- (Gehorsams-)Übungen
basic education Grunderziehung
basket Hundekorb
Basque Shepherd Dog Baskischer Schäferhund
Basset Basset
Basset Bleu de Gascogne Basset Bleu de Gascogne
Basset d'Artois Basset d'Artois
Basset Fauve de Bretagne Basset Fauve de Bretagne, Fahlroter Bretonischer Niederlaufhund
Basset Griffon Vendeen Basset Griffon Vendéen
Basset Hound Basset
Batak Dog Batakenhund
bathe baden
battery farming Massentierhaltung
battue Treibjagd, Drückjagd
Bavarian Mountain Hound Bayerischer Gebirgsschweißhund
Bavarian Schweisshund Bayerischer Gebirgsschweißhund
bawl at someone anbrüllen
bay Hetzlaut; Laut geben
baying of hounds at work Geläut (Jagdlaut)
be (get) annoyed sich ärgern

be a foregone conclusion vorprogrammiert sein (Konflikt)
be above the average über dem Durchschnitt liegen
be absent fehlen
be acquainted with kennen, vertraut sein mit
be afraid (of) sich ängstigen
be ashamed sich schämen
be astonished at staunen über
be at someones mercy jemandes Willkür ausgeliefert sein
be below the average unter dem Durchschnitt liegen
be changing sich im Wandel befinden
be damaged Schaden nehmen
be defeated unterliegen
be easy to get along with verträglich sein
be free and easy zwanglos (Verhalten)
be good for fördern, förderlich sein
be happy sich freuen
be ill-advised schlecht beraten sein
be in a good (bad) mood gut (schlecht) gelaunt sein
be kindred souls seelenverwandt sein
be lame hinken
be neglected verwahrlosen
be on the safe side sicherheitshalber
be paralysed with fear erstarren vor Schreck
be placed (e.g. third) sich platzieren als (z.B. Dritter)
be pressed for time unter Zeitdruck stehen
be profitable sich lohnen
be ready bereitstehen
be safe in Sicherheit sein
be scared at the idea of contact Berührungsängste haben
be sent off Platzverweis erhalten
be served as eingesetzt sein als
be still growing im Wachstum befinden
be suited for taugen für
be terrified of panische Angst haben vor
be the boss das Sagen haben
be under pressure to succeed unter Erfolgszwang stehen
be worth sich lohnen
beach Strand
Beagle Beagle
Beagle Harrier Beagle-Harrier
bear gebären
beard Bart
Bearded Collie Bearded Collie, Beardie
bearing-down pains Presswehen
beast of prey Raubtier

beater Treiber(in) auf der Jagd
Beauceron Beauceron
beaver dachsfarben, biberfarben
become friends anfreunden
become isolated vereinsamen
become stabilized sich stabilisieren
become stunted verkümmern
Bedlington Terrier Bedlington-Terrier
Bedouin Shepherd Dog Beduinenhirtenhund
beef Rindfleisch
beef dog chew Ochsenziemer
beef extract Fleischextrakt
beefy fleischig
beeper Piepser
beesting tail Vorstehhundrute
beg betteln
begin to have confidence Zutrauen fassen
beginner Anfänger(in)
beginner teams Anfänger-Team
behave sich verhalten
behave badly sich daneben benehmen
behaviour, us: behavior Verhalten
behaviour, abnormal Verhaltensstörung
behaviour, allelomimetic Nachahmung
behaviour, alternative Alternativverhalten
behaviour chain Verhaltenskette
behaviour for attract attention aufmerksamkeitsheischendes Verhalten
behaviour, incompatible unvereinbares Verhalten
behaviour, learned erlerntes Verhalten
behaviour, long-duration anhaltendes Verhalten
behaviour, restructured Ersatzhandlung
behaviour, specific arttypisches Verhalten
behaviour, submissive unterwürfiges Verhalten
behaviour, superstitious abergläubisches Verhalten
behaviour, supression of Unterdrückung von Verhaltensweisen
behaviour, trained antrainiertes Verhalten
behaviour, undesired unerwünschtes Verhalten
behaviour, unwanted unerwünschtes Verhalten
behaviour modification Verhaltensänderung
behaviour modification training Verhaltenstraining

behaviour therapy Verhaltenstherapie
behavioural disorder Verhaltensauffälligkeit
behavioural pattern Verhaltensmuster
behavioural periods (soziale) Entwicklungsphasen
behavioural science Verhaltensforschung
behavioural scientist Verhaltensforscher(in)
being afraid of gun fire/ noises Schussangst/ Geräuschangst
being attacked by one's own dog Eigenangriff
being left alone allein gelassen werden
Belgian Cattle Dog Bouvier des Flandres, Flämischer Treibhund
Belgian Draught Dog Belgischer Zughund
Belgian Griffon Belgischer Griffon, Griffon Belge, Kleiner Brabanter
Belgian Groenendael Groenendael
Belgian Laekenois Laekenois
Belgian Malinois Malinois
Belgian Mastiff Belgischer Karrenhund
Belgian Sheepdog Belgischer Schäferhund
Belgian Short-Haired Pointer Belgische Bracke
Belgian Tervueren Tervueren
belligerent streitlustig
belly Unterleib
belong to dazugehören
belong together zusammengehören
below average unterdurchschnittlich
belt Gürtel
belton farbige Tüpfelung
Bergamasco Herder Bergamasker
Bergamese Shepherd Bergamasker
Bernese Hound Berner Laufhund
Bernese Mountain Dog Berner Sennenhund, Gelbbackler
best in field Tagesbeste(r)
best in group Gruppensieger(in)
best of breed Rassenbeste(r)
best of day Tagesbeste(r)
best of show Tagesbeste(r)
beware of the dog! Vorsicht – Bissiger Hund!
Bhotia Bhotia
biceps Bizeps
Bichon Bolognese Bologneser
Bichon Frise Bichon Frisé
bicolour zweifarbig
bicycle Fahrrad

bicycle path Radweg
big game Hochwild
binoculars Fernglas
bird dog Hühnerhund, Vogelhund
bird of prey Raubvogel
birth canal Geburtsweg
Bisben (Himalayan Bisben) Bisben
biscuits Hundekuchen
bitch Hündin
bitchiness Hündinnentyp
bitchy hündinnenhaft
bite Biss; beißen, zubeißen
bite Bissen (Happen)
bite and teeth inspection Zahnkontrolle
bite arm (mondioring) Beißarm (Ringsport)
bite inhibition Beißhemmung
bite off abbeißen
bite wound Bisswunde
black schwarz
black and silver schwarz-silbern
black and tan schwarz-beige, schwarz-loh(farben), schwarz-rot
Black and Tan Coonhound Schwarz-Roter Waschbärenhund, Black-and-Tan Coonhound
black and tan saddled fuchsfarben mit schwarzem Sattel
Black Fell Terrier Patterdale Terrier
Black Forest Hound Slowakische Bracke
Black Mouth Cur Schwarzlippiger Cur
black overlay Ruß (Fellfarbe)
Black Russian Terrier (Schwarzer) Russischer Terrier
blackened schwarz gewolkt, berußt (Fellfärbung)
blackening schwarze Wolkung
bladder Blase, Harnblase
bladed flach
blame tadeln
blame somebody for something jemandem anlasten
blank cartridge Platzpatrone
blank looks verständnislose Blicke
blanket Decke
blanket for the dog Hundedecke
blaze Blesse
bleed bluten
blind blind
blind (protection work, mondioring) Versteck (Schutzdienst), Blende (Schutzdienst, Ringsport)
blind obedience Kadavergehorsam
blink zwinkern
block abblocken
block off absperren

blocky geblockt; massiv
blond blond
blood Blut; Schweiß (Jagd)
blood blister Bluterguss
blood count Blutbild
blood line Blutlinie
blood pressure Blutdruck
blood trail Schweißfährte, Wundfährte
bloodcurdling markerschütternd
bloodhound Schweißhund
bloodhound like hubertoid
bloodshot blutunterlaufen
blow Schlag (Hieb)
blue blau
blue and tan blau mit loh
blue belton schwarze Tüpfelung auf weiss
Blue Gascony Basset Basset Bleu de Gascogne
Blue Gascony Griffon Griffon Bleu de Gascogne
blue merle blue-merle, grau marmoriert
Blue Picardy Spaniel Blauer langhaariger Vorstehhund Picardie, Épagneul Bleu de Picardie
blue roan blau gestichelt, schwarz-schimmel
blue speckled blau fleckig
blue tan blau mit loh
blue-black blauschwarz
blue-mottled blau scheckig
Bluetick Coonhound Bluetick Coonhound
blunt muzzle stumpfer Fang
blunted abgestumpft (z.B. Gefühle)
boar hound Saupacker, Saurüde, Packerhund
board elections Vorstandswahl
board meeting Vorstandssitzung
boarding kennel Hundepension
Bobtail Bobtail, (Alt)englischer Schäferhund
body Leib, Rumpf
body language Körpersprache
body wrap (TTouch) Körperbandage (TTouch)
Bohemian Griffon (Cesky) Fousek, Tschechischer Rauhhaariger Vorstehhund, Böhmischer Rauhbart
Bohemian Terrier Tschechischer Terrier, Czesky Terrier
boil Geschwür
bolt sprengen (z.B. Fuchs aus dem Bau)
bomb detection dog Sprengstoffspürhund
bone Knochen
bone meal Knochenmehl
bones of the hip Hüftknochen

bone-shaped in Form eines Knochens, knochenförmig
booked-up ausgebucht
booster (shot) Nachimpfung
boot Stiefel
booty Beute
Bordeaux Mastiff Bordeaux-Dogge
border area Grenzbereich
Border Collie Border Collie, Working Sheepdog
Border Terrier Border Terrier
borderline case Grenzfall
bored gelangweilt
borrelia infection Borreliose
borrow something (from) sich etwas leihen (von)
Borzoi Barsoi, Russischer Windhund
Bosnian Rough-Coated Hound Bosnische Rauhaar Bracke
Boston Terrier Boston Terrier
bottle Flasche
bottle-raising Flaschenaufzucht
bottom Hinterteil
bottom line Bauchlinie, untere Linie
Boulet Griffon Boulet Griffon
bounce Elastizität
Bourbonnais Pointer Bourbonnais Vorstehhund
Bouvier Bouvier des Flandres
bowel movement Stuhlgang
bowl Schüssel
Boxer Boxer
Boykin Spaniel Boykin Spaniel
Bracco Italiano Italienische Bracke
brace Paar; Zweierkoppel
braid something etwas flechten
braided tug toy Flechtseil, Zottel, Zerrseil (Spielzeug)
brain Gehirn
brain teaser Denkaufgabe
brainwork geistige Arbeit
branch Stange (Geweih)
brave mutig, tapfer
bravery Mut, Tapferkeit
brawl for sich raufen
Brazilian Greyhound Brasilianischer Windhund, Veadeiro Catarinense
Brazilian Terrier Brasilianischer Terrier
Brazilian Tracker Brasilianischer Laufhund
breach of trust Vertrauensbruch
break Pause, Ruhepause
break Knick
break away (from) sich losreißen (von)
break-off Abbruch (Sport)
breast Brust(drüse)
breastbone Brustbein
breasts Gesäuge
breath Atem

breathe atmen
breathe hard schnaufen
bred out (from their bloodline) herausgezüchtet (aus der Blutlinie)
bred-by class Zuchtklasse
breech delivery Steißgeburt
breed Rasse
breed sich vermehren, verpaaren; züchten
breed characteristic(s) Rassekennzeichen
breed club (us) Zuchtverein, Rassezuchtverein
breed council Rassenkommission
breed disqualification Ausschlussfehler
breed society (engl.) Zuchtverein, Rassezuchtverein
breed standard Rassestandard
breed warden Zuchtwart(in)
breeder Züchter(in)
breeder's class Zuchtgruppenwettbewerb
breeder's group Zuchtgruppe
breeders' association Zuchtverband
breeding Zucht
breeding activity Nachzucht
breeding animal Zuchttier
breeding goal(s) Zuchtziel(e)
breeding notification Deckmeldung
breeding particulars Zuchtdaten
breeding program Zuchtprogramm
breeding stock Zuchtmaterial
Briard Briard
bridge of the nose Nasenrücken
brindle wolfsstreifig
brindled gestromt
brindled spots Porzellanscheckung
brindling Stromung, Tigerung
bring bringen, apportieren, herbeibringen
bring somebody relief jemandem Linderung verschaffen
bring something back etwas wiederbringen, etwas zurückholen
bring up aufziehen
bringsel Bringsel
brisk munter, lebhaft
bristle (up) sträuben (Fell)
bristle coat Stichelhaar, Drahthaar
bristle-coated drahthaarig
British Sheepdogs Britische Hütehunde
Brittany (Spaniel) Bretonischer Vorstehhund

Brittany Fawn Griffon Falbfarbiger Rauhaariger Bretonischer Laufhund
Brittany Spaniel Épagneul Breton
broad in skull breit zwischen den Ohren
broad jump Weitsprung
Broholm Mastiff Broholmer
broken from deer rehrein
broken from hare hasenrein
broken piece Scherbe
broken-coated stichelhaarig
Broken-Haired Black and Tan Terrier Altenglischer Rauhaarterrier
bronchitis Bronchitis
Bronze Age Dog Bronzehund
bronze coloured bronzefarben
brood bitch Zuchthündin
brood-bitch class Nachzuchtgruppe
brood-tending behaviour Brutverhalten
brown braun
brownish yellow braun-gelb
bruise Prellung
brush Bürste, bürsten
brush out ausbürsten, auskämmen
brush tail Bürstenrute
Brussels Griffon Brüsseler Griffon, Griffon Bruxellois
brutality Brutalität
buckle on umschnallen
buckskin lederfarben
Buenos Aires Hairless Dog Buenos Aires Nackthund
build bauen, aufbauen
building Gebäude;
bulb of the glans Schwellkörper, Eichel (anatomisch)
Bulgarian Hound Bulgarische Bracke
bulging hervorstehend, hervortretend
bulging eyes kugelförmige Augen
bulky klobig
bull Stier
Bull Terrier Bullterrier
Bulldog Bulldogge, Bullenbeißer
Bullmastiff Bullmastiff
bump rempeln
bunny Hasenattrappe, Hetzattrappe, künstlicher Hase
burrow dog Bauhund, Erdhund
burrow work Erdarbeit
burrowing Erdarbeit
bursting with energy energiegeladen
bury verscharren
bush Strauch
bushy buschig
bustle Trubel

butterfly ears
Schmetterlingsohren
butterfly nose
Schmetterlingsnase
buttock Keule
buttocks Gesäß
button ear Knopfohr
buy kaufen
buy something from abkaufen
buyer Käufer(in)
by degrees stufenweise
by force mit Gewalt
by way of trial versuchsweise
bystanders Umstehende

C

caesarean Kaiserschnitt
Cairn Terrier Cairn Terrier
calendar of events Veranstaltungskalender
call Appell
call someone back jemanden zurückrufen
call someone names beschimpfen
calliper Körmaß
callus Liegeschwiele, Schwiele
calm ruhig
calm down besänftigen
calming signal Beschwichtigungssignal
calmness Gelassenheit
Cameroons Dog Kamerunhund
camouflage tarnen
camp campieren
camper Reisemobil
can take a lot einstecken können
Canaan Dog Canaan Hund, Kanaanhund
Canadian Eskimo Dog Kanadischer Eskimohund
Canarian Warren Hound Podenco Canario
Canary Dog Perro de Presa Canario, Kanarische Dogge, Bardino
cancellation Absage
cancer (medical) Krebs (medizinisch)
Cane Corso Cane Corso
canid Canide, Kanide
canine Hunde-, hunde-
canine (tooth) Eckzahn
canine distemper Hundestaupe, Staupe
canine infectious hepatitis ansteckende Leberentzündung
canine leptospirosis Stuttgarter Hundeseuche

canine parainfluenza virus Parainfluenza-Virus
canine tooth Fangzahn
canned food Dosenfutter
canter leichter Galopp
capable of being interbred kreuzbar
capable of development entwicklungsfähig
capture erbeuten
car crate Autobox
car dog blanket Autoschondecke
car safety fence Hundeschutzgitter, Auto-
car safety net Hundeschutznetz, Auto-
car sickness Reisekrankheit, Reiseübelkeit
caramel karamellfarben
carbohydrate Kohlehydrat
care Sorgfalt
care of the environment Umweltschutz
careful behutsam, schonend, sorgfältig
carefulness Achtsamkeit
careless achtlos
carelessness Achtlosigkeit
carnivore Fleischfresser, Raubtier
Carolina Dog Carolina Hund
carp back Karpfenrücken
carpal joint Karpalgelenk, Vorderfußwurzelgelenk
carpal pad Karpalballen
Carpathian Sheepdog Carpatin
carriage Tragen (der Ohren, des Kopfes usw.)
carried flat (tail) flach getragen (Rute)
carrion Aas
carry a leg hinken
carsick reisekrank
cart dog Zughund
cartilage Knorpel
cask Tonne
cast Farbton
cast somebody out of verstoßen aus
castrate kastrieren
castration Kastration
cat Katze
Catahoula Leopard Dog Louisiana Catahoula
Catalan Sheepdog Gos d'Atura Catalan, Katalonischer Schäferhund
catalogue Katalog
catch fangen, auffangen; ergreifen (z.B. Beute)
catching ansteckend
cattle Vieh
cattle dog Treibhund

Caucasian Owtcharka Kaukasischer Owtscharka, Steppenowtscharka
caudal kaudal
caudal vertebra Schwanzwirbel
cause Ursache
cavalettis (agility) Kavalettis (Agility)
Cavalier King Charles Spaniel Cavalier King Charles Spaniel
Celtic Hound Keltenbracke, Segusier
central theme Leitgedanke
central thought Leitgedanke
centre of gravity Schwerpunkt
centre of ring Ringmitte
cereals Getreide; Hundeflocken
cerebellum Kleinhirn
cerebrum Großhirn
ceremonial address Festrede
ceremony Festakt
certificate Urkunde, Zertifikat, Leistungsnachweis, Prüfungsnachweis
certificate of aptitude for the international beauty championship CACIB Zeugnis der Anwartschaft auf das internationale FCI-Schönheitschampionat CACIB
certificate of aptitude for the international utility championship CACIT Zeugnis der Anwartschaft auf das internationale FCI-Arbeitschampionat CACIT
certificate of correct bite Gebissbescheinigung
certificate of proficiency Sachkundenachweis
certificate towards a title Anwartschaft
certification Bescheinigung
certified helper geprüfte(r) Schutzdiensthelfer(in)
cervical vertebrae Halswirbel
Cevennes Shepherd Languedoc-Schäferhund, Berger du Languedoc
chain Kette
chain anketten
chain collar Kettenhalsband
chain link collar Gliederhalsband
chain to anketten
chair Stuhl
chairman (chairwoman) of the board Vorstandsvorsitzende(r)
challenge Herausforderung, herausfordern
challenge certificate CC (GB) Zeugnis der Anwartschaft auf das Schönheitschampionat

challenge cup Wanderpokal
champion class Championklasse
championship Championat, Meisterschaft
chance Zufall
chance of success Erfolgschance
change Wandel, umwandeln
change of food Futterumstellung
change of pace Wechsel der Gangart
change ones' view umdenken
changing behaviour Verhaltensänderung
character Wesen, Wesensart
characteristic Kennzeichen, Merkmal
characteristic of the breed rassetypisch
chase verfolgen, hetzen
chase a ball Ball jagen
chase away verjagen, wegjagen
chase instinct Hetztrieb, Jagdtrieb
chase one's tail die eigene Rute jagen
chat Plauderei
cheat schummeln
check überwachen
check cord lange Feldleine
cheek Backe, Wange
cheek bone Jochbein
cheek muscle Wangenmuskel
cheer somebody up zusprechen, aufmuntern
cheerful fröhlich
cheerleading Aufmunterungen rufen
cheerless freudlos
cherry nose Fleischnase
Chesapeake Bay Retriever Chesapeake Bay Retriever
chest Brust
chestnut kastanienbraun
chestnut roan braunschimmel
chew kauen, zerkauen
chew on (or up) benagen
chewing stick Kaurolle
chief breed warden Oberzuchtwart
Chihuahua Chihuahua
Chika Chinesischer Windhund
chin Kinn
chin whiskers Ziegenbart
china eye Glasauge
Chinese Crested Dog Chinesischer Nackthund, Chinesischer Schopfhund
Chinese Fighting Dog Char Pei
Chinese Greyhound Tschika, Chinesischer Windhund
Chinese Hound Chinesischer Meutehund
Chinese Temple Chin Chinesischer Tempelhund
Chinook Chinook

Chippendale front französischer Stand
chiselled ziseliert; gemeißelt
chiselling Ziselierung
chocolate schokolade(nbraun)
choice Wahl(möglichkeit)
choke chain Würgekette, Würgehalsband
choke collar Zughalsband
chops hängende, lose Haut, die Falten an den Lefzen und am Kiefer bildet
choroid membrane Aderhaut (des Auges)
Chow Chow Chow Chow
Chrysanthemum Dog Shi Tzu, Tibetanischer Löwenhund
circle left/ right Kreis nach links/ rechts
circle round umkreisen
circulate umlaufen
circumspection Umsicht
circumstances Begleitumstände, Gegebenheit
circus dog Zirkushund
clamped (tail) eingeklemmt (Rute)
clamped between legs (tail) eingezogen, zwischen den Beinen (Rute)
clash with somebody mit jemandem zusammenstoßen
class Klasse, Gruppe
classic example Paradebeispiel
classification Klassifizierung
classify klassifizieren
claw Kralle, Klaue
clay court Sandplatz
clean putzen; sauber
clean outline saubere Linienführung
cleanliness Reinlichkeit
clearing Lichtung
cleft palate Spaltrachen
clever schlau
click and treat Click und Belohnung
click one's tongue schnalzen mit der Zunge
clicker Clicker
clicker training Clickertraining
climb (over) klettern (über)
climbing jump (over scaling wall) Klettersprung (Schrägwand)
clip Schur, scheren
clip (tail) kupieren (Rute)
clipboard Klemmbrett
clippers Scherapparat, Schermaschine
clockwise Uhrzeigersinn
cloddy bodennah
close eng anliegend
close hocks hackeneng, enghessig

close moving gait bodenenger Gang
close of entry Meldefrist
close season Schonzeit
close together nahe beieinander
close-coupled kurzlendig
closed behind Hinterläufe, bodeneng
closed hunting season Schonzeit
closed tunnel (agility) Sacktunnel (Agility)
cloudburst Platzregen
cloudiness of the eye Augentrübung
cloudiness of the eye lens Linsentrübung
clove of garlic Knoblauchzehe
club insignia Abzeichen, Logo
club mate Vereinskamerad(in)
clubhouse Vereinsheim/-haus
Clumber Spaniel Clumber Spaniel
coach Trainer(in)
coarse ohne Adel, ohne Eleganz, grob
coarse head Kopf ohne Adel
coat Haarkleid, Fell
coat care Fellpflege
coat change Haarwechsel
coat colouring Fellfärbung
coat loss Haarwechsel
cobby gedrungen, kompakt
Cocker Spaniel Cocker Spaniel
coddle verhätscheln
coincidence Zufälligkeit
cold bag (or box) Kühltasche
cold pack kalter Umschlag
collapsed tunnel Stofftunnel, weicher Tunnel
collapsible water bowl faltbarer Wassernapf
collar Halsband, Halsung
collar bone Schlüsselbein
collect sammeln
collie eye anomaly, CEA Collieaugenanomalie
colostrum Kolostralmilch, Erstmilch, Vormilch
colour, us: color Farbe
colour at birth Geburtsfarbe
colour therapy Farbtherapie
colour variety Farbschlag
colouring Färbung
comb Kamm
combination Kombination
combine (with) kombinieren (mit)
combined with gemeinsam mit
come herankommen
Come! (verbal command) Hier! (Hörzeichen)
come close nahe kommen
come in heat in die Läufigkeit kommen
come in season läufig werden

ome into conflict with n Konflikt geraten mit
ome off well/ bad (sport) vegkommen, gut/ schlecht (Sport)
ome to a head zuspitzen
oming to terms with the past Vergangenheitsbewältigung
ommand Hörzeichen, Kommando, Befehl
ommand-based training konventionelles Training
ommanding from a distance Leiten auf Distanz
ommemorative publication Festschrift
omment on kommentieren
commercial food Fertignahrung
commercially prepared balanced dog food Vollnahrung
communal pad Sohlenballen
communicate kommunizieren
communication Kommunikation, Verständigung
communication problems Verständigungsprobleme
communication system Kommunikationssystem
compact gedrungen, kompakt
companion Gefährte, Gefährtin
companion dog Begleithund, Gesellschaftshund
companion dog test Begleithund-Prüfung
compared to im Vergleich zu
compatible with vereinbar mit
compensation Kompensation
compete teilnehmen (im Sinne von wetteifern, konkurrieren)
compete with somebody Rang streitig machen
competence Kompetenz .
competent fachkundig, kompetent, sachverständig; zuständig
competition Wettbewerb, Konkurrenz
competition, indoor- Hallenwettbewerb
competition, outdoor- Wettbewerb im Freien
competitive sport Leistungssport
competitor Teilnehmer(in), Konkurrent(in)
complacency Selbstgefälligkeit
complacent selbstgefällig
complete vervollständigen
complete and balanced diet Komplettfutter
complete and balanced food Alleinfutter(mittel)
completed (e.g. training) abgeschlossen (z.B. Ausbildung)
completion Vervollständigung
complex vielschichtig

complex of problems Problemkreis
complicated verzwickt
composed gelassen
compound Gehege, (Tier-)
comprehend verstehen
comprehensible verständlich
comprehension Begriffsvermögen
compulsion psychischer Zwang
compulsory training Training über Zwang, Starkzwangausbildung
concave eingesenkt
conceal verschweigen
concede zugestehen
conceive aufnehmen
concentrate (on) sich konzentrieren (auf)
concentration Konzentration
conclude from folgern aus
concussion (of the brain) Gehirnerschütterung
condition Kondition
conditioning (of behaviour) Konditionierung (von Verhalten)
cone Kegel (Markierungs-), Pylone (Markierungs-)
cone-shaped konisch
conference Sitzung
confidence Vertrauen, Zuversicht
confident of victory siegessicher
confiding zutraulich
confidingness Zutraulichkeit
conflict Konflikt
conformation Habitus
conformation judge Zuchtrichter, Formwertrichter(in)
conformation score Formwertnote
conformity Übereinstimmung
confront somebody with konfrontieren mit
confrontation Konfrontation
confuse verwirren
confuse (with) verwechseln (mit)
confusion Verstörtheit; Verwechslung
congenial to geistesverwandt
Congo Dog Basenji
conjunctiva Bindehaut
conjunctivitis Bindehautentzündung
connection Zusammenhang
consanguinity Blutsverwandtschaft
consequence Konsequenz
consider erwägen
consider the pros and cons Vor- und Nachteile abwägen
consistency (in behaviour) Konsequenz
consolidate vertiefen (Lehrstoff)

consommé Fleischbrühe
constipation Verstopfung
constricted gait gebundenes Gangwerk, unfreies Gangwerk
constrictor muscle Schließmuskel
contact dermatitis Kontaktdermatitis
contact zone (agility) Kontaktzone, Sicherheitszone (Agility)
contagion Ansteckung
contagious ansteckend
containing vitamins vitaminhaltig
contentious streitig
contentment innere Zufriedenheit
context Kontext
Continental Toy Spaniel Papillon, Épagneul Nain Continental, Kontinentaler Zwergspaniel
contingencies of reinforcement Zufallsbestätigung
continue fortbestehen, weiterführen, fortführen
continue fighting weiterkämpfen
continuity Kontinuität
continuously kontinuierlich
contract of sale Kaufvertrag
contractions Wehen
control of Kontrolle über (im Sinne von Beherrschung)
controversial issue Streitfrage
contusion Verstauchung, Prellung, Quetschung
convene versammeln
convince überzeugen
convulsion Zuckung
Coonhound Waschbärenhund, Coonhund
cooperate kooperieren
cooperation Kooperation, Mitarbeit, Zusammenarbeit
cooperative kooperativ
cope bewältigen,
cope a situation einer Situation gewachsen sein
cope with verkraften
copper toxicosis Kupfervergiftung
coprophagy Kotfressen
copulation Deckakt, Paarung
cord Strick
corded zottelhaarig
corded coat Zottelhaar
corded hair Schnürenhaar
corded poodle Schnürenpudel
Corgi Corgi
corkscrew tail Korkenzieherrute
cornea Hornhaut
corner of the mouth Fangwinkel, Mundwinkel

corner-cutting (heelwork) Ecken schneiden/ nicht ausgehen (Fußarbeit)
corner-cutting (tracking) Winkel verkürzen/ schneiden (Fährtenarbeit)
cornflakes Maisflocken
corny feet Verhornungsstörung (Pfote)
correction Einwirkung, Korrektur
correction, aversive Einwirkung, aversive
cosset hätscheln
costal arch Rippenbogen
counsellor Berater(in)
counter (sport) kontern (Sport)
counter-argument Gegenargument
counter-attack (sport) Konter (Sport)
counter-example Gegenbeispiel
country breed Landrasse, Landschlag
country lane Feldweg
country of origin Herkunftsland
country road Landstraße
coupling Lende
courage Mut
courage and hardness TSB (Trieb, Selbstsicherheit, Belastbarkeit)
courage test (protection work) Mutprobe (Schutzdienst)
courageous mutig
course hetzen
course (agility) Parcours (Agility)
course Lauf (Wettrennen)
course of training Schulungskurs
coursing Windhundjagd
coursing on hare Hasenhetze
court Platz
court balzen
courting Balz
Couteulxtype Basset Hound Couteulx Basset Hound
cover absichern
cover Überzug
cover belegen, decken (im Sinne von züchten)
cover something up überspielen (Fehler, Schwächen)
cover up verwehen (Spuren), zudecken
cower kauern, sich ducken
cow-hocked kuhhessig
coyote Kojote
crack Knacks
crack Knall (Schuss)
crack knallen (mit Peitsche)
crackling knistern
cramp Krampf
cranium Schädel

crate Hundetransportbox
craving for admiration Geltungsbedürfnis
cream creme(farben)
creaseless faltenlos
creature Geschöpf, Lebewesen
credit point Pluspunkt
crest Schopf
Crimean Hound Krimwindhund
cringe kriechen; kauern, sich ducken
crisp gekräuselt
criteria Kriterien, Anforderungen
criteria shifting Anforderung ändern/ senken
criticism Kritik
criticize beanstanden, kritisieren
Croatian Sheepdog Kroatischer Schäferhund
crook Hütestab (Hakenstock)
crook tail Hakenrute
crooked verkrümmt
crooked legged krummbeinig
crop kupieren (Schwanz, Ohren)
crop up plötzlich auftauchen
cross Mischling, Bastard; kreuzen (züchten)
cross bite Kreuzbiss
crossbreed Mischling, Bastard
crosscheck Gegenprobe
crosswind Seitenwind
crouch (down) sich ducken
croup Kruppe
crowd of people Menschenmenge
crown Krone
crucial experience Schlüsselerlebnis
cruciate (ligament) Kreuzband
cruel grausam
cruelty Grausamkeit
cruelty to animals Tierquälerei
crunch point Knackpunkt
cry Hetzlaut
cry of fear Angstschrei
cryptorchidism Kryptorchismus
cuddle schmusen
cue Signal (Hör- oder Sichtzeichen)
cue to stop Signal zum Aufhören
cull ausmerzen
Cumberland Sheep Dog Cumberland Schäferhund
cup Pokal
cup winner Pokalsieger(in)
curiosity Neugier
curious about neugierig auf
curl (up) the lips Lefzen hochziehen
curled gelockt
curling inward eingerollt
curly lockig, gelockt

Curly Coated Retriever Curly Coated Retriever, Kraushaariger Retriever
current zeitgemäß
current intensity Stromstärke
curry striegeln
curry comb Striegel
curtain (Lhasa Apso) über die Augen fallende Stirnlocke
cushioned gepolstert
customs dog Zollhund
cut Schnittwunde
cut down zurückschrauben (Ansprüche)
cute niedlich
cut-up aufgezogen
cycle track Radfahrweg
cyclic zyklisch
cyclist Radfahrer(in)
cylindrical epithelion Zylinderepithel
cynology Hundekunde, Kynologie
cynophile Hundeliebhaber(in)
Czech Miniature Pinscher Prager Rattler
Czech Mountain Dog Böhmischer Berghund
Czechoslovakian Wolfdog Tschechoslowakischer Wolfshund

Dachshund
Teckel, Dackel, Dachshund
daily täglich
Dalmatian Dalmatiner
dam Muttertier
damage Schaden, schaden
damp and cold nasskalt
Dandie Dinmont Terrier
Dandie Dinmont Terrier
danger Gefahr
dangerous gefährlich
Danish Broholmer
Altdänische Dogge, Broholmer
Danish Dachsbracke
Dänische Dachsbracke
dappled (mehrfarbig) gescheckt
dare to approach or to come
sich heranwagen
dark (or black) mask
dunkle Maske
dark beige biberfarben
dark brown dunkelbraun
dark red dunkelhirschrot
dark reddish brown
kastanienbraun
dark stippled dunkel gestichelt
dauntless unerschrocken
day of fasting Fastentag
daybreak Tagesanbruch
dazzler Blender
dead leaf herbstlaubfarben
deaf taub
deafness Taubheit
death howler Todverbeller
decide entscheiden
decision Entscheidung
decoy Helfer (Ringsport)
decoy Lockvogel
decoy track Verleitungsfährte
deep tief
deep chested tiefbrüstig
deep red tiefrot
deer Hirsch, Reh, Rehwild
deer track (or trail)
Rotwildfährte
defecate koten, sich lösen

defecation Kotabsatz
defence Verteidigung, Gegenwehr
defence drive Selbsterhaltungstrieb
defence of territory Revierverteidigung
defenceless wehrlos
defencelessness Wehrlosigkeit
defend verteidigen
defend oneself (against) sich wehren (gegen)
defensive bite Verteidigungsbiss
defensive reaction Abwehrreaktion
defiance Trotz
deficiency Mangel
deficiency symptom Mangelerscheinung
definition Definition
degree of relationship Verwandtschaftsgrad
dehydration Austrocknung
delay Verzögerung, verzögern
delivery Apport, Bringübung, Bringen
delivery to hand in die Hand geben
delouse entlausen
demand for Forderung nach
demanding fordern
demanding too much überfordern
dematting comb Entfilzungskamm, Filzkamm, Schneidekamm
demodectic mange Haarbalgmilbenausschlag, Demodex-Räude
demonstrate zeigen
den Bau
dense dicht
dentition Stellung und Anzahl der Zähne, Zahnstellung
deny leugnen
departure Abreise
dependent (on) abhängig (von)
deplorable state of affairs Missstand
deposit Anzahlung
depression Vertiefung (Gelände)
depth of chest Brusttiefe
descendent Nachkomme
descent Abstammung
describe beschreiben, schildern
description Schilderung
desensitize desensibilisieren
Desert Afghan Steppenafghane
Desert-Type Afghanhound Wüstenafghane
desirable wünschenswert
desire to take Greifwille, Beutetrieb
desired erwünscht
despair verzweifeln
despairing verzweifelt

despondency Verzagtheit
destroy zerstören
destruction Zerstörung
destruction instinct Zerstörungstrieb
detangling spray Kämmhilfe-Spray
detectable nachweisbar
deteriorate sich verschlechtern
deterioration Verschlechterung
determination Zielstrebigkeit
determination in trailing Spurwille
determination of stud value Körung
determined zielstrebig
devastate verwüsten
devastation Verwüstung
develop entwickeln
develop further weiterentwickeln
development Entwicklung
devotion Ergebenheit
devour verschlingen, fressen
dew(drop) Tau(tropfen)
dewclaw Afterklaue (oder -kralle), Wolfskralle
dewlap Kehlhaut, Wamme
diamond-shaped rautenförmig
diaphragm Zwerchfell
diarrhoea Durchfall
diarrhoea with vomiting Brechdurchfall
die a natural death natürlichen Todes sterben
die of starvation verhungern
die of thirst verdursten
difference Unterschied
different from anders als
difficult schwierig
difficulty Schwierigkeit
dig buddeln,scharren
digest verarbeiten (Eindrücke); verdauen
digestibility Verdaulichkeit
digestion Verdauung
digging Buddeln
digitigrade animal Zehengänger
dignity Würde
diligence Fleiß
diligent fleißig
direction Richtung
direction of the wind Windrichtung
director of judges Leistungsrichterobmann(-obfrau) LRO
directory Adressbuch
dirt Schmutz
dirty schmutzig
disagreeable unsympathisch
disappear verschwinden
disappoint enttäuschen
disappointment Enttäuschung
disapproval Missbilligung
disapprove (of) missbilligen, ablehnen

disapproving Ablehnung
disc Scheibe
discharge Ausfluss
discipline Disziplin
discontinue the fight (protection work) Kampf einstellen (Schutzdienst)
discordant disharmonisch, unharmonisch
discover entdecken
discs Disc-Scheiben
disdain verschmähen
dish face Sattelnase
dished eingedellt
disinformation Desinformation
dislike (of, for) Abneigung (gegen)
dislocation Verrenkung
dismissal Disqualifikation
dismissed (coursing) disqualifiziert
disobedience Ungehorsam
disobedient unfolgsam, ungehorsam
disobey an order Verweigern eines Kommandos
disobey someone Gehorsam verweigern
displaceable bar Abwurfstange
displacement (or sparking-over) activity Übersprungshandlung, Ersatzhandlung
displacement activity Ersatzhandlung, Übersprungshandlung
display behaviour Imponiergehabe
disposed geartet
disposition Naturell, Veranlagung
dispute someones' right of... streitig machen
disqualification Disqualifikation
disqualified disqualifiziert
disqualifying fault Ausschlussfehler, disqualifizierender Fehler
disregard Missachtung; missachten, unbeachtet lassen
disruptive element Störfaktor
distance Distanz
distance control Distanzkontrolle, Kontrolle auf Distanz
distemper teeth Staupezähne
distichiasis doppelte Wimpernreihe
distinct phase Prüfungsdisziplin/-Sparte/-Abteilung
distinguish (from) unterscheiden (von)
distinguished hervorragend, edel
distraction Ablenkung
distress yelp Schmerzschrei
distribute verteilen

distribution Verteilung
distrust misstrauen
distrust (of) Misstrauen (gegen)
distrustful misstrauisch
disturb stören
disturbance Störung
ditch Wassergraben
dive tauchen
divide teilen, zerteilen
do a good job
gute Arbeit leisten
do something without being forced to etwas ohne Zwang tun
do without verzichten auf
Dobermann Dobermann
dock kupieren (Körperteil)
docked tail Stummelrute
doctor Arzt
document Urkunde, Dokument; dokumentieren
documentation Dokumentation
doe Ricke
dog Hund
dog, savage scharfer Hund
dog behaviourist
Hunde-Verhaltensexperte, Hundepsychologe
dog biscuit Hundekuchen
dog bowl Fressnapf, Futternapf
dog box Hundetransportbox
dog cart Hundekarren, Hundewagen
dog catcher Hundefänger
dog class Trainingseinheit, Übungsstunde
dog club Hundeverein
dog collar Hundehalsband
dog cushion Hundepolster
dog dancing Dogdancing (Sport: Tanzen mit dem Hund)
dog dealer Hundehändler(in)
dog fancier Hundefreund(in)
dog fight Beißerei, Rauferei, Hundekampf
dog food Hundefutter
dog handler Hundeführer(in)
dog house Hundehütte
dog in white (mondioring)
Probehund (Ringsport)
dog licence disk
Hundesteuermarke
dog lover Hundeliebhaber(in)
dog owner Hundehalter(in), Hundebesitzer(in)
dog person Hundler(in), Hundeliebhaber(in), (Hundesportler/-aussteller)
dog psychologist
Hundepsychologe
dog race or racing
Hunderennen
dog shampoo Hundeshampoo
dog show Hundeschau, Zuchtschau, Schönheitswettbewerb

dog show racket audiotape Geräusch-Kassette mit Prüfungslärm
dog sled(ge) Hundeschlitten
dog sport career hundesportliche Laufbahn/ Werdegang
dog sport(s) Hundesport
dog supplies Hundebedarfsartikel
dog tag Hundesteuermarke
dog that can find and retrieve wounded game (hunting) Verlorenbringer (Jagd)
dog trailer Hundeanhänger (Auto-, Fahrrad-)
dog training Hundeausbildung
dog training court or site Hundeübungsplatz
dog walk (agility) Laufsteg (Agility)
dog whistle Hundepfeife
dog with pincer bite Aufbeißer
dog with undershot mouth Vorbeißer
dogdom Hundewelt
dogery Hundewelt
dogging Jogging mit Hund
doggy rüdenhaft
doghouse Hundehütte
Dogo Argentino Dogo Argentino
dogs breeding Hundezucht
dog-sitting Hundebetreuung
dogs basket Hundekorb
dogs bed Hundebett
dogsport(s) Hundesport
domesticate domestizieren
domesticated domestiziert
domesticated dog Haushund
dominance Dominanz
dominance fight Machtkampf
dominant überlegen sein
dominate dominieren
domineering herrschsüchtig
domineeringness Herrschsucht
dope dopen
doping Doping
dot Punkt, Fleck
double coat Stockhaar
double-bar jump (agility) doppelte Hürde (Agility)
double-coated stockhaarig
doubt Zweifel, anzweifeln, zweifeln
down (or drop) while in motion Ablegen aus der Bewegung
down and stay Ablegen und Bleiben
down with recall Ablegen nach Herankommen
Down! (verbal command) Platz! (Hörzeichen)
down-faced ramsnasig
downfaced head Winkelkopf

Down-Stay! (verbal command) Platz-Bleib! (Hörzeichen)
downward trend Abwärtstrend
drag zerren, schleppen
drag hunt Schleppjagd
drag something off etwas wegschleppen
draw ziehen
draw a conclusion Schlussfolgerung (ziehen)
draw attention to sich bemerkbar machen
drawn-up aufgezogen
dreadful abscheulich
dress code Kleiderordnung
drift off abdriften
drill team Formation
drink trinken, saufen
drink (noisily) schlabbern (laut)
dripping wet tropfnass
drive Trieb, Schub
drive (live-stock) treiben (Vieh)
drive (us) Drückjagd
drive past vorbeifahren
drive somebody into a corner in die Enge treiben
drive somebody out of jemanden vertreiben aus
drive somebody/ something away jemanden/ etwas vertreiben
drool sabbern, speicheln
drooping croup abfallende Kruppe
drooping stance kraftloser Stand
drop ablegen
drop (an object) Auslassen (eine Sache)
drop (protection work) Ablassen (Schutzdienst)
drop back (heelwork) nachhängen (Fußarbeit)
Drop it! (verbal command) Aus! (Hörzeichen)
drop on recall Ablegen nach Herankommen
dropped tail Hängerute
Drover Bullenbeißer
drug (sniffer) dog Drogenspürhund
drug detection dog Rauschgiftsuchhund
dry trocken (Kopf usw.)
dry dog food Trockenfutter
dry supplementary food Trockenergänzungsnahrung
dryness Trockenheit
duel Zweikampf
dugs Gesäuge
dull glanzlos
dumbbell (stick) Apportierb(l)ock, Bringholz
dummy Dummy, Apportier-dummy

dung Losung (vom Wild), Mist (Tierkot), Dung
duodenum Zwölffingerdarm
Dupuy Pointer Dupuy Vorstehhund
durable dauerhaft
during the day tagsüber
Dutch Longhaired-Shepherd Holländischer Langhaar Schäferhund
Dutch Roughcoated-Shepherd Holländischer Rauhaar Schäferhund
Dutch Sheepdog Schapendoes
Dutch Shepherd Holländischer Schäferhund
Dutch Shorthaired-Shepherd Holländischer Kurzhaar Schäferhund
Dutch Smoushond Smoushond
Dutch Steenbrak Holländische Steinbracke
Dutch Water Spaniel Friesischer Wasserhund, Wetterhound
dwarfism Zwergwuchs
dye färben (z.B. Haar)
dysplasia Dysplasie

E

each other zueinander
eager eifrig
eager to learn lernbegierig
eagerness Eifer (Arbeitswille/ Begierde)
ear Ohr
ear, cropped kupiertes Ohr
ear flap Ohrlappen
ear infection Ohrenentzündung
ear inflammation (medical) Otitis (medizinisch)
ear leather Ohrmuschel
ear mite Ohrmilbe
ear opening Ohrschlitz
ear too large and/ or heavy schweres Ohr
earache Ohrenzwang
earage Behang
ear-mite infestation Ohrräude
earn (title) erlangen (Ausbildungskennzeichen)
ear-pinch Ohrkneifen (Zwangsausbildung)
ears, low set tief angesetzte Ohren
earth dog Bauhund, Erdhund
easily spielend leicht
easily digestible leicht verdaulich
East Siberian Laika Ostsibirische Laika
east-west-feet auswärts gedrehte Pfoten
easy to train gelehrig
easy to understand leicht verständlich
eat essen, fressen
eclampsia Eklampsie
ectoparasite Ektoparasit
ectropion Ektropium, Hängelid
Ecuador Bush Dog Ecuador Waldhund
eczema Ekzem
edge of the forest Waldrand
effect Wirkung
effective wirksam, wirkungsvoll

effectiveness Wirksamkeit
efficiency Arbeitsleistung, Leistungsfähigkeit
efficiency contest Leistungswettbewerb
effort Versuch (Bemühung)
egg cell Eizelle
egg-shaped eiförmig
ego-boost Selbstbestätigung
Egyptian Sheepdog Ägyptischer Schäferhund, Armant
ejaculate Ejakulat
ejaculation Ejakulation
elation Hochgefühl
elbow Ell(en)bogen
elbow cyst Ellbogenbeule, Liegebeule
elbow dysplasia Ellbogendysplasie
elbow joint Ellbogengelenk
electronic collar (for training purposes) Teletakt-Gerät
elegant elegant
element of surprise Überraschungsmoment
element of uncertainty Unsicherheitsfaktor
eligible teilnahmeberechtigt
eliminate beseitigen (Missstände)
eliminate sich entleeren, sich versäubern
elimination Ausscheidung; Beseitigung
Elkhound Elchhund
emaciated abgemagert
embryo Embryo
embryonic embryonal
emergency (situation) Notlage
emergency measure Notmaßnahme
emetic Brechmittel
eminently in hohem Maße, überaus
emotion Regung (Gefühl)
emotional life Gefühlsleben
emotional outburst Gefühlsausbruch
emotional state Seelenzustand
empathize with sich einfühlen
empathy Einfühlungsvermögen
emphasize Nachdruck verleihen
empowering (the dog) zugestehen, erlauben (dem Hund)
empty leer
encounter feindliche Begegnung
encourage ermuntern
encouragement Ermunterung
encyclopaedia Lexikon
endbrain Endhirn
endoparasite Endoparasit
endurance Stehvermögen, Ausdauer
endure erdulden
endure something über sich ergehen lassen
enemy Feind(in)

nergetic energisch
nergy Energie
nergy blockade
:nergieblockade
nergy demand Energiebedarf
nergy flow Energiefluss
English Bulldog
Englische Bulldogge
English Cocker Spaniel
Englischer Cocker Spaniel
English Coonhound
English Coonhound
English Foxhound
Englischer Fuchshund
English saddle clip
englische Schur
English Setter
Englischer Setter, Laverack Setter
English Shepherd
English Shepherd
English Springer Spaniel
(Englischer) Springer Spaniel
English Toy Spaniel King Charles Spaniel, Zwergspaniel
English Toy Terrier
Black and Tan Toy Terrier, English Toy Terrier
enjoyment Freude, Genuss, Vergnügen
enter anmelden (einen Hund zur Prüfung)
enter a protest against
Protest einlegen gegen
enter in (trial/ competition/ koerung) anmelden bei (Wettkampf/ Körung)
enteritis Darmentzündung
enthusiasm Enthusiasmus
entire nicht kastriert/ nicht sterilisiert
entire male dog
nicht kastrierter Rüde
Entlebuch Mountain Dog
Entlebucher Sennenhund
entrance Eingang
entrance of the tunnel
Tunneleingang
entropion Entropium
entropion Roll-Lid
entry Anmeldung; Starterfeld; Teilnehmerzahl
entry fee Meldegebühr (oder -geld)
entry form Meldeschein
environment Umgebung, Umwelt
environmental impact
Umwelteinfluss
environmental safety Umwelt-sicherheit
envy (at food) Futterneid
epididymis Nebenhode
epilepsy Epilepsie
equipment Gerät (für Wettkampf/ Parcours); Ausrüstung

erect (ears) aufgestellt (Ohren)
erectile tissue Schwellkörper
eruption Durchbruch (der Zähne)
escalate eskalieren
escalation Eskalation
escape Flucht, flüchten, entkommen
escape route Fluchtweg
establish etablieren
esteem Wertschätzung
Estonian Hound Estländische Bracke
Estrela Mountain Dog Estrela Berghund, Portugiesischer Berghund der Serra da Estrela
ethical ethisch
ethics Ethik
Eurasian Eurasier
Eustachian tube Eustachische Röhre
euthanasia Euthanasie, Sterbehilfe
euthanize einschläfern
evaluate a dog as his stud potential kören/ ankören
evaluation of breeding potential Zuchtwertschätzung
even bite Zangenbiss
evening Abend
eventful erlebnisreich
event calendar Ausstellungskalender
ever so often x-fach
everything alles
evolution Evolution
exam nerves Prüfungsangst, Prüfungsnervosität
examination Prüfung
examination as to suitability for breeding Ankörung, Zuchttauglichkeitsprüfung, Zuchtzulassungsprüfung
examination fee Prüfungsgebühr
examination table Behandlungstisch
examine (with fingers) abtasten
example Beispiel
excessive übertrieben
excessive angulation Überwinkelung
excessive breeding Überzüchtung
exchange Tausch, tauschen
excited aufgeregt
excitement Aufregung
exciting spannend
exclude ausscheiden
excrement(s) Kot, Exkremente
excrete ausscheiden
excretion Ausscheidung
exemplary vorbildlich

exercise Auslauf; Übung (Aufgabe)
exercise (a dog) Gassi gehen
exercise area Abkotstelle, Versäuberungsplatz, Hundekotplatz
exercise run (or enclosure) Auslaufplatz
exercise tolerance Ausdauer
exhausted erschöpft, abgekämpft
exhibit ausstellen
exhibition Ausstellung
exhibitor Aussteller(in)
existence Fortbestand
existential dread Lebensangst
expect erwarten
expect something of somebody jemandem etwas zumuten
expectancy Erwartungshaltung
expectant erwartungsvoll
expectation Erwartung
expenditure (of) Aufwand
expense allowance Aufwandsentschädigung
experience Erfahrung, erleben
experienced routiniert, erfahren
experimental animal Versuchstier
expert opinion Sachverständigengutachten
explain erklären, erläutern
explanation Erklärung, Erläuterung
explore erkunden
expression Ausdruck
expression, gentle freundlicher, sanfter Gesichtsausdruck
expression, oriental orientalischer Ausdruck
expressive ausdrucksvoll
extending distance Distanz erweitern
extension Raumgriff
extensor (muscle) Streckmuskel
external parasite(s) Ungeziefer
extinction Löschung (eines Verhaltens)
extinction burst Löschungstrotz
extinguish (behaviour) löschen (Verhalten)
extraneous cue unbewusstes Signal
extremity Gliedmaße
eye Auge
eye contact Blickkontakt
eye level Augenlinie
eye lid Lid
eyes, deep-set tiefliegende Augen
eyes, haw offene Augen
eye mark Augenfleck
eye muscle Augenmuskel
eye rim Lidrand
eye socket Augenhöhle

eyeball Augapfel
eyebrow Augenbraue
eyelash Wimper
eyelid Augenlid
eyesight Sehvermögen
eyes, slanting schräg gestellte Augen

F

face somebody zuwenden (das Gesicht)
facial expression Gesichtsausdruck
facial mask Gesichtsmaske
facts of the case Sachverhalt
fading Ausschleichen (z.B. Körperhilfen)
fading cue Signal ausschleichen/ abschwächen
fading puppy syndrome Welpensterben
fading stimuli Reiz abschwächen, ausschleichen
faeces Kot
fail scheitern
fail to do something versäumen etwas zu tun
failure Misserfolg, Versagen
failure rate Durchfallquote
fair fair
fairness Fairness
fall stürzen
fall ill erkranken
fallacy Trugschluss, Irrtum
fallow fahl(gelb)
fallow deer Damwild
false pregnancy Scheinschwangerschaft
false rib Asternale Rippe, falsche Rippe
family Familie
family background Familienverhältnisse
family descent Abstammung
family dog Familienhund
family environment familiäres Umfeld
family tree Stammbaum
farewell Abschied
farewell scene Abschiedsszene
farm dog Hofhund
fashionable (dog) breed Modehund
fast pace/ gait schnelle Gangart
fat dick, fat

fate Schicksal
father Vater(tier)
fatty fett(reich)
fauces Schlund
fault (sport, show) Fehler (Sport, Ausstellung)
faultless (sport) fehlerfrei (Sport)
faulty fehlerhaft
faulty bite Gebissfehler
faulty temperament Wesensschwäche
favour favorisieren
fawn rehbraun, gelbbraun, rehfarben, rehrot, weißgelb, hellbraun, falb
fawn Rehkitz
fawn brindle dunkel gestromt
fear (of) Angst (vor), Furcht (vor)
fear biter Angstbeißer
fear biting Angstbeißen
fear of being alone Angst vor dem Alleinsein
fear of death Todesangst
fearful angstvoll
fearless unerschrocken, furchtlos
feather Feder
feathered (ears, legs, body) befedert (Ohren, Beine, Körper)
federal hunting law Bundesjagdgesetz
feed füttern, verfüttern
feeding Fütterung
feeding bottle Milchflasche
feel empfinden, spüren
fellow Gefährte/ Gefährtin
felted filzig
female (dog) Hündin
femoral artery Oberschenkelschlagader
fence Einzäunung, Gatter, Zaun
fence in einzäunen
feral dog Wildhund
fertile fruchtbar, zeugungsfähig
fertility Fruchtbarkeit, Zeugungsfähigkeit
Fetch! (verbal command) Bring!, Hol's! (Hörzeichen)
fever Fieber
fibula Wadenbein
field Feld; Sparte
field committee Schiedsgericht
Field Spaniel Field Spaniel
field trial Arbeitsprüfung, Feldjagdsuche, Gebrauchshund-wettbewerb
field trial director (or chairman/ -woman) Rennleiter(in)
fight Rauferei, raufen, kämpfen
fight against ankämpfen gegen
fight for kämpfen um
fight or flight Angriff oder Flucht
fighting kämpfend, kämpferisch
fighting dog Kampfhund
fighting drive Kampftrieb

fighting spirit (sport) Kampfgeist (Sport)
figure eight (e.g. heelwork) in Form einer 8 (z.B. Fußarbeit)
Fila Brasileiro Fila Brasileiro, Brasilianische Dogge
fill füllen
fill someone with fear Angst einflössen
film camera Filmkamera
film report Filmbericht
final course Endlauf
final result Endergebnis
final run Endlauf
final stage Endphase
final whistle Abpfiff
find a way to communicate gemeinsame Sprache finden
Find! (verbal command) Such! (Hörzeichen)
Find! (protection work) Revier! (Schutzdienst)
fine-tuning Feinabstimmung
finger toothbrush Fingerzahnbürste
finish Abschlussgrundstellung
Finnish Hound Finnenbracke, Finnischer Laufhund
Finnish Lapphund Finnischer Lapphund
Finnish Spitz Finnenspitz
fire Feuer
firehouse dog Feuerwehrhund
firework Feuerwerkskörper
fireworks Feuerwerk
firm stramm
firm grip spray Anti-Rutsch-spray für Hundepfoten
first of all zuallererst
first-aid man (woman) Sanitäter(in)
first-class erstklassig
fish eye Fischauge
fist Faust
fistula Fistel
fit vital
fit of anger Zornausbruch
fitness of the older dog Altersfrische
fitness training Konditionstraining
flabbiness Schlaffheit
flabby schlaff
flag Fahne(nrute)
flagpole tail Fahnenmastrute
flake Flocke
flank Seite, Flanke, Weiche
flap (of dog door) Schwingklappe (an der Tür)
flare Blesse; Laterne
flat Wohnung
flat croup waagerechte Kruppe
flat foot Plattfuß, Spreizfuß (-pfote)
flat-chested flachbrüstig
flatcoated schlichthaarig

Flat-Coated Retriever Flat Coated Retriever
flat-muscled flach bemuskelt
flaw in one's reasoning Denkfehler
flawless (show) makellos (Ausstellung)
flea Floh
flea (and tick) collar Parasitenhalsband
flea allergy Flohallergie
flea collar Flohhalsband
flea powder Ungezieferpuder
flea shampoo Ungeziefershampoo
flea spray Ungezieferspray
flee from fliehen vor
flesh marks fleischfarbene Flecken (Nasenschwamm)
fleshy fleischig
flews Lefzen
flexi-leash Flexi-Leine, Ausziehleine, Abrollleine
flexor (muscle) Beugemuskel
flight distance Fluchtdistanz
flight reflex (or response) Fluchtreflex
flock of sheep Schafherde
flood of words Redeschwall
floodlight Scheinwerfer
floodlights Flutlicht
floppy disk, soft bite Frisbeescheibe aus Softmaterial
Florentine Spitz Volpino Italiano
fluencies Geläufigkeitsübungen, Routineübungen
fluency (e.g. exercises) Geläufigkeit (z.B. in Übungen)
flush aufscheuchen, aufstöbern
fluttering lips Flatterlippen
fly (at) sich stürzen auf
flyball Flugball
flyball (sport) Flyball (Sportart)
flyball box Flyball-Apparat
flyball racing Flyball-Wettbewerb
foam Schaum, Geifer
foam with rage vor Wut schnauben
focus on something sich konzentrieren auf etwas, etwas fixieren, anstarren, fokussieren
focus point Konzentrationspunkt
foetal membranes Eihäute
foetus Fötus
fold Falte, Knick
folding ring gates (e.g. obedience) faltbarer Ringbegrenzungszaun (z.B. Obedience)
folding target stick faltbarer Targetstick
follicular mange Akarusräude, Haarbalgmilbenausschlag
follow folgen, nachgehen

follow (or work) a track ausarbeiten (einer Fährte), absuchen (einer Fährte)
follow and hold (protection work) Verfolgen und Stellen (Schutzdienst)
food Futter
food additive Futterzusatz
food allergy Futterallergie
food dish Fressnapf, Futternapf
food drive Futtergier, Futtertrieb
food refusal Futterverweigerung
food, solid festes Futter
food supplement Futterzusatz
food supply Futterversorgung
food treats Futterbelohnung
foot Fuß (Pfote)
footpath Steg, Wanderweg
footprint Fußabdruck
footwear Schuhwerk
forbidden verboten
force erzwingen
force Wucht; Zwang, Gewalt
force do something zwingen, etwas zu tun
force of habit Macht der Gewohnheit
force something (upon) etwas aufzwingen
forechest Vorbrust
forecourt Vorplatz
foreface Gesichtsschädel; Vorgesicht; Schnauze, Fang
forefinger Zeigefinger
forehead Stirn
foreign word Fremdwort
forelock Stirnlocke
forequarters Vorderhand, Vorhand
foresighted vorausschauend
foreskin Vorhaut
forest Wald
forestall etwas zuvorkommen
forester Förster(in)
forget vergessen
formulation of a problem Problem(stellung)
fortify oneself sich stärken
fortunately erfreulicherweise
forward planning Vorausplanung
Forward! (verbal command) Voran! (Hörzeichen)
forward-looking zukunftsweisend
foster mother Amme
foster mothering Ammenaufzucht
foul colour Fehlfarbe
foul judge (dog racing) Bahnbeobachter(in) (Hunderennen)
four-legged vierbeinig
Fox Collie Fox Collie
Fox Terrier Fox Terrier
fox' den Fuchsbau

Foxhound Foxhound
foxy fuchsähnlich, fuchsartig
foxy-red fuchsrot
freckle Sommersprosse, Fleckchen
free of matting filzfrei
freedom of action Handlungsfreiheit
freedom of will Willensfreiheit
freely moving frei beweglich
freeze (in a position) erstarren, verharren
French Black and White Hound Französischer Schwarz-Weißer Laufhund
French Bulldog Französische Bulldogge, Bully
French front französischer Stand
French Orange and White Hound Französischer Orange-Weißer Laufhund
French Pointer Französischer Vorstehhund, Französische Bracke
French Shorthaired Sheepdog Schäferhund der Beauce, Beauceron, Bas Rouge
French Spaniel Épagneul Français, Französisch Langhaar, Französischer Spaniel
French Tricolour Hound Französischer Dreifarbiger Laufhund
French-English Hound Anglo Français
friend Freund(in)
friendliness Zutraulichkeit
friendly zutraulich
friendship Freundschaft
frighten erschrecken
frightened verängstigt
from a distance aus der Ferne
from behind hinterrücks
from the dogs' point of view aus der Hundesicht
front Front
front, narrow schmale Front
front, pinched schmale Front (fehlerhaft)
front angulation Vorderhandwinkelung
front leg Vorderlauf
front paw Vorderpfote, Vorderfuß
front position Vorsitz
frontal frontal
frontal bone Stirnbein
frontal groove Stirnfurche
frontal line Stirnstrich
frosty weather Frostwetter
froth Schaum, schäumen
frustrate frustrieren
frustration Frust(ration)
full body suit (mondioring) Ganzkörperhetzanzug, Vollanzug (Ringsport)

full dentition Vollzahnigkeit
full of expression (eyes, work) ausdrucksvoll (Augen, Arbeit)
full of gaps lückenhaft (z.B. Gebiss)
full speed volles Tempo
full-grown voll entwickelt
fun Spaß
functional zweckmäßig
fungus infection Pilzbefall
fur change Fellwechsel
furniture Möbel

gait Gang, Gangart, Gangwerk
gait, erratic unsicherer Gang
gait, floating schwebender Gang
gait, free freier, ungehemmter Gang
gait, hackney steppender Gang
gait, normal normaler Gang
gait, quick schneller Gang
gait, rolling schaukelnder, wiegender Gang
gait, springy federnder Gang
gaiting fault fehlerhafte Gangart
gallop Galopp, galoppieren
game mutig
game Wild
game park Wildpark
game preserve Wildgehege
game trail (hunting) Wildwechsel (Jagd)
garden fence Gartenzaun
gastric torsion Magendrehung
gastroenteritis Magen-Darm-Katarrh, Brechdurchfall
gathering (live-stock) eingattern (Vieh)
gender Geschlechts-, geschlechts-,
gene Gen
genealogy Genealogie, Abstammung
general allgemein
general appearance allgemeines Erscheinungsbild, Gesamterscheinung
general knowledge Allgemeinwissen
general meeting Mitgliederversammlung
general narcosis Vollnarkose
general outline Linienführung
general public Allgemeinheit, Öffentlichkeit
generalization Generalisierung, Absichern von Verhalten
generalize verallgemeinern
generation Generation

generic term Oberbegriff, Sammelbegriff
genetic disposition genetische Veranlagung
genetically damaging erbgutschädigend
genetics Genetik
genital Geschlechts-, geschlechts-,
genitals Genitalien, Geschlechtsteile
genotype Erbgut
gentle friedlich, sanft
gentle to poultry geflügelfromm
gentleness Behutsamkeit, Sanftmut
German Broken-Coated Pointer Deutsch Stichelhaar
German commands deutsche Kommandos
German Hound Deutsche Bracke, Olper Bracke, Sauerländer Bracke
German Hunt Terrier Deutscher Jagdterrier
German Longhaired Pointer Deutscher Langhaariger Vorstehhund
German Long-Haired Pointer Deutsch Langhaar
German Mastiff Deutsche Dogge
German national winner deutsche(r) Bundessieger(in)
German Pinscher Deutscher Pinscher
German Sauerland Hound Holzbracke
German Sheeppoodle Schafpudel
German Shepherd Dog Deutscher Schäferhund
German Short-Haired Pointer Deutsch Kurzhaar (Deutscher Kurzhaariger Vorstehhund)
German Spaniel Deutscher Wachtelhund
German Spitz Deutscher Spitz
German Toy Spitz Deutscher Zwergspitz
German Wirehaired Pointer Deutsch Drahthaar
gestation Trächtigkeit
gestation (period) Tragezeit (Schwangerschaft)
gesture Geste, Handbewegung
get a (sound) thrashing Prügel beziehen
get a thrashing Hiebe bekommen
get along with each other sich verstehen
get dirty sich schmutzig machen
get excited (about) sich ereifern

Get him! (verbal command in protection work) Fass! (Hörzeichen beim Schutzdienst)
get out of danger sich in Sicherheit bringen
get rid of rewards Belohnungen abbauen
get rid of the food Futterbelohnung abbauen
get something back etwas wiederbekommen
get something through durchsetzen
get to the bottom of ergründen
get used to sich daran gewöhnen
get worked up about sich hineinsteigern
giant breed riesenwüchsige Rasse
Giant German Spitz Deutscher Großspitz
Giant Schnauzer Riesenschnauzer
Giant Spitz Großspitz
girth Umfang, Körperumfang
give (or administer) a booster shot nachimpfen
give a command Kommando geben
give a short bark kurz verbellen, blaffen
give birth (to) gebären
give someone a dressing-down abkanzeln
give someone a friendly nod jemandem freundlich zunicken
give someone instructions jemanden instruieren
give something back etwas zurückgeben, hergeben
give tongue Laut geben (Bellen)
giving tongue Waidlaut
giving tongue to a scent Fährtenlaut, Spurlaut geben
gland Drüse
glans (penis) Eichel
glass cupboard (cabinet) Vitrine
glass eye Glasauge
glaucoma Glaukom
Glen of Imaal Terrier Glen of Imaal Terrier
gloss Glanz
glossy glänzend
gloves Handschuhe
gnaw zernagen
gnaw (on) nagen (an)
Go (out)! (verbal command) Voran/ Voraus! (Hörzeichen)
go away weggehen
go deer-stalking auf die Pirsch gehen
go for a walk spazieren gehen
go hungry hungern

go in(to) hineingehen
go mouldy schimmeln
go on weitergehen, weitermachen
go on working weiterarbeiten
go over abtasten
go stalking anpirschen
go through puberty pubertieren
go wrong fehlschlagen
goal Ziel, End-
goal behaviour Zielverhalten, Zielübung
go-behind finish Abschlussgrundstellung (um Hundeführer herum)
goitre Kropf
gold Gold
gold brindle goldgestromt
gold sable zobelfarben
golden goldrot
Golden Retriever Golden Retriever
golden yellow goldbraun, löwenfarbig
gone wild verwildert
Good boy/ girl! Braver Hund!
Good dog! Guter Hund!, Brav!
good nose Spürsinn
Good sport! Weidmannsheil!
Gordon Setter Gordon Setter, Schottischer Setter
Gotland Hound Gotland Stövare
grade Prädikat
gradually allmählich
graminivorous Gras fressend
grandfather Großvater
grandmother Großmutter
grandparents Großeltern
granuloma Granulom
grass Rasen, Gras
grave folgenschwer
gravid trächtig
graze weiden
grazing shot Streifschuss
great großartig
Great Anglo-French Hound Grand Anglo Français, Großer Anglo-Französischer Laufhund
Great Dane Deutsche Dogge
Great Pyrenees Pyrenäen Berghund
great suspense Hochspannung (Erwartungshaltung)
Great Swiss Mountain Dog Großer Schweizer Sennenhund
greediness Gefräßigkeit
greediness for Gier nach
greedy gefräßig
greedy for gierig
Greek Hare Hound Hellinikos Ichnilatis, Griechischer Laufhund, Griechische Bracke
Greek Sheepdog Griechischer Schäferhund

green dog außer Konkurrenz vorgeführter Hund
Greenland Dog Grönlandhund
greeting ritual Begrüßungszeremonie
grey grau, ergrauen
grey and fawn grau-kupferrot
grey spots Porzellanscheckung
grey tiger Grautiger (Farbe)
grey-black mixed schwarz-grau meliert
Greyhound Greyhound
Griffon Griffon
Griffon Nivernais Griffon Nivernais
grip (protection work) Griff (Schutzdienst)
grizzle ergrauen, graumeliert
grizzling Ergrauen
groom pflegen
groomer's Schursalon
grooming Fellpflege
grooming shears Hundeschere, Trimmschere
grooming shop (poodle parlour) Hundesalon
grooming table Trimmtisch
gross (muscles or bone) überentwickelt (Muskeln oder Knochen)
ground Gelände, Terrain
ground colour Grundfarbe
ground obstacles Grundgeräte, Basisgeräte
group Gruppe
group exercise Gruppenübung
group of people Personengruppe
grow up aufwachsen
growl knurren
growth Wachstum
guarantee sicherstellen
guard bewachen
guard dog Wachhund
guard dog, chained Kettenhund
Guatemalan Hairless Dog Guatemalischer Nackthund
guess erraten
guide dog (for the blind) Blinden(führ)hund
gun Gewehr
gun dog Jagd(gebrauchs)hund
gun shyness Schussunsicherheit
gunfire test Überprüfung der Schussfestigkeit
gun-shy schussscheu
gust of wind Windstoß

H

habit Gewohnheit
habituation Gewöhnung
habituation to the environment Umweltgewöhnung
hackles Nackenhaare
hackles, raised aufgestellte Nackenhaare
hackles up Nackenfell sträuben
haemorrhage Blutsturz
hair Haar
hair on back Rückenhaar
hair root Haarwurzel
hair with wavy undercoat Wellhaar
hairless dog haarloser Hund
Hairless Dog Nackthund
Halden Hound Haldenstover
half-brother Halbgeschwister
half-hearted halbherzig
half-sister Halbgeschwister
half-truth Halbwahrheit
half-turn (e.g. heelwork) halbe Drehung, Winkel (z.B. Fußarbeit)
hallmarks Charakteristika
Hallstrom Dog Hallstromhund
Hamilton Hound Hamiltonstövare
hand position (performance) Handhaltung (bei Vorführung)
hand raising künstliche Welpenaufzucht
hand shy handscheu
hand signal Handsignal, optisches Signal, Sichtzeichen
handle handhaben, umgehen
handler Hundeführer(in), Vorführer(in), Führer(in)
handlers' track Eigenfährte, Führerfährte
handling Vorführung
handling competition Vorführungswettbewerb
handling with dogs Umgang mit Hunden
hanging ear Hängeohr, Schlappohr

hanging ears Behang
Hannoverian Hound
Hannoverscher Schweißhund
happen sich zutragen
hard hart
hard cheese Hartkäse
hard pad syndrome
Hartballenkrankheit
hardening Abhärtung
hardness Härte
hardwearing strapazierfähig
hardwood dumbbell
Hartholz-Apportiergegenstand
hare/ rabbit Hase
Hare-Hound Hasenhund
harlequin harlekin, graugefleckt
harm someone jemandem Leid zufügen
harmful substance Schadstoff
harmless harmlos, ungefährlich
harmlessness Harmlosigkeit
harmonious harmonisch
harmonize harmonieren
harmony Harmonie
harness Geschirr, Brustgeschirr
harsh (coat) harsch (Fell)
hasty fluchtartig; vorschnell
haunch Hüfte, Keule
haunch bone Hüfthöcker
Havana Silk Dog
Havaneser, Bichon Havanais
have a favourable effect on
sich vorteilhaft auswirken auf
have a hereditary handicap
vorbelastet, erblich
have a relapse rückfällig werden
have a stool koten, sich lösen
Hawaiian Poi Dog
Polynesischer Eingeborenenhund
hazel haselnussbraun
he has a lot to catch up on
er hat viel nachzuholen
he has a way with dogs
er kann mit Hunden umgehen
he's slightly cracked
er hat einen Knacks weg (geistig)
head Kopf
head collar Halti® (Kopfhalfter)
head halter „promise collar"
Kopfgeschirr
head planes Kopflinien
head position Kopfhaltung
heal (up) abheilen;
zuwachsen (Wunde)
health Gesundheit
health certificate
Gesundheitszeugnis
healthy gesund
heap of rubble Trümmerhaufen
hear hören
hearing ear dog
Gehörlosenhund
hearing range Hörweite
heart Mut; Herz
heart ventricle Herzkammer
heat Hitze; Läufigkeit, Östrus

heat stroke Hitzschlag
heavy bone, of derbknochig
heel bei Fuß gehen; Ferse
heel position Grundstellung
Heel! (verbal command) Bei Fuß! (Hörzeichen)
heeling off-lead Freifolge
heeling on lead Leinenführigkeit
heelwork Fußarbeit, Fußgehen
height Stockmaß
height Höhe (Größe)
height at shoulders Schulterhöhe, Widerristhöhe, Risthöhe
help helfen
help someone on jemandem weiterhelfen
helper (protection work) Helfer(in), Figurant(in) (Schutzdienst); Schutzdiensthelfer(in)
helper evaluation Beurteilung des Schutzdiensthelfers
helper evaluation form Beurteilungsbogen für die Arbeit des Schutzdiensthelfers
helpful hilfreich
helpless hilflos, ratlos
helplessness Hilflosigkeit, Ratlosigkeit
hepatitis Hepatitis, Leberentzündung
herd hüten
herder Hütehund
herding (live-stock) hüten (Vieh)
herding breeds Hütehundrassen
herding trial Hütehundwettbewerb
herding work Hütearbeit
hereditary erblich
hereditary (or genetic) make up Erbmasse
hereditary defect Erbfehler
hereditary disease Erbkrankheit
heredity Erbanlage, Vererblichkeit
hermaphroditism Zwittertum
herniated disc syndrome Dackellähme
heron Reiher
Hertha Pointer Hertha Pointer
hesitate zaudern
hesitating zögernd
hidden versteckt
hidden sleeve (protection work) Unterzieharm (Schutzdienst)
hide sich verkriechen
hide behind verstecken hinter
hide from sich verstecken vor
hiding place Versteck
hierarchy Hierarchie, Rangordnung
high drive working triebstark arbeiten

high in withers abfallende Oberlinie
high jump Hochsprung
high legged hochbeinig
high off the ground hochgebaut
high on leg hochläufig
high pain threshold Schmerzunempfindlichkeit
high value, of hochwertig
higher-ranking member of the pack ranghöheres Rudelmitglied
high-performance leistungsstark
high-performance sports Spitzensport
high-stepping tänzelnd
high-voltage Starkstrom
hike wandern
Himalayan Sheepdog Bhotia
hind Hinter-, hinter-,
hind (or rear) leg Hinterlauf
hip Hüfte
hip bone Hüfthöcker
hip dysplasia Hüftgelenksdysplasie
hip socket Beckenpfanne
history Geschichte, Vorbericht
hit out at the dog nach dem Hund schlagen
hobby Hobby
hobby breeder Liebhaberzüchter
hobbyhorse Steckenpferd
hocks Sprunggelenke
hocks, weak durchgetretene Sprunggelenke, weiche Sprunggelenke
hold and bark (protection work) Stellen und Verbellen (Schutzdienst)
hold out ausstrecken, darbieten
hold the grip (protection work) Griff halten (Schutzdienst)
hollow of the knee Kniekehle
Holstein Hound Holsteiner Bracke
home territory Heimbereich
homoeopathy Homöopathie
hookworm Hakenwurm
horde Rotte
hormone Hormon
horn of the uterus Gebärmutterhorn
horse Pferd
horse droppings Pferdeäpfel
hostile (to) feindselig (gegen)
hostile behaviour feindliches Verhalten
hostility Feindseligkeit
hot pack warmer Umschlag
hound Jagdgebrauchshund
hound at hetzen (auf)
hound glove Putzhandschuh
hound hunting in pairs Paarjäger
hour Stunde

housebroken (us) stubenrein, zimmerrein
house-dog Wohnungshund
household obedience Gehorsam für den Hausgebrauch
house-train stubenrein machen
house-trained stubenrein, zimmerrein
housing conditions Wohnverhältnisse
Hovawart Hovawart
howl heulen, jaulen
howling Geheul
hue Farbton
humane choke collar gestopptes Zughalsband
humanize vermenschlichen
humerus Oberarmknochen, Oberarmbein
humorous humorvoll
humorless humorlos
Hungarian Cattle Dog Pumi
Hungarian Foxhound Pannonischer Spürhund
Hungarian Greyhound Magyar Agar, Ungarischer Windhund
Hungarian Hound Siebenbürger Bracke, Erdélyi kopó
Hungarian Pointer Magyar Vizsla, Ungarischer Vorstehhund
hunger Hunger
hunt jagen, hetzen
hunt about stöbern
hunt by sight Sichthetze
hunt fox or hare with scenthounds brackieren
hunt game (or birds) in heavy cover buschieren
hunt master Jagdleiter
hunter Jäger
hunting Jagd
hunting breeds Jagdhundrassen
hunting collar Schweißhalsung (Jagd)
hunting dog Jagd(gebrauchs)hund
hunting ground Jagdrevier
hunting instinct Jagdtrieb
hunting kennel Jägerhof
hunting leash Riemen (Jagd)
hunting licence Jagdschein
hunting season Jagdzeit
hunting test Jagdhundprüfung
hunting together gemeinsames Jagen
hunting training Jagdtraining
hunting with a pack of hounds Meutejagd
huntress Jägerin
huntsman like weidmännisch
hurdle Hürde
hurt wehtun
hybrid Hybride, Mischling
hybrid vigour Vitalität beim Mischling
hydrocephalus Wasserkopf

hydrophobia Wasserscheu
hydrophobia Tollwut
Hygenhund Hygenhund
hyoid bone Zungenbein
hyperrefined überzüchtet
hypersensitive überempfindlich
hysteria Hysterie

Ibizan Hound
Podenco Ibicenco, Xarnelo
Iceland Dog
Islandspitz, Islandhund
icy eisig
icy cold Eiseskälte
id tag Hundemarke
idea Einfall (Gedanke)
identify (article) verweisen (Fährtengegenstand)
identifying verweisen (Fährtengegenstand)
ideological weltanschaulich
ideology Weltanschauung
ignore ignorieren, überhören
illegal ungesetzlich
Illyrian Sheepdog Sarplaninac
imaginative einfallsreich
imaging sich vorstellen
imbalance Unausgeglichenheit, Unausgewogenheit
imitate nachahmen
imitation Nachahmung
immature unfertig
immediate obedience Appell
immediate objective Nahziel
immediately unmittelbar, sofort
immobile unbeweglich
immune immun
immunity Immunität
immunization Immunisierung, Impfung
impaction of the anal glands
verstopfte Analdrüse
impair beeinträchtigen
impairment Beeinträchtigung
impatient ungeduldig
impolite unhöflich
importance of Bedeutung von
impress beeindrucken, imponieren
imprint Abdruck (z.B. Fuß-)
imprint prägen
imprint (dog, behaviour)
prägen (Hund, Verhalten)

imprinting Prägung (Junghund, Welpe)
improper unsachgemäß
improve verbessern; sich verbessern
impulse Regung (Anwandlung); Stromstoß
in (out of) sight in (außer) Sicht
in a false pregnancy scheinschwanger
in a straight line geradlinig
in dealing with im Umgang mit
in heat läufig
in line with the body parallel zum Körper
in many places vielerorts
in need of a rest ruhebedürftig
in repose in Ruhestellung
in reverse order umgekehrte Reihenfolge
in season läufig
inactive inaktiv
inadequate unangemessen
inappetence Futterverweigerung, Appetitlosigkeit
inattention Unaufmerksamkeit
inattentive unaufmerksam
inborn angewölft
inbreed angeboren, eingezüchtet
inbreeding Inzestzucht
incalculable unberechenbar
incident Vorfall
incisor Schneidezahn
incompatibility (e.g. with dogs) Unverträglichkeit (z.B. mit Hunden)
incompatible unvereinbar
incompetent inkompetent
inconsistency Inkonsequenz
inconsistent inkonsequent
increase Steigerung; steigern, sich steigern
increase in performance Leistungssteigerung
increment Zuwachs
incubation period (or time) Inkubationszeit
independence Selbstständigkeit
Indian Miniature Hairless Dog Sonangi
indicate verweisen
indication (of) Indiz, Hinweis auf
indifference Desinteresse, Teilnahmslosigkeit
indifference to gunshot Schussfestigkeit
indigestibility of food Futterunverträglichkeit
indiscriminate wahllos
individual distance Individualdistanz
induce veranlassen
ineffective unwirksam, wirkungslos

inexperienced unerfahren
infect anstecken, infizieren
infected infiziert, vereitert
infected anal glands Analbeutelentzündung
infection Infektion, Ansteckung
infectious infektiös, übertragbar (medizinisch), ansteckend
infectious disease Infektionskrankheit
inferior unterlegen
inferiority Unterlegenheit
infertile unfruchtbar, zeugungsunfähig
infertility Zeugungsunfähigkeit, Unfruchtbarkeit
infinitely variable stufenlos regelbar
infirmity (of old age) Altersschwäche
inflammation Entzündung
influence Beeinflussung, beeinflussen
influence of the weather Witterungseinflüsse
inform of/ about informieren über
informality Zwanglosigkeit
infusion of new blood Blutauffrischung
ingenious occupation sinnvolle Beschäftigung
ingredients Zutaten
inguinal area Leistengegend
inguinal hernia Leistenbruch
inhalation narcosis Inhalationsnarkose
inherit erben
inherited angeboren, ererbt
inherited defect Erbmangel
inhibited gehemmt
inhibition against biting Beißhemmung
inhumane breeding practice(s) Qualzucht
inject injizieren
injection Spritze, Injektion
injury (to) Verletzung (an)
inner life Seelenleben
inquire anfragen
inquire about sich erkundigen über
insecure unsicher
insecurity Unsicherheit
insemination Besamung
insensitive unempfindlich
inserted (tail) angesetzt (Rute)
insertion (e.g. tail, ear) Ansatz (z.B. Rute, Ohren)
insignificant unerheblich
insist on bestehen auf, sich versteifen auf
insoluble unlösbar
instinct Instinkt, Trieb
instinct to protect Wehrtrieb
instinctive instinktiv

instinctive behaviours Instinktverhalten
instinctive drift Instinkt-Drift
instruct anleiten
instruction Instruktion, Weisung, Anleitung; Vorschrift
instructive lehrreich
instructor Trainer, Übungsleiter
insurance Versicherung
integrate sich eingliedern
integration Eingliederung
intelligence Klugheit
intend doing beabsichtigen zu tun
intention Absicht
interaction Wechselwirkung
interbreed kreuzen (im Sinne von züchten)
interbreeding Kreuzung
interdigital Zwischenzehen
interdigital space Zwischenzehenraum
interest in Interesse an
intermediate behaviours Übersprungsverhalten
internalize verinnerlichen
international trial regulations IPO
interpersonal zwischenmenschlich
interpret dolmetschen
interpretation Deutung
interrelation Wechselbeziehung
interrupt unterbrechen
intervene dazwischentreten, eingreifen
intervertebral disc Bandscheibe
intestinal diet Magen-Darm-Diät
intestine Eingeweide
intimidate einschüchtern
intimidating (or threatening) posture Drohstellung
intimidation Einschüchterung
intimidation display Imponiergehabe
intolerance (of food) Unverträglichkeit (Futter)
intonation Tonfall
introduce einführen
introduction Einführung
inured (to) abgehärtet sein (gegen)
invalid ungültig
inventive erfinderisch
investigate untersuchen, erforschen
investigation Untersuchung
invitation to play Spielaufforderung
involuntary (or submissive) urination unterwürfiges Urinieren
irascible jähzornig
Irish pattern irische Zeichnung
Irish Red and White Setter Irischer Rot-Weißer Setter

Irish Setter (Irish Red Setter) Irish Setter
Irish Terrier Irischer Terrier
Irish Water Spaniel Irischer Wasserspaniel
Irish Wolfhound Irischer Wolfshund
irregular ungeregelt
irreverent respektlos
irritability Reizbarkeit
isabella isabellfarben
isolating the problem Problem herausarbeiten/ isolieren
isolation Vereinsamung
Istrian Sheepdog Istrischer Schäferhund, Krasky Ovcar
Istrian Shorthaired Hound Istrische Kurzhaar Bracke
Istrian Wirehaired Hound Istrische drahthaarige Bracke
Italian Coarsehaired Pointer Spinone Italiano
Italian Greyhound Italienisches Windspiel, Zwergwindhund
Italian Hound Italienischer Laufhund, Segugio Italiano
Italian Pointer Italienischer (kurzhaariger) Vorstehhund, Italienische Bracke
Italian Roughcoated Pointer Italienischer Rauhaariger Vorstehhund
Italian Spinone Spinone Italiano
Italian Spitz Italienischer Spitz, Volpino Italiano
Italian Truffle Dog Lagotto
itch jucken
itch mite Sarcoptesmilbe
ivory elfenbeinfarbig

J

Jack Russell Terrier Jack Russell Terrier
jackpot (extra dose of primary reinforcer) Jackpot (besondere Belohnung)
Jamthund Großer Schwedischer Elchhund
Japan Chin Chin, Japan Chin
Japanese Fighting Dog (Tosa Inu) Tosa Inu, Japanischer Kampfhund
Japanese Spaniel Chin, Japan Chin
Japanese Spitz Japanischer Spitz, Nihon Supittsu
Japanese Terrier Japanischer Terrier, Nihon Teria
jaw Kiefer
jejunum Leerdarm (oberster Teil des Dünndarms)
jerk on the leash Leinenruck, an der Leine rucken
jerky ruckartig
jet black tiefschwarz
jogging Jogging, joggen
joint Gelenk
joint responsibility Mitverantwortung
joint socket Gelenkspfanne
jointly responsible mitverantwortlich
jostle rempeln
journey Reise
joy (at) Freude (über)
joy of barking Bellfreudigkeit
joy of retrieving Bringfreude
joyful freudig
judge richten (bewerten); Richter(in)
judge, evaluate beurteilen, bewerten
judge's orders Richteranweisung
judge's sheet, judge's commentary Richterbericht
judge's table Richtertisch
judging Beurteilung

jump Sprung, Hürde; springen
jump back zurückspringen
jump over überspringen
jump to conclusions voreilige Schlüsse ziehen
Jump-Fetch! (verbal command) Hopp-Bring! (Hörzeichen)
jumps (agility) Hürden (Agility)
junior Junghund
junior class Jugendklasse
junior handling competition Vorführungswettbewerb für Jugendliche
Jura Hound Jura Laufhund
juvenile Junghund, jugendlich
juvenile period Junghundstadium

K

Kai-Inu Kohshu Tora, Kai
Kaikadi Kaikadi
Kalagh Kalagh
Kangal Dog Kangal
Kangaroo Dog Australischer Windhund
Karelian Bear dog Karelischer Bärenhund
Karelo-Finnish Laika Karelisch-Finnische Laika
keen of scent feinnasig
keep a diary Tagebuch führen
keep still stillhalten
keep track Spur halten
Keeshond Keeshond
kennel Box, Hundebox, Hundetransportbox
kennel (building) Zwinger
kennel cough Zwingerhusten
kennel help Zwingerwart, Tierpfleger
kennel name Zwingername
kennelling Zwingerhaltung
kennel-name registration Zwingernamenschutz
kennels Zwinger
Kentucky Shell Heap dog Kentucky Muschelhaufenhund
Kerry Beagle Kerry Beagle
Kerry Blue Terrier Irish Blue Terrier, Kerry Blue Terrier
key ring Schlüsselring
kibble Trockenfutter
kick Tritt, Stoß (Fuß); treten, stoßen
kidney Niere
kidney failure Nierenversagen
kill töten
kind-hearted gutherzig
King Charles Spaniel King Charles Spaniel, Toy Spaniel
Kirghiz Greyhound Kirgisischer Windhund
Kishu Inu Kishu Inu
kneading Milchtritt
knee (joint) Knie(gelenk)

kneecap Kniescheibe
kneel down knien
knock down umreißen (umstoßen)
knock off (working) aufhören (zu arbeiten)
know kennen
knowledge Erkenntnis
knuckle Knöchel
knuckled-up aufgeknöchelt
knuckling over überknickend, vorgebogen
koerklassing ankören
koerung Körung
Komondor Komondor
Kong® (toy) Kong® (Spielzeug)
Kooichi Dog Kooichi
Kooiker Dog Kooikerhondje
Korean Gindo dog Koreanischer Gindo
Korthals Griffon Französischer Rauhaariger Vorstehhund, Korthals Griffon
Kromfohrlander Kromfohrländer
Kurdish Greyhound Kurdischer Windhund
Kuri dog Kuri
Kurland Hound Kurländischer Bracke
Kuvasz Kuvasz

L

labial commissure Mundwinkel
labour-inducing injection Wehenspritze
Labrador Retriever Labrador Retriever
lachrymal gland Tränendrüse
lack of ... Mangel
lack (or loss) of appetite Appetitlosigkeit
lack of communication Kommunikationsschwierigkeiten
lack of concentration Konzentrationsschwäche
lack of food Nahrungsmangel
lack of pigmentation Pigmentmangel
lack of plan Planlosigkeit
lack of space Platzmangel
lack of stamina Konditionsschwäche
lack of time Zeitmangel
lack of understanding Verständnislosigkeit
lacking energy energielos
lacking refinement grob
lacking self-control unbeherrscht
Laconian Greyhound Lakonier
Laekenois Laekenaar, Laekenois
Laika Laika
lake See
Lakeland Terrier Lakeland Terrier
lamb Lamm
lamb clip Schäfchenschur
lame lahm
Lancashire Heeler Lancashire Heeler
land mine dog Minensuchhund
Landseer Landseer
lank(y) mager
lap (up) auflecken
lap dog Schoßhund
Lapponian Herder Finnischer Vallhund

Large Blue Gascony Hound Großer Blauer Laufhund der Gascogne
Large Gascon Saintongeois Großer Gascon Saintongeois
large intestine Dickdarm
Large Munsterlander Großer Münsterländer
Large Spanish Hound Sabueso Espanol de Monte
laryngitis Kehlkopfentzündung
larynx Kehlkopf
Larzac Spaniel Épagneul Larzac, Larzac Vorstehhund
lashing tail schwingende Rute
late developer Spätentwickler(in)
late squeal Spätfolgen
latency Latenz, Verborgenheit
latent latent, verborgen
lateral seitlich
Latvian Hound Lettische Bracke
lave-eared langohrig
law of learning Lerngesetz
law of least effort Gesetz des geringsten Aufwandes
law of nature Naturgesetz
lawn Rasenplatz
lay of shoulder Schulterlage
laying and brooding period Setz- und Brutzeit
layman Laie
laziness (e.g. in jumping) Faulheit, Trägheit (z.B. beim Springen)
lead, us: leash Leine
lead (or leash) training Leinengewöhnung
lead dog Leithund, Leittier beim Schlittenhundesport
lead poisoning Bleivergiftung
leader Leithund
leader of the pack Rudelführer(in)
leadership Führung
lean mager
leap into freedom Freisprung
leap on springen auf
leap up aufspringen
learn lernen
learnable erlernbar
learned behaviour erlerntes Verhalten
learning process Lernprozess
leased bitch Miethündin
leash, engl.: lead Leine
leash law Leinenzwang
leashed, leaded angeleint
leather Leder
leather Ohrlappen
leather article (scent discrimination) Ledergegenstand (Geruchsunterscheidung)
leather collar Lederhalsband
leather leash Lederleine

lecture Vortrag
lecture hall Vortragssaal
Left Turn! (verbal command) Links um! (Hörzeichen)
leg Lauf, Bein
leg cuff (mondioring) Beinmanschette (Ringsport)
legality Legalität
leggy hochläufig
lemon zitronengelb
lemon belton gelbe Tüpfelung auf weiss
lend leihen
length of stay Verweildauer
lengthy langwierig
lens Linse
Leonberger Leonberger
leonine löwenartig
Leopard Cur Leopard Cur
Leopard Tree Dog Leopard Cur
leptospirosis Leptospirose
levator muscle Hebemuskel
level Niveau, Prüfungsstufe
level gerade
level bite Zangenbiss
Levesque Levesque Laufhund
lice infestation Lausbefall
licence, us: license Genehmigung, Zulassung
licensed zugelassen
lick lecken
lick (up) schlecken, (auf-)
lick granuloma Leckdermatitis
lick off ablecken
licking über den Fang lecken
licking the corner of the mouth Mundwinkellecken
lie liegen
lie low sich versteckt halten
life partnership Lebensgemeinschaft
life span Lebensdauer
life story Lebensgeschichte
life task Lebensaufgabe
lifeless temperamentlos
lifelong lebenslang
lifework Lebenswerk
lift his leg Bein heben/ urinieren
lifting paw Pfote heben
ligament Band
light brown hellbraun, fahl(gelb)
light fawn sandweiß
light food Schonkost
light grey silbergrau, mausgrau
light red hellhirschrot
light wheaten hellweizenfarben
light yellow hellgelb
lightly wounded leicht verwundet
lightweight Leichtgewicht
limb Glied
limber up aufwärmen
limited hold Zeitfenster
line breeding Linienzucht
line judge Zielrichter(in)

lion clip klassische Schur
lion coloured löwenfarbig, löwengelb
lip Lippe
lipfold dermatitis Lefzenekzem
lipoma Lipom
lips meeting exactly guter Lefzenschluss
listless lustlos, schlapp, unlustig
listlessness Teilnahmslosigkeit
literature Literatur
Lithuanian Hound Litauische Bracke
litter Wurf
litter of one Einlingswelpe
litter size Wurfgröße, Wurfstärke
littermate Geschwister, Wurfgeschwister
Little Lion Dog Löwchen
live as one of the family Familienanschluss haben
live together Zusammenleben
lively munter, lebhaft
liver schokolade(nbraun), leberfarben
liver Leber
liver belton braune Tüpfelung auf weiss
liver roan braunschimmel
liver sausage Leberwurst
live-stock Vieh(bestand)
live-stock guarding dog Herdenschutzhund
living conditions Lebensbedingungen
living space Lebensraum
locating Ortung
locating the aggressor (or agitator) (protection work) Streife nach dem Scheintäter (Schutzdienst)
lock (up) abschließen
lock jaw Kieferklemme; Tetanus
lock jaws sich verbeißen
lock up einsperren
lockable abschließbar
lodge a complaint Einspruch erheben/ einlegen
lodge a protest reklamieren
log gefällter Baumstamm
logical folgerichtig
logos Logo
loin Lende
loin region Nierenpartie
loll (e.g. tongue) heraushängen (z.B. Zunge)
loneliness Alleinsein, Einsamkeit
lonely einsam
long apron (protection work) Hetzschürze (Schutzdienst)
long back überlanger Rücken
long bone Röhrenknochen

long down (obedience) Platz-Bleib-Übung (Obedience)
long jump (agility) Weitsprung (Agility)
long leash lange Leine (Longe)
long sit (obedience) Sitz-Bleib-Übung (Obedience)
long-coupled lange Lendenpartie
longhaired langhaarig
Longhaired Dachshund Langhaardackel
longish halblang
long-nosed langköpfig
long-term objective Fernziel
look after sich kümmern (um)
look ahead vorausdenken
look around sich umsehen
look away wegsehen
look like ähneln
look on zusehen
look up aufblicken
loose locker, lose
loose in elbows ellbogenweit
loose lips offener Lefzenschluss
lose one's temper Selbstbeherrschung verlieren
loser Verlierer(in)
loss of confidence Vertrauensverlust
loud geräuschvoll, lautstark
loudspeaker Lautsprecher
louse (plural: lice) Laus
louse egg Nisse
lout Rüpel
lovable liebenswert
love and attention Streicheleinheiten
love of exercise Bewegungsfreudigkeit
loveless lieblos
low in withers ansteigende Oberlinie
low set ears tief angesetzte Ohren
low set tail tief angesetzte Rute
lower eyelid Unterlid
lower jaw Unterkiefer
lower jawbone Kinnlade
low-fat fettarm
low-fat curd cheese Magerquark
low-performance leistungsschwach
Lucas Terrier Lucas Terrier
Lucerne Hound Luzerner Laufhund
Lucerne Short-Legged Hound Luzerner Niederlaufhund
lucky hit Zufallstreffer
lumbar vertebra Lendenwirbel
lung Lunge
lung torsion Lungendrehung
lunge at anfallen, angreifen, sich stürzen auf
lure Lockmittel, Verlockung; Reiz

lure Hasenattrappe, Hetzattrappe, künstlicher Hase
lure (with titbit) locken (mit Leckerbissen)
lure coursing Coursing
lure machine Hasenmaschine
lusterless hair (or coat) stumpfes Fell
lustreless glanzlos
Lymes' disease Lyme-Krankheit
lymph Lymphe
lymphosarcoma Lymphosarkom

M

Mackenzie River Dog MacKenzie River Hund
Mahratta Greyhound Marathen Windhund
maiden jungfräulich
main meal Hauptmahlzeit
main point Schwerpunkt
Majorca Sheepdog Mallorca Schäferhund
make machen
make a find Geruchsspur finden
make perfect perfektionieren
make public öffentlich bekannt machen
make rapid progress schnell Fortschritte machen
maladjusted verhaltensgestört
male dog Rüde
malformation Missbildung
malformed missgebildet
Malinois Malinois, Mechelaar
Mallorquin Bulldog Perro de Presa Mallorquin
malnutrition Unterernährung
Maltese Malteser, Angorahund
maltreat misshandeln, schinden, quälen
maltreatment Misshandlung
mammal Säugetier; Milchdrüse
mammary gland Brustdrüse
mammary gland tumour Mammatumor, Milchdrüsentumor
Manchester Terrier Manchester Terrier
mandarins beard Kinnbart
mane Mähne
mange Räude
mangle Mangel
mangle zerfleischen
mangy räudig
Manila Spaniel Philippinischer Spaniel
manipulate manipulieren
manipulation Manipulation
manner Art (und Weise)
manoeuvrable lenkbar

mantle Satteldecke, Mantel
manual manuell
many-sided vielseitig
maraud wildern (durch Hunde)
Maremma Sheepdog Maremma Abruzzenhund
mark markieren; Prädikat
mark of confidence Vertrauensbeweis
mark out abstecken (Gelände)
marking Markierung, markieren
markings Abzeichen
marquee Festzelt
marrow (medical) Mark (medizinisch)
marrow-bone Markknochen
mask Maske
mask, dark (or black) dunkle Maske
masked mit Maske
masseter muscle Kaumuskel
massive massiv
master Herr(chen) eines Hundes
Mastiff Mastiff, Dogge
mastiff-type or mastiff-like mastiffartig, molossoid
mastitis Brustdrüsenentzündung
mat verfilzen, verkleben
mate Verpaarung
material damage Sachschaden
maternal instinct Mutterinstinkt
mating Paarung, Verbindung
mating call Lockruf
mating of related individuals Engzucht
mating season Paarungszeit, Balzzeit
matted filzig
matter for conflict Konfliktstoff
matting Verfilzung
maxilla Oberkiefer
maximum number of points Höchstpunktzahl
meadow Wiese
meaning Bedeutung
measuring device Körmaß
meat Fleisch
medicinal power Heilkraft
medicine Arznei
medium mittelgroß
Medium Vendeen Griffon Kleiner Rauhaariger Laufhund der Vendée, Briquet Griffon Vendéen
Medium-Sized Schnauzer Mittelschnauzer
meet begegnen, treffen
meeting Begegnung, Treffen, Jagdtreffen
melon pips Vieraugenflecken
meeting point Treffpunkt
member Mitglied
member of the board Vorstandsmitglied

member of the family Familienmitglied
membership Mitgliedschaft; Mitgliederzahl
membership card Mitgliedsausweis
membership fee Mitgliedsbeitrag
memory Erinnerung, Gedächtnis
meningitis Hirnhautentzündung
meniscus Meniskus
mental anguish Seelenqual
mental training Mentaltraining
merciless erbarmungslos, schonungslos
merle merle
mesocephalic mittellangköpfig
messenger dog Meldehund
metacarpal bones Vordermittelfußknochen
metacarpals Fessel
metal Metall
metatarsus Hintermittelfuß
method Methode
metritis Gebärmutterentzündung
mewl fiepen
Mexican Hairless Dog Mexikanischer Nackthund, Xoloitzcuintle
microchip Mikrochip
microchip identification Chip-Kennzeichnung, Transponder-Kennzeichnung
microphone Mikrophon
Mid-Asiatic (Russian) Shepherd Mittelasiat
mid-brain Mittelhirn
Middle Asian Owtcharka Mittelasiatischer Owtscharka
Middle-Sized Anglo-French Hound Mittelgroßer Anglo-Französischer Laufhund
middleweight Mittelgewicht
midge Mücke
midsize mittelgroß
Mikawa Inu Mikawa Inu
military dog Militärhund
milk Milch
milk (or temporary or deciduous) tooth Milchzahn
milk fever Milchfieber
milk sugar Milchzucker
milk teeth Milchgebiss
mimicry Nachahmung
minced meat Hackfleisch
mincing trot verkürzter Trab
mine Mine
mine detection dog Minensuchhund
minerals Mineralsalze
Miniature Bull Terrier Miniatur Bullterrier, Zwergbullterrier

Miniature Dachshund Kaninchenteckel, Kaninchendachshund
miniature dog Kleinhund, Zwerghund
Miniature Pinscher Rehpinscher, Zwergpinscher
Miniature Schnauzer Zwergschnauzer
minimum age requirement Mindestalter, Zulassungsalter
mink oil Nerzöl
miscarriage Fehlgeburt
misery Elend
misjudgement Fehleinschätzung
mismarked fehlfarbig
mismating Fehldeckung
mismating shot Abtreibungsspritze
mistake Fehler, Irrtum
mistraining schlechtes Training
mistress Frauchen (eines Hundes)
misunderstand falsch verstehen, missverstehen
misunderstanding Missverständnis
misunderstood unverstanden
mite Milbe, Made
mite infestation Milbenbefall
mixed breed Mischling
mix-up Verwechslung
mo(u)lt Haarwechsel
mo(u)lting period Haarungsperiode
mobile beweglich
mock at spötteln über
mock fight Scheinkampf
mockery Spott
mocking spöttisch
mode of operation Wirkungsweise
model Leitbild
modelled gemeißelt
modification Modifikation
modify abwandeln, modifizieren
molar Backenzahn, Mahlzahn
mollycoddle verzärteln
Molossian Dog Molosser
molossoid molossoid, doggenartig
Mongolian Dog Mongolischer Hund
mongrel Promenadenmischung, Köter
monorchid Monorchide
monotonous eintönig
mop dog Wuschelhund
Moscow Longhaired Toy Terrier Moskauer Langhaariger Zwergterrier
Moscow Watchdog Moskauer Wachhund
mother Muttertier, Mutter
motion Bewegung

motion exercises Übungen aus der Bewegung
motion sickness Reisekrankheit
motionless reglos
motivate motivieren
motivation Motivation
mottled geschimmelt
mould Schimmelpilz
mount aufspringen, besteigen
mount (of) aufreiten (auf)
Mountain Afghan (Hound) Bergafghane
Mountain Cur Mountain Cur
Mountain Dog Berghund, Sennenhund
mourn trauern, betrauern, nachtrauern
mourner Leidtragende(r)
mourning for Trauer um
mouse (plural: mice) Maus
mouse hole Mauseloch
mouse-grey mausgrau
mouser Mäusefänger
mousetrap Mausefalle
moustache Schnauzbart, Schnurrbart
mouth Fang, Schnauze, Maul
mouth the game die Beute knautschen
move towards streben zu
moving slowly verlangsamte Bewegung
mucous membrane Schleimhaut
mud Schlamm
muddy matschig, schlammig
Mudhol Hound Mudhol Windhund
Mudi Mudi
multicoloured vielfarbig
multitude Vielzahl
municipal area Stadtgebiet
Munsterlander Münsterländer
muscle of the eyelid Lidmuskel
muscle tone Muskeltonus
muscles Muskulatur, Muskeln
muscular system Muskulatur
musculo-skeletal system Bewegungsapparat
mush Matsch
musher Schlittenführer, Musher
mushing Hundeschlittenfahren
music therapy Musiktherapie
mustard senffarben
mutilate verstümmeln
mutilation Verstümmelung
mutt Mischling
mutual wechselseitig
muzzle Schnauze, Fang; Beißkorb, Maulkorb; Maulkorb anlegen
muzzle area Fangpartie
muzzle band Schnauzenband
mycosis Pilzkrankheit

nail clippers Krallenzange, Krallenstanze
nail file Krallenfeile
name plate Namensschild
nape Genick
nape (of the neck) Nacken
narrowchested schmalbrüstig
nasal bone Nasenbein
nasal cavity Nasenhöhle
nasal plane Nasenspiegel
nasal septum Nasenscheidewand
national champion Landesmeister(in)
national flag Nationalflagge
national team Nationalmannschaft
national training director Obmann(-frau) für Ausbildung und Sport OFS
native language Landessprache
natural natürlich, naturgemäß
natural authority natürliche Autorität
natural jumping rhythm natürlicher Springrhythmus, -ablauf
natural preserve Landschaftsschutzgebiet
nature Natur
naturopathy Naturheilkunde
naughtiness Unartigkeit
naughty unartig
Navarro Pointer Navarro Vorstehhund
navel Nabel
Neapolitan Mastiff Mastino Neapoletano
near to nahe bei
nearness Nähe
necessary erforderlich
neck Hals
neck, cloddy kurzer Hals
neck ruff Halskrause, Kragen

need a lot of affection liebebedürftig
neglect Vernachlässigung, Verwahrlosung; vernachlässigen, verwahrlosen lassen
neglected verwahrlost
neighbour Nachbar(in)
nematode Fadenwurm
Nenets Herding Laika Nenzen Rentierhütehund
neonatal period vegetative Entwicklungsphase
nephritis Nierenentzündung
nerve Nerv
nerve-racking nervtötend
nerves Nervigkeit
nervous nervlich; nervös, schreckhaft
nervous system Nervensystem
nervousness Nervosität
nest Bau, Nest
nesting Lagerbildung, Nestbau
neuritis Nervenentzündung
neutrality Neutralität
New Guinea Singing Dog Neuguinea Dingo
New Ireland Dog Neuirland Eingeborenenhund
New Zealand Native Dog Neuseeländer Eingeborenenhund
New Zealand Sheepdog Neuseeländer Schäferhund
Newfoundland Dog Neufundländer
nibble (at) anknabbern
nidation Nidation
nipple Zitze, Brustwarze
nit Nisse
No! (verbal command) Nein! (Hörzeichen)
nobility Adel
nod (to) nicken, zunicken
noise Krach, Lärm
non-level bite Spaltgebiss
nonplussed verdutzt
non-qualifying score kein Qualifikationswettkampf
non-socialized nicht sozialisiert
non-stop pausenlos
non-violence Gewaltlosigkeit
non-violent gewaltfrei, gewaltlos
Nootka Dog Nootka Schäferhund
nordic nordisch
Nordic Spitz Norbottenspitz
Norfolk Retriever Norfolk Retriever
Norfolk Terrier Norfolk Terrier
normalize normalisieren
normally normalerweise
Northwest Indian Greyhound Rampur Windhund
Norwegian Buhund Norwegischer Buhund

Norwegian Elkhound Norwegischer Elchhund
Norwegian Hound Norwegischer Laufhund, Dunker
Norwegian Puffin Dog Lundehund, Norwegischer Vogelhund
Norwich Terrier Norwich Terrier
nose Nase
nose band Nasenband
nose leather Nasenschwamm
nostril Nasenloch
not for competition außer Konkurrenz
not to know what to expect Erwartungsunsicherheit
not typical untypisch
notepad Notizblock
notice bemerken
notoedric mange Kopfräude
Nova Scotia Duck Tolling Retriever (Toller) Nova Scotia Duck Tolling Retriever
novice Neuling
Nubian Dog Nubischer Nackthund
nudge stupsen, anstupsen
nuisance Plagegeist
number Anzahl
numbered agility cones nummerierte Agility-Kegel/ Pylonen
nurse säugen; Krankenschwester
nutrition Ernährung
nylon collar Nylonhalsband
nylon leash Nylonleine

obedience Gehorsam, Folgsamkeit, Unterordnung
obedience exercise Unterordnungsübung
obedience ring Unterordnungsring
obedience training Unterordnungsarbeit, Erziehung
obedience trial Unterordnungswettbewerb
obedience work Gehorsamsarbeit
obedient folgsam, fügsam, gehorsam sein
obese fettleibig
obey, listen gehorchen
object Sache; Ziel
object, to reklamieren, einwenden
object of exchange Tauschobjekt
objection Einspruch
objective Zielsetzung, Zielvorstellung
obligatory registration Meldepflicht
observation Beobachtung, Wahrnehmung
observe beobachten
observer Beobachter(in)
obstacle Hindernis, Gerät
obstinacy Starrsinn
obstinate dickköpfig, starrköpfig, widerspenstig
obtain erhalten, erringen, erzielen
obtrusive zudringlich
obtuse stumpfwinkelig
occasion Anlass
occasionally gelegentlich
occlusion Zahnschluss
oedema Ödem
oesophagus Speiseröhre
oestrus Östrus

oestrus-prevention injection Antiläufigkeitsspritze
off-colour Pigmentverlust; Fehlfarbe
offence Verstoß
offering behaviour Verhalten anbieten
official amtlich
official speaker Festredner
off-lead freilaufend
off-lead training Training mit unangeleintem Hund
offspring Nachzucht; Nachkomme
ointment Salbe
Old Danish Pointer Altdänischer Hühnerhund (Vorstehhund), Gammel Dansk Honsehund, Bakhund
Old English Sheepdog Bobtail, (Alt)englischer Schäferhund
Old English Terrier, Welsh-Terrier Altenglischer Terrier, Welsh Terrier
Old Fighting Dog of Cordoba Perro de Pelea Cordobés
Old Spanish Pointer Perdigueiro Navarro
old-fashioned altmodisch, unzeitgemäß
olfactory capacity Geruchsvermögen
olfactory nerve Geruchsnerv
olfactory organ Geruchsorgan
omnipresent allgegenwärtig
on a lead (or leash) angeleint
on the one hand einerseits
on the right hand side rechts
one-day trial Eintagesprüfung
one-man dog Einmannhund
open class offene Klasse
open coat offenes Haarkleid
open foot Spreizfuß (-pfote)
open trailing spurlautes Jagen
open tunnel (agility) flexibler Tunnel (Agility)
opinion Meinung
opinion (on) Ansicht (über)
opportunity Gelegenheit
opposition Gegenwehr, Gegenüberstellung
optic nerve Sehnerv
optimize optimieren
orange (coat) orange (Fellfarbe)
orange belton orange Tüpfelung auf weiss
orange roan orangeschimmel
orb Augapfel
orbit Augenhöhle
orchitis Hodenentzündung
order Reihenfolge
order someone around jemanden herumkommandieren
order, rang-order Rangordnung
organism Organismus
organize veranstalten

organizer Ausrichter, Veranstalter
orientate orientieren
orientation Orientierung
original scorebook Original-Leistungsheft/-buch/-urkunde
original track Ansatzfährte
ossify verknöchern
osteoporosis Osteoporose
otodectes mite Otodectes (Ohrmilbe)
otter tail Otterrute
Otterhound Otterhund
out at elbows ellbogenweit
out of the ribbons unplatziert
Out! (verbal command) Aus! (Hörzeichen)
out, release Auslassen/ Ablassen
outbreeding Auskreuzung
outburst of rage Wutanfall
outcrossing Blutauffrischung, Einkreuzung, Fremdpaarung
outdoor run Gehege
outgoing freundlich
outline Umriss
outside the law außerhalb der Legalität
outsider Außenseiter(in)
outsize Übergröße
outskirts of the town Stadtrand
oval oval
ovary Eierstock
over angulated überwinkelt
over exercised übertrainiert
over trained übertrainiert
Over! (verbal command) Hopp! (Hörzeichen)
overanxious überängstlich
overbite Rückbiss, Unterbiss, Hinterbiss
overbuilt überbaut
overcome (e.g. fear) überwinden (z.B. Angst)
overdo things sich zuviel zumuten
overfeed überfüttern
overhead trolley cable Laufdraht
overlaid gewolkt
overloaded überladen
overnose wrinkle Stirnfalte
overpower überwältigen
overreach übertreten
overreact überreagieren
overshot (bite) hinterständig
overshot mouth Hinterbiss
overshot pasterns vorgebogene Fesselgelenke
overzealous übereifrig
oviduct Eileiter
ovulation Eisprung, Ovulation
own track Eigenfährte
owner Herr(chen) eines Hundes
owners' failure Fehler des Hundeführers

pablum Schmelzflocken
pace Passgang; Schritt
pack Rudel
pack (of hounds) Meute (Hunde-)
pack animal Rudeltier
pack hound Meutehund
pad Ballen
padded stick Schlagstock, Softstock
padding Wattierung
paddle mähen
paddock Pferdekoppel
pain Schmerz
pain threshold Schmerzgrenze
pained gequält
painful schmerzhaft
palate Gaumen
pale-yellow fahl(gelb)
palisade (protection work, mondioring) Schrägwand (Schutzdienst, Ringsport)
palpebral fissure Lidspalte
pancreas Bauchspeicheldrüse
panic Panik
pant hecheln
papers Papiere
Papillon Papillon
Papuan Dog Papuahund
paradoxical paradox
parasite Parasit, Schmarotzer
parent (animal) Elterntier
parent person Bezugsperson
parent umbrella organization Dachverband
parental elterlich
parenthood Elternschaft
parents Eltern
Pariah Dog Pariahund
park Park
Parson Jack Russell Terrier Parson Jack Russell Terrier
partial success Teilerfolg
participants Teilnehmer(in), Prüfungsteilnehmer(in)
partition Zwischenwand

partly teils
partly unpigmented nose Wechselnase
partridge Rebhuhn
parvo infection Parvovirose
pass Passierschein
pass (in racing) überholen
pass by vorbeigehen
pastern (Vorder-)Mittelfuß, Fessel
pat tätscheln
patch Platte
patched gescheckt
patella Kniescheibe
patience Geduld
patient geduldig
Patterdale Terrier Patterdale Terrier
pattern Muster
pause area (agility) Stoppzone (Agility)
pause box (agility) Anhaltezone (Agility)
pause for reflection Denkpause
pause table (agility) Tisch (Agility)
paw Pfote
pawing pföteln
pay attention to achten auf, beachten
peace of mind Seelenruhe
peaceable friedfertig
peak condition Hochform
peak performance Spitzenvorführung, Vorführung der Spitzenklasse
peaked cap Schirmmütze
pearl white perlweiß
Peat Bog Dog Torfhund
peculiarity Eigenart
pediculosis Lausbefall
pedigree Abstammungsnachweis, Papiere, Ahnentafel
pedigree dog Rassehund
peg Anbindepflock
Pekingese Pekinese
pellets kleinkörniges Trockenfutter
pelvis Becken
penalty Punktabzug
pencil (of hair) Büschel
pendulous ears Behang
pendulous lips Hängelefzen
penis Penis
penknife Taschenmesser
pennant Fahne(nrute)
pepper pfefferfarben
perceive wahrnehmen
perceptible wahrnehmbar
perception Wahrnehmung
perceptive faculty Wahrnehmungsvermögen
perfect vervollkommnen
perfection Perfektion, Vervollkommnung

perform leisten (vollbringen, erfüllen); vorführen
performance Leistung, Vorführung
performance breeding Leistungszucht
performance degree (or title) Leistungszeichen
performance diet Leistungsfutter
performance level Leistungsstand
performance principle Leistungsprinzip
performance test Leistungsprüfung
performance title Ausbildungskennzeichen (AKZ)
performance-enhancing leistungssteigernd
performance-oriented leistungsbezogen
peridontal disease Zahnfleischentzündung
perineum Damm
period of development Entwicklungsphase
period of development of group organization Rudelordnungsphase
period of imprinting Prägungsphase
period of socialization Sozialisierungsphase
peritoneal hernia Dammbruch
peritoneum Bauchfell
permission Erlaubnis
permit erlauben, etwas zulassen
permit to be bred Zuchtzulassung
permitted zulässig
Perro de Pastor Mallorquin Perro de Pastor Mallorquin
perspiration Schweiß
perspire schwitzen
Peruvian Hairless Dog Peruanischer Nackthund, Inca Orchid Moonflower dog, Perro sin Pelo del Perú
pesky nervig
pet Heimtier; streicheln, hätscheln
pet dog Familienhund
pet ear and nose trimmer Ohr-Trimm-Messer
pet first aid kit Erste-Hilfe-Ausrüstung für Tiere
pet owner Tierhalter(in)
pet store Tierhandlung
phalanges Zehenknochen
Pharaoh Hound Pharaonenhund, Kelb tal Fenek
pharmacy Apotheke
pharynx Rachen
phase Phase

Philippine Islands Dog Philippinenhund
philtrum Oberlippenspalt
phobia Phobie
photophobia lichtscheu
Phu-Quoc Dog Phu Quoc Hund
physical physisch
physical fitness körperliche Fitness
physical force körperliche Einwirkungen
Picardie Spaniel Langhaariger Vorstehhund der Picardie
Picardy Sheepdog Picard, Berger de Picard
Picardy Spaniel Épagneul Picard
pick up (e.g. a scent or an article on the track) aufnehmen (z.B. Geruch oder Gegenstand auf der Fährte)
piebald scheckig
piece of advice Ratschlag
pied tricolour dreifarbig gescheckt
pigeon blue taubenblau
pigeon-toed pfoteneng
pigment Pigment
pigmentation Färbung
pile Strich
pill Tablette
Pillenween Terrier Pillenween Terrier
pin brush Drahtbürste
pincer bite Zangengebiss, Aufbiss
pinch einklemmen, kneifen, zwicken
pinch collar Stachelhalsband, Korallenhalsband, Stachelwürger
pink nose rosa Nase
pink papers (SV) rote Papiere (Leistungszucht SV)
Pinscher Pinscher
pipe tunnel (agility) fester Tunnel (Agility)
pistol Pistole
pit dog Kampfhund
pitiful erbarmenswert
pivot Drehpunkt
pivot point of the seesaw (agility) Kipp-Punkt der Wippe (Agility)
placard Plakat
place Ort; platzieren
place at stud zur Zucht einstellen
placement Platzierung, Reihung
placenta Plazenta
placid sanftmütig, ruhig
plan planen
plan something ahead Vorausplanen
plaque Zahnstein

plaster cast Gipsverband
platelet Blutplättchen
platform Podest
play ·Spiel, Belohnungsspiel
play hide-and-seek Versteck(en) spielen
play instinct Spieltrieb
play something down verharmlosen
playful verspielt
playing spielerisch
playmate Spielkamerad(in)
plead (for) plädieren (für)
pleasant angenehm, erfreulich
plenary assembly Vollversammlung
pliant elastisch
Plott Hound Plotthund
pluck ausrupfen
plume Fahne(nrute)
plume like buschig
plumed tail befederte Rute
pneumonia Lungenentzündung
poach wildern (durch Personen)
poacher Wilddieb, Wilderer
point Höcker
point of buttocks Sitzbeinhöcker
point of intersection Schnittpunkt
point system Punktesystem
pointed ear Spitzohr
pointer Vorstehhund
Pointer (English Pointer) Pointer
Pointing Longcoated Griffon Französischer Langhaariger Vorstehhund, Griffon Boulet
pointless zwecklos
points Fellzeichnung
poison Gift, vergiften
poisoned bait Giftköder
poisoning Vergiftung
poisonous gift(halt)ig
Poitevin Poitevin
pole Stange
police dog Polizeihund, Dienstgebrauchshund, Diensthund
Poligar Sighthound Poligar Windhund
Polish Greyhound Polnischer Windhund
Polish Hound Polnische Bracke, Ogar Polski
Polish Lowland Sheepdog, PON Polski Owczarek Nizinny, PON, Polnischer Niederungshütehund
Polish Mountain Dog Podhalaner
Pomeranian Pommernspitz
Pomeranian Sheepdog Pommerscher Hütehund
pond Teich
Pont-Audemer Spaniel Épagneul du Pont Audemer, Pont Audemer Spaniel

Poodle Pudel
poor in vitamins vitaminarm
popular beliebt
portable jump zerlegbare Sprunghürde
Portugese Pointer Perdigueiro Portugues
Portuguese Cattle Dog Portugiesischer Treibhund
Portuguese Hound Podengo Portugues
Portuguese Pointer Portugiesischer Pointer, Portugiesischer Vorstehhund
Portuguese Sheepdog Portugiesischer Schäferhund
Portuguese Water Dog Portugiesischer Wasserhund
Posavac Hound Savetal Bracke
position Stellung, Körperhaltung
positive motivational training method Trainingsmethode über positive Motivation
positive reinforcement positive Bestätigung, positive Verstärkung
possibility Möglichkeit
post Pfosten
posterior hinter
posture imponieren; Körperhaltung, Haltung
posture, submissive Demutshaltung, demütige Körperhaltung
posturing Imponiergehabe
power Macht, Stärke
powerful kraftvoll
practicable durchführbar, machbar
practice, us: practise Praxis, Übung, Gewohnheit, Schulung,
practice dog-competition Training unter Wettkampf-bedingungen
practice jump Übungssprung
practice matches Training unter Wettkampfbedingungen
practise üben, trainieren
praise Lob, loben
prance tänzeln
prancing tänzelnd
precaution measure Vorsichtsmaßnahme
precious stone therapy Edelsteintherapie
precise exakt
precondition Vorgabe, Bedingung
predator Beutegreifer, Raubtier
predatory instinct Beutetrieb
pre-digested vorverdaut
predominant vorwiegend
predominant breed bevorzugte Rasse

prefer bevorzugen
preference (for) Vorliebe (für)
pregnancy Trächtigkeit
pregnant (being ...) trächtig (sein)
prehistory Vorgeschichte
prejudice Vorurteil
preliminary examination Vorprüfung
preliminary exercise Vorübung
preliminary report Vorbericht
preliminary stage Vorstufe
preliminary talk Vorbesprechung
premature vorzeitig
premature birth Frühgeburt
premium list Ausschreibung; Prämierungsliste
premolar Prämolar
preparation Vorbereitung
prepare vorbereiten
prepare for vorbereiten auf
preparedness for defence Verteidigungsbereitschaft
prescribe verschreiben
prescription (medical) Rezept (medizinisch)
present vorführen
present oneselfs' best advantage von seiner besten Seite zeigen
presentation ceremony Siegerehrung
president Vorsitzende(r), Vorstand
press down niederdrücken
pressure Zwang, Druck
pressure to perform Leistungsdruck
prevent verhindern, vorbeugen
previous knowledge Vorkenntnisse
previous training Vorausbildung
prey Beute
prey animal Beutetier
prey chasing behaviour Beutefangverhalten
prey drive Beutetrieb
prey motivated beutemotiviert
price Preis, Kaufpreis
prick (ears) aufrichten, spitzen (Ohren)
prickear Stehohr
primary primär
primitive type Urtyp
principal feature (of exercise) Hauptanforderung (der Übung)
privilege Sonderrecht, Vorrecht
prize Ehrenpreis
prize winner Preisträger(in)
probability Wahrscheinlichkeit
probable wahrscheinlich
problem Problem
problem behaviour Problemverhalten

problem dog Problemhund
problem solving Problemlösung
process of development Entwicklungsprozess
procreate zeugen (fortpflanzen)
prod Stups, stupsen
proestrus Vorbrunst
professional handler Berufsvorführer(in)
profile Profil
profuse reichlich, üppig
progenitor Elterntier
progeny Nachzucht
progeny group Nachzuchtgruppe
progression (e.g. in training) Fortschritt (z.B. im Training)
promise word Zusage
promising erfolgversprechend, vielversprechend
promote fördern
promotion of one's public image Selbstdarstellung
prompt action schnelles Handeln
pronged collar Korallenhalsband
pronounced ausgeprägt
proof Beweis
proofing Absichern von Verhalten (Generalisieren)
prostate gland Vorsteherdrüse, Prostata
protect (from) beschützen (vor)
protection Schutz
protection clothes (protection work) Schutzanzug, Hetzkleidung (Schutzdienst)
protection dog Schutzhund
protection of animals Tierschutz
protection pants (protection work) Schutzhose (Schutzdienst)
protection sleeve cover with handle (protection work) Hetzarmüberzug mit Schlaufe (Schutzdienst)
protection suit (mondioring) Schutzanzug (Ringsport)
protective (leather) pants (protection work) Schutzdiensthose aus Leder
protective sleeve (protection work) Hetzärmel (Schutzdienst)
protective suit (protection work) Schutzanzug (Schutzdienst)
protective vest (protection work) Schutzjacke (Schutzdienst)
protectiveness Schutztrieb
protein Eiweiß, Protein
protest Protest, protestieren
protruding hervortretend, vorstehend
proud stolz, auch: läufig

provable beweisbar
provoke provozieren
psyche Psyche
psychic(al) psychisch
psychograph Psychogramm
psychological psychologisch
psychological intimidation Psychoterror
psychology of learning Lernpsychologie
puberty Pubertät(sphase)
pubic bone Schambein
public Publikum
puddle Pfütze
Pudelpointer Pudelpointer
Pug Mops, Carlin
pug nose Stumpfnase
Puli Puli
Pulka Pulka
pull zerren; ziehen, zuziehen (Halsband)
pull down niederziehen
pull tab Kurzführer (Leine)
pulmonary alveolus Lungenbläschen
pulmonary artery Lungenarterie
pulsation Puls(schlag)
pulse Puls
pulse rate Pulsschlag
pulse rate, high erhöhter Pulsschlag
pulse rate, low niedriger Pulsschlag
punch Schlag (Faust)
punish bestrafen, strafen
punishable strafbar
punisher bestrafende Person
punishment Strafe, Bestrafung
pupil Schüler
pupil (anatomic) Pupille (anatomisch)
puppy Welpe, Junges
puppy class Welpenkurs, Jüngstenklasse
puppy clip jugendliche Schur
puppy collar Welpenhalsband
puppy food Welpennahrung
puppy formula Welpenmilch
puppy kindergarten Welpenschule
puppy licence Welpenschutz
puppy pen Welpengitter
puppy sleeve (protection work) Junghundarm (Schutzdienst)
puppy test Welpentest
puppy training Welpenerziehung
purchase kaufen
purebred reinrassig
purpose Zweck
pursue hetzen
purulent eitrig
pus Eiter
push Stoß, stoßen
push forward sich vordrängen

push someone around
jemanden herumstoßen
push someone under
unterbuttern
pushed-in nose
zurückgesetzte Nase
pussy eitrig
put down einschläfern
put on a chain anketten
put someone under pressure
auf jemanden Druck ausüben
put to flight in die Flucht schlagen
put to sleep einschläfern
put under a taboo Tabu setzen
put (undesired) behaviour on cue (unerwünschtes) Verhalten auf Signal setzen
put up resistance
sich widersetzen
putting together with
zusammentun mit
pyometra
Gebärmuttervereiterung
Pyrenean Mastiff Mastin d'Aragon, Mastin de los Pirineos, Spanischer Pyrenäenhund
Pyrenean Sheepdog
Pyrenäen Schäferhund

quadruped Vierbeiner
qualification Qualifikation
qualified qualifiziert
qualify for sich qualifizieren
qualifying round Qualifikationsrunde
qualifying scores Qualifikationswettkampf/ -prüfung
quality Qualität, Erstklassigkeit
quality of life Lebensqualität
quarantine Quarantäne
quarrelsome streitsüchtig
quarry Beute
quarter revieren, suchen, absuchen
quick munter, lebhaft, flink
quick release hook Panikhaken
quick to learn gelehrig
quick-tempered aufbrausend
quiet leise
Quiet! (verbal command) Aus! Ruhig! (Hörzeichen)
quirk Marotte
quiver beben, zittern
quotation Zitat
quote zitieren

rabid tollwütig
rabies Tollwut, Hundswut
rabies shot Tollwutschutzimpfung
raccoon dog Marderhund
race Lauf, Rennen
race course Rennbahn, Windhundrennbahn
racing blanket Renndecke
racing collar Windhundhalsband
racing dog Rennhund
racing kennel Rennhundzwinger
racing muzzle Maulkorb für das Rennen
radiograph Röntgenbild
radius (medical) Speiche (medizinisch)
rage Wut
rain Regen
raincoat Regenmantel
raise sträuben (Fell)
raise aufziehen
raising Aufzucht
rally style obedience Obedience Rallye
rams head Ramsung
rams nose Ramsnase
random zufällig
random mating Zufallspaarung
random reinforcement Bestätigung nach Zufallssystem
range of use Verwendungsbereich
rank Rang
rank order Rangordnung
rare breed seltene Rasse
rash (disease) Ausschlag (Krankheit)
rat tail Rattenschwanz
Rat Terrier Ratten Terrier
rating Stellenwert
rattle scheppern
raw roh

rawhide Büffelhaut, Ochsenziemer
rawhide bone Büffelhautknochen
reach Schrittlänge
reach, within (out of) Reichweite, in (außer)
reachy neck Hals in guter Länge
react reagieren
reaction Reaktion
read lesen
readiness to take to water Wasserfreudigkeit
reading matter Lektüre
ready to fight kampfbereit
ready to start startbereit
reality Realität
realization Einsicht
realize/ carry out realisieren
rear aufziehen
rear Hinter-, hinter-,
rear (or hind) foot (or paw) Hinterpfote
rear (or hind) leg Hinterlauf
rear angulation Hinterhandwinkelung
rear-end consciousness Hinterhand-Bewusstheit/ Koordination
rearing Aufzucht
reasoned durchdacht
rebel (against) aufbegehren (gegen)
rebuke Zurechtweisung; zurechtweisen
recall Abruf; abrufen, heranrufen
recall exercise Abrufübung
receptive paarungsbereit
receptiveness Deckbereitschaft, Deckungswilligkeit
recipe Rezept
recognition Anerkennung
recognizable erkennbar
recognize erkennen
recognize as a breed als Rasse anerkennen
recognized titles for attendance at anerkannte AKZ zur Teilnahme an
recognized by anerkannt durch
recoil from zurückschrecken vor
recommend weiterempfehlen
reconstruct rekonstruieren
record time Rekordzeit
recover from sich erholen
recovery Erholung
rectal rektal
rectum Mastdarm, Rektum
red rot
red (or tan) markings Brand
Red and White Irish Setter Rotweißer Irischer Setter
red brindle rotgestromt
Red Deer Dingo Red Deer Dingo

red fawn rotfalb, blond
red grizzle rotmeliert
red mange Räude
red merle rot merle
red roan rot gestichelt
red sesame rotsesam
red speckled rotfleckig
red wheaten rotweizenfarben
Redbone Coonhound Redbone Coonhound
reddish rötlich
reddish grey rötlich grau
reddish yellow rotgelb
reddish-brown leberfarben
redirected behaviour Übersprungshandlung
red-mottled rotscheckig
reduce verringern, mindern, reduzieren
reducing diet Abmagerungsdiät
reed stick Rohrstock
re-education Umerziehung
refine verfeinern
refined edel
reflect widerspiegeln, reflektieren
reflex Reflex
reflex action Reflexbewegung
reflex, conditioned bedingter Reflex
refresh erfrischen, auffrischen
refresher course Auffrischungskurs
refusal Verweigerung
refuse verwehren, versagen, verweigern; sich weigern
refuse something flatly etwas strikt ablehnen
refutable widerlegbar
regenerate regenerieren
regeneration Regeneration
regenerative power Regenerationsfähigkeit
register eintragen, registrieren
registration fee Meldegebühr (oder -geld)
regulation Reglement
regulations Prüfungsordnung
regurgitate hervorwürgen
regurgitate (food for pups) vorwürgen (Futter für Welpen)
rehabilitate resozialisieren
reiki-treatment Reiki-Behandlung
reinforce bestätigen, verstärken
reinforcement Bestätigung, Verstärkung
reinforcement, conditioned konditionierte Bestätigung
reinforcement, continious kontinuierliche Bestätigung
reinforcement, negative negative Bestätigung
reinforcement, postitive positive Bestätigung
reinforcement, variable variable Bestätigung

reintegration Wiedereingliederung
relapse Rückfall
relapsing rückfällig
related (to) verwandt (mit)
related by blood blutsverwandt
relation Verhältnis
relationship Beziehung
relax sich entspannen, ausruhen
relaxation Entspannung
relaxation exercise Entspannungsübung
relaxed entspannt, ungezwungen
relearn umlernen
release entlassen, loslassen
release (a hunting dog from leash) schnallen (des Jagdhunden)
release (from leash) ableinen
release from erlösen von
release reward Belohnungsspiel als Auflösung einer Übung
release word Entlassungswort, Wort für das Auflösen der Übung
reliability Zuverlässigkeit
reliability ratio festes System
reliable verlässlich, zuverlässig
relieve lindern
remain neutral sich neutral verhalten
remain on the spot verharren
remark Bemerkung
remedy abuses Missstände abschaffen
remedy things Abhilfe schaffen
remind erinnern
rename umbenennen
renunciation Verzicht
repeat wiederholen
repeated breeding nachdecken
repertoire Repertoire
repertoire cuing Verhaltensketten bilden
repetition Wiederholung
replaceable ersetzbar
replacement Austausch, Ersatz
replacement scorebook Ersatzleistungsheft
replete gesättigt
repress unterdrücken
repression Unterdrückung
require verlangen
require a great deal of energy großer Energie-Aufwand
requirement Anforderung, Erfordernis, Bedürfnis
rescue Rettung
rescue dog Rettungshund
research Forschung
reservation Buchung
reserve Zurückhaltung
reserved zurückhaltend
reshape umformen
residential area Wohngebiet
residual risk Restrisiko

resist sich sträuben
respect Respekt, respektieren
respect for each other voreinander Achtung haben
respectability Achtbarkeit
respectable achtbar
respectful achtungsvoll, respektvoll
respiratory tract Atmungstrakt
respondent conditioning klassische Konditionierung, Konditionierung nach Pawlow
response Reaktion
responsibility Verantwortlichkeit
responsible verantwortlich, verantwortungsbewusst
rest ruhen
resting place Ruheplatz
restless ruhelos, unruhig
result Ergebnis
retained testicle Bauchhoden, Leistenhoden
retina Netzhaut
retrain abtrainieren
retraining Umschulung, Umverknüpfung
retrieve apportieren
retrieve on flat Apportieren/Bringen auf ebener Erde
retrieve over jump Apportieren/Bringen über die Hürde
retriever Retriever, Apportierhund
retriever bag Apportiersack
retrieving buck Bringsel
return Rückkehr, zurückkehren
return to the wild state verwildern
return to handler zum Hundeführer zurückkehren
return to normal sich normalisieren
revaccination Auffrischungsimpfung, Wiederholungsimpfung
revenue stamp Steuermarke
reverse umgekehrt
reverse scissors bite umgekehrtes Scherengebiss
reward Belohnung, belohnen
rewarding lohnend
Rhodesian Ridgeback, African Lion Hound Rhodesian Ridgeback
rib Rippe
rib, false falsche Rippe
rib, true echte Rippe
rib cage Brustkorb
ribbon Band
rich chestnut red mahagonirot
rich colour intensive Farbe
rich in vitamins vitaminreich
rickets Rachitis
riding to hounds Parforcejagd

right of pre-emption Vorkaufsrecht
right to live Lebensberechtigung
Right Turn! (verbal command) Rechts um! (Hörzeichen)
ring Ring
ring conditions Bedingungen im Ring (Wettkampf)
ring gates (e.g. obedience) Ringbegrenzungszaun (z.B. Obedience)
ring steward Ringsekretär(in), Ringwart(in)
ring steward Sonderleiter(in)
ring steward (obedience) Wettkampfleiter(in) (Obedience)
ring tail Ringelrute
ring wise dog ringerfahrener, routinierter Hund
ringed gerollt
riot stick Beißwurst
rise to the occasion sich der Situation gewachsen zeigen
rise up sich sträuben
risk Risiko
ritual Ritual, rituell
rival Rivale, Rivalin
rivalry Rivalität
road to success Weg zum Erfolg
roadside Straßenrand
roan Schimmel
roan gestichelt
rocky felsig
roll sich wälzen
root of the muzzle Schnauzenwurzel
root of the tail Schwanzwurzel
ropy tail knotige Rute
rose ear Rosenohr, Windhundohr
Roseneath Terrier Roseneath Terrier
rosette Rosette
rotator muscle Drehmuskel
Rothbury Terrier Rothbury Terrier
Rottweiler Rottweiler
Rough Collie Schottischer Schäferhund, Langhaar Collie
rough-coated rauhaarig
roughness Rohheit
roundworm Nematode, Spulwurm, Fadenwurm
roundworm infestation Askaridenbefall
routine Routine
routinization Routiniertheit
rowdy Raufbold, Rowdy
rub kraulen
rub down frottieren
rubber brush Gummibürste
rubber floor matting Antirutsch-Bodenbelag
rubbish Müll
rubbish can Mülleimer
ruby rubinrot, kastanienrot

rucksack Rucksack
rude rüpelhaft
rudimentary grundlegend; unvollkommen, verkümmert
rule Regel, Spielregel
Rumanian Sheepdog Rumänischer Hirtenhund
Rumanian Shepherd Dog Mioritic Hirtenhund
rump Kruppe
run Rennen
run away davonlaufen, weglaufen
run back zurücklaufen
run behind hinterherlaufen
run down hetzen
run off losrennen
runner-up Zweitplatzierte(r)
running gait Laufschritt
running line Laufdraht
runny nose Nasenkatarrh, Schnupfen
run-off Entscheidungslauf
rush something übereilen
rush up zustürzen auf
rush up at zuspringen auf
russet rotbeige
russet gold dunkelsemmelfarben
Russian Bear Dog Medelan
Russian Harlequin Hound Russischer Harlekin Hund
Russian Hound Kostromá Bracke, Russische Bracke
Russian Parti-coloured Hound Anglo-Russische Bracke, Russische Gescheckte Bracke
Russian Sheepdog Owtscharka, Russischer Hirtenhund
Russian Spaniel Russischer Jagdspaniel
Russian Wolfhound Barsoi, Russischer Windhund
Russo-European Laika Russisch-Europäischer Laika
rust braunrot
rustiness rostfarbener Schimmer
rutting season Brunftzeit

Saarloos Wolfhound Saarloos Wolfshund
sabled gewolkt
sabled (coat) berußt (Fellfärbung)
sabre tail Säbelrute
sacral vertebra Kreuzbeinwirbel
sacrum Kreuzbein
saddle Sattel, Mantel
saddle back Sattelrücken
safe geborgen
safe distance Sicherheitsabstand
safety Geborgenheit, Sicherheit
safety belt Sicherheitsgurt
safety light collar blinkendes Sicherheitshalsband
safety measure Sicherheitsmaßnahme
safety sensation Sicherheitsgefühl
sagging durchhängend
Saint Bernard Bernhardiner, St. Bernhardshund
Saint Germain Pointer Saint Germain Vorstehhund
Saint Hubert Hound St. Hubertus Hund
Saint Usuge Spaniel Épagneul St. Usuge, St. Usuge Vorstehhund
sales contract Kaufvertrag
saliva Speichel
salivate sabbern
salmon Lachs
salt and pepper pfeffer und salz(farben)
Saluki Saluki
salve Salbe
Samoyed Samojede
samoyed smile Samojedenlächeln
sanction Sanktion, sanktionieren
sandbag (agility) Sandsack (Agility)
sandy sandfarben, sandig
Sanshu Dog Sanshu Inu

Sar Planinac Illyrischer Schäferhund
sarcoptic mange Sarcoptesräude, Grabmilbenräude
satisfied zufrieden, überzeugt
sausage Wurst
save retten
save the situation Situation retten
sawdust Sägemehl
scabious räudig
scale Schuppe (Haut-)
scaling wall (protection work, agility) Schrägwand (Schutzdienst, Agility), Palisade (Ringsport), Steilwand
scallywag Schlingel
scalp Kopfhaut
scar Narbe
scatter verstreuen
scent Duftstoff, Geruch, Duftfahne
scent Spur (Jagd), Fährte; Witterung, wittern, riechen
scent discrimination Geruchsunterscheidung
scent dog Fährtenhund
scent mark Duftmarke
scent trail of unwounded game Gesundfährte
scent work Nasenarbeit
scenthound Spürhund, Bracke
scenting Nasenarbeit
scentless witterungslos
sceptic Skeptiker(in), Zweifler(in)
sceptical skeptisch
scepticism Skepsis
schedule Plan, Schema
schematic schematisch
schematize schematisieren
Schiller Hound Schiller-Stövare
Schipperke Schipperke
school ausbilden, abrichten
schooling Ausbildung, Abrichtung
schutzhund trial (or test) Schutzhundprüfung
scientific naturwissenschaftlich
scimitar tail Schwertrute
scissors bite Scherengebiss
scissors hook Scherenkarabiner
sclera Lederhaut
scold someone schimpfen
scooting with back on the floor Schlittenfahren mit dem Hinterteil über den Boden
score Wertung
score sheet Bewertungsblatt
scoreboard Anzeigetafel für die Ergebnisse
scorebook Leistungsheft
scoring considerations Wertungsaspekte
scoring issue Wertungsergebnis

scoring systems Wertungssystem, Punktesystem
Scottish Deerhound Deerhound, Schottischer Hirschhund
Scottish Terrier Schottischer Terrier
scrambled mouth durcheinanderstehende Schneidezähne
scratch kraulen, scharren, kratzen, zerkratzen
screening for genetic defects Erbfehlerermittlung
scribbling pad Kladde
scrotum Hodensack, Skrotum
scruff Nacken
scruff-shake Genick schütteln
scruple Skrupel
scuffle rangeln
scurf Schuppen
Sealyham Terrier Sealyham Terrier
search Suche, suchen
search and rescue dog Rettungshund, Trümmersuchhund
search for wounded game Nachsuche, Verlorensuche
search for game stöbern
search for wounded game on blood trail (hunting) Nachsuche (Jagd)
Search! (verbal command) Such! Revier! (Hörzeichen)
searching dog Suchhund
season Brunst, Läufigkeit, Östrus
season Jahreszeit, Saison
sebaceous gland Talgdrüse
secluded abgeschieden
seclusion Abgeschiedenheit
second dentition Zahnwechsel
secondary sekundär
section Teilstück
sedate sedieren
seeing eye dog Blindenführhund
seek revieren, suchen
Seek! (verbal command) Such! (Hörzeichen)
seek refuge in attack die Flucht nach vorn antreten
seek refuge with (from) Schutz suchen bei (vor)
seeking for help hilfesuchend
seesaw (agility) Wippe (Agility)
selection Zuchtwahl
selective selektiv
selectively bred hochgezüchtet
selectively bred breed Hochzuchtrasse
self-assessment Selbsteinschätzung
self-coloured nose Nase in der Farbe des Haarkleides
self-confidence Selbstbewusstsein, Selbstsicherheit

self-confident selbstbewusst, selbstsicher
self-control Selbstbeherrschung
self-deception Selbstbetrug
self-defence Selbstverteidigung
self-discipline Selbstdisziplin
self-esteem Selbstwertgefühl
self-inflicted injury Selbstbeschädigung
self-knowledge Selbsterkenntnis
self-masked Maske in der Fellfarbe
self-will Eigenwille
semicircular canal Bogengang
semi-drop (ear) halb gekippt
semi-moist dog food Halbfeuchtfutter
seminal duct Samenleiter
seminar Seminar, Kurs
semi-pricked ear Kippohr
send out vorausschicken
sense of hearing Gehör, Gehörsinn
sense of humor Humor, Sinn für Humor
sense of sight Gesichtssinn
sense of smell Geruchssinn
sense of touch Tastsinn
sensitive einfühlsam, empfindlich, sensibel
sensitive to noise lärmempfindlich
sensitiveness Sensibilität
sensitivity Empfindlichkeit
sensitize sensibilisieren
sepsis Blutvergiftung
septic septisch
sequence Sequenz
series of tests Versuchsreihe
serum Impfstoff
service dog Assistenzhund (für Behinderte)
set (e.g. tail, ear) Ansatz (z.B. Rute, Ohren etc.)
set eingesetzt
set a dog on someone den Hund auf jemanden hetzen
set (on) high hoch angesetzt
set forward shoulder vorgeschobene Schulter
set limits to Grenzen setzen
Setter Setter
settle in sich eingewöhnen
sexual Geschlechts-, geschlechts-,
shade Farbton
shaded gewolkt, schattiert
shading Wolkung
shading on the face Schattenmaske
shadow Schatten
shady schattig
shaggy ruppig
shake schütteln, sich schütteln
shake hands Pfötchen geben
shampoo Shampoo

shank Unterschenkel
shape Kondition; Formen eines Verhaltens, formen
Shar Pei Shar Pei, Chinesischer Faltenhund
sharp (fierce) scharf (aggressiv)
sharpness Schärfe
shave off abrasieren
shaved ausgeschoren
shearing tooth Reißzahn
shed (hair) haaren
shedding Haarwechsel
sheepdog Schäferhund
sheepdog trial Hütehundwettbewerb
shepherd Schäfer
shepherd (dog) Schäferhund
Shepherd Spitz Hütespitz
Shetland Sheepdog Sheltie, Shetland Schäferhund
she-wolf Wölfin
Shi Tzu Shi Tzu, Tibetanischer Löwenhund
Shiba Inu Shiba Inu
shift the motivation Motivationslage verändern
Shikari dog Schikari
Shikoku (Inu) Kohchi Ken, Shikoku Inu
Shilluk Greyhound Shilluk Windhund
Shiloh Shepherd Dog Shiloh Schäferhund
shine Glanz, erstrahlen
shining glänzend
shipping crate Transportbox
shock Schock, Schreck
shoo away scheuchen
shoptalk Fachsimpelei
short lead (or leash) Kurzführer
short muzzle Kurzkopf
short-acting narcosis Kurznarkose
shortage Knappheit, Mangel
short-backed kurzrückig
short-faced kurzköpfig
short-haired kurzhaarig
Short-Haired Miniature Dachshund Kurzhaar Zwergdachshund
Short-Haired Vizsla Vizsla Kurzhaar
short-legged niederläufig, kurzläufig
Short-Legged Hound Basset
short-legged hound Niederlaufhund
short-muzzled kurzschnauzig
short-nosed kurznasig
short-stepping kurztrittig
shot Spritze, Injektion
shot Schuss, knallen (mit Pistole)
shotgun pellet Schrotkorn
shoulder Schulter
shoulder blade Schulterblatt

shoulder joint Schultergelenk
shoulder, set forward vorgeschobene Schulter
shoulder, laid back zurückgelegte Schulter
shout schreien
shout at anschreien
shout someone down jemanden niederbrüllen
show Ausstellung; ausstellen, herzeigen
showcase Ausstellungsvitrine
show clip Ausstellungsschur
show dog Ausstellungshund
show judge Formwertrichter(in)
show lead Vorführleine, Ausstellungsleine
show regulations Ausstellungsordnung, Zuchtschauordnung
show ribbon Formwertband
show ring Ausstellungsring, Rassering
show schedule Ausstellungskalender
show teeth Lefzen hochziehen
show training Ausstellungstraining, Ringdressur
show-assessed merit Formwert
show-dog breeding Schönheitszucht
shower Regenschauer
showing one's teeth Zähnefletschen
showmanship Vorführkunst
shrink back zurückscheuen
Shropshire Terrier Shropshire Terrier
shy scheu
shyness Scheuheit
Siberian Husky Husky, Sibirischer Husky
sibling Geschwister
Sicilian Greyhound Sizilianischer Windhund
sickle tail Sichelrute
side Flanke, Seite
side effects Nebenwirkungen
sidelong glance Seitenblick
sideways seitwärts
sight Sicht
Sight Hound Windhund, Sichthund
sight hound collar Windhundhalsband
sign Zeichen
sign of Anzeichen für
sign of fatigue Ermüdungserscheinung
sign of old age Alterserscheinung
signal Signal, signalisieren
signal collar reflektierendes Halsband
signature cover Kenndecke
signpost beschildern
signposting Beschilderung

silence Stille
silence of game Wildruhe
silent geräuschlos, leise, stumm
silent heat versteckte Läufigkeit, stiller Östrus
silhouette Außenlinie
silky seidig
silly ideas Flausen
silver grausilber, silber(farben), silbrig
silver-fawn schiefergrau
similar (to) ähnlich (mit)
similarity (to) Ähnlichkeit (mit)
simple einfach
simplification Vereinfachung
simplify vereinfachen
sinew Sehne
sinewy sehnig
single bar jump (agility) einfache Hürde (Agility)
singles stake Solorennen
single-tracking (gait) Schnurgang
sink its teeth into sich verbeißen
sire zeugen (Fortpflanzen)
sit back and watch untätig zusehen
sit up (and beg) Männchen machen
Sit! (verbal command) Sitz! (Hörzeichen)
sit-in-motion Absitzen aus der Bewegung
sit-stay Hinsetzen mit Sitzenbleiben
Sit-Stay! (verbal command) Sitz! Bleib! (Hörzeichen)
situation Situation
size of entry Meldezahl
sketchy knowledge lückenhaftes Wissen
skill Fertigkeit, Fähigkeit
skimmed milk Magermilch
skin Haut
skin disease Hautkrankheit
skin eruption Ausschlag
skin on head Kopfhaut
skull Schädel, Gehirnschädel
Skye Terrier Skye Terrier
slacken (speed) verlangsamen (Tempo)
slalom Slalom
slanted abfallend
slanting schräg, abfallend
slate schiefer(blau)
slaver sabbern
sled dog Schlittenhund
sled dog race Schlittenhundrennen
sledge Schlitten
sleep schlafen
sleepy schläfrig
sleet Schneeregen

sleeve (protection work) Schutzarm (Schutzdienst)
sleeve dog Schoßhund
slew feet auswärts gedrehte Pfoten
slicker Striegel
slide Rutsche, rutschen
slightly built leicht gebaut
slim schlank
slip Flüchtigkeitsfehler
slip off abrutschen
slipped hock lockeres Sprunggelenk
slippery rutschig
slope Neigung
sloping abfallend
Sloughi Sloughi, Arabischer Windhund
Slovac Cuvac Slovensky Cuvac
Slovakian Hound Slowakische Bracke, Slowakische Schwarzwildbracke
Slovakian Pointing Griffon Slowakischer Raubart, Slowakischer Rauhaariger Vorstehhund
Slovakian Sheepdog Slowakischer Hirtenhund
slow langsam
slow down verlangsamen, verzögern
slow pace langsame Gangart
slowness Langsamkeit
sluggishness Trägheit
slush Schneematsch
Smalands Hound Smalandsstövare
small klein
Small (German) Spitz Kleinspitz
Small African Greyhound Kleiner Afrikanischer Windhund
Small Anglo-French Hound Kleiner Anglo-Französischer Laufhund
Small Bernese Hound Berner Niederlaufhund
Small Blue Gascony Griffon Kleiner Blauer Griffon der Gascogne
Small Blue Gascony Hound Kleiner Blauer Laufhund der Gascogne
small domestic animals Kleinvieh
Small French Pointer Kleiner Französischer Vorstehhund
small game Niederwild
Small Gascon Saintongeois Kleiner Gascon Saintongeois
Small German Spitz Deutscher Kleinspitz
small intestine Dünndarm
Small Munsterlander Kleiner Münsterländer Vorstehhund, Heidewachtel

Small Polish Hound
Kleiner Ogar Polski
Small Portuguese Hound
Portugiesischer Niederläufiger Laufhund
Small Spanish Hound
Sabueso Espanol Lebrero
Small Swiss Hound
Schweizer Niederlaufhund
Smaller Jura Hound
Jura Niederlaufhund
smear (medical) Abstrich (medizinisch)
smell Geruch, riechen
smile at anlächeln, belächeln
smile at someone zulächeln
Smithfield Collie
Smithfield Collie
smoke Rauch
smoke detection dog
Rauchmeldehund
Smooth Collie Kurzhaar Collie
smooth ear Lederohr
smooth work (live-stock)
ruhige Arbeit (z.B. am Vieh)
smooth-coated glatthaarig
smooth-haired glatthaarig
snack Belohnungsleckerli
snap schnappen, zuschnappen
snap at abschnappen, abbeißen, schnappen nach
snappish, vicious bissig
snarl knurren, fauchen
snarling Zähne fletschend
sneak schleichen
sniff beschnuppern, schnüffeln, schnuppern
snoop around herumschnüffeln
snore schnarchen
snout Schnauze, Fang
snow Schnee
snow flurry Schneegestöber
soaking wet patschnass
sociable umgänglich
social sozial
social animal soziales Tier
social deprivation
Sozialdeprivation
social rank soziale Stellung
socialization Sozialisation
socialize sozialisieren
socially acceptable
sozialverträglich
socks weiße Fesseln
soft weich
soft back weicher Rücken
soft bite floppy disc
Frisbeescheibe aus Softmaterial
Soft Coated Wheaten Terrier
Soft Coated Wheaten Terrier
softly sachte
softness Sanftheit
sole owner Alleinbesitzer(in)
solid einfarbig
solid food festes Futter
solid white reinweiß

solitary hunter Alleinjäger, Solojäger
Solling Bloodhound Solling Leitbracke
solution Lösung
solvable lösbar
Somerset Harrier Somerset Harrier
Sonangi Alunk
soothe (pain) lindern (Schmerz)
sorrow Leid
sorting aussortieren
soul Seele
sound Geräusch; gesund, erbgesund
soundless lautlos
soundness Erbgesundheit
South Russian Ovtcharka Südrussischer Owtscharka
South Russian Sheepdog Südrussischer Owtscharka
South Russian Steppen Hound Steppenwindhund
Southern Harrier Southern Harrier
sovereign souverän
sovereignty Souveränität
space Abstand; Platz (Raum)
space of time Zeitraum
Spaniel Spaniel
Spanish Greyhound Spanischer Windhund, Galgo Espanol, Levrier Espanol
Spanish Hound Spanischer Laufhund
Spanish Mastiff Spanische Dogge, Sabueso Espanol, Mastin Leones, Mastin Machego
Spanish Pointer Spanischer Vorstehhund, Perdiguero Burgales
Spanish Water Dog Spanischer Wasserhund, Perro de Agua Espanol
speak sprechen
Speak! (verbal command) Laut! (Hörzeichen)
special arrangement Sonderregelung
special case Sonderfall
special field Fachgebiet, Spezialgebiet
specialize in sich spezialisieren
specialized dictionary Fachwörterbuch
specialized literature Fachliteratur
specialized training Spezialausbildung
specialty show Sonderschau, Spezialzuchtschau
species Art (biologisch)
specific behaviours arttypisches Verhalten
speckle Tüpfel, Tupfen

speckled geschimmelt, gesprenkelt
speckling Tüpfelung
spectator Zuschauer(in)
speechless sprachlos
speed Geschwindigkeit, Tempo
speediness Schnelligkeit
spell of bad weather Schlechtwetterperiode
sperm bank Samenbank
spike collar Stachelhalsband, Korallenhalsband
spinal process Dornfortsatz
spine Wirbelsäule
spine of scapula Gräte
spiral stake Anbindepflock, Anbindehaken, Bodenhaken
spirited munter, lebhaft
spittle Speichel
splash Fleck, Sprenkel; plantschen
splay feet offene Zehen
splayed out gespreizt
spleen Milz
splendid fellow Prachtkerl
split dazwischen drängen, splitten
split nose Spaltnase
split ring Splentring
splitting up splitten
splotched gesprenkelt
spoil verhätscheln, verwöhnen
spoilt verzogen (verwöhnt)
spondylosis Spondylose
sponsor Veranstalter, Ausrichter
sport Sport
sport of schutzhund Schutzhundsport
sport of water trial Wassersuche
sports ground Sportplatz
spot Fleck
spot (bitch in season) tröpfeln (während Läufigkeit)
spotted getüpfelt, getupft
spotted nose Schmetterlingsnase
spotting Blutung (der läufigen Hündin)
spotting Scheckung
sprain Verstauchung
spread streuen
spread-bar jump (agility) dreifache Hürde (Agility)
spreading Ausbreitung
spring from herunterspringen
spring hook Karabinerhaken
spring of ribs Rippenwölbung
springer Stöberhund
square Viereck
squat hocken, sich hinhocken
squeak quietschen
squeaker (toy) Quietschventil (im Spielzeug)
squeeze quetschen
St. Hubert Hound Bluthund
St. John's Dog St. Johns Hund

St. Louis Gray Dog Grauer St. Louis Hund
Stabijhoun Stabijhoun
stability Stabilität
stable Stall
stacked aufgebaut
stadium Stadion
Staffordshire Bull Terrier Staffordshire Bullterrier
stage Stufe
stage fright Lampenfieber
stage in labour Austreibungsphase, Nachgeburtsphase
stage of development Entwicklungsstufe
staghound Hetzhund
stagnate stagnieren
stagnation Stagnation
staircase Treppe
stale track (or line) erkaltete Fährte
stalk Pirsch, pirschen, anpirschen
stamina Ausdauer
stance Stand, Stellung (des Körpers)
stand still stillstehen
Stand! (verbal command) Steh! (Hörzeichen)
standard Standard
standard in breed Rassestandard
standard course time (agility) Standardzeit (Agility)
Standard German Spitz Deutscher Mittelspitz
standard of performance Leistungsniveau
Standard Poodle Königspudel, Großpudel
Standard Schnauzer Schnauzer
standing heat Hochbrunst
stand-off hair (or coat) abstehendes Haarkleid
Stand-Stay! (verbal command) Steh! Bleib! (Hörzeichen)
stare at anstarren
staring (hair or coat) struppig (Fell)
staring eye(s) starrer Blick
staring hair gesträubtes Haar
start Start, Ausgangspunkt
start the dog tracking den Hund auf die Fährte ansetzen
start of tracking Abtritt am Beginn der Fährte
starting box Startbox, Startkasten
starting flag (tracking) Startpfahl (Fährtenarbeit)
starting line Startlinie
starting position (obedience) Ausgangsposition (Obedience)
starting team Startmannschaft
state Zustand
state of anxiety Angstzustand

state something clearly etwas klarstellen
station wagon Kombiwagen
statistical statistisch
statistics Statistik
status Stellung (Ansehen/ Rang)
status symbol Statussymbol
statutes and articles Vereinssatzung
statutory satzungsgemäß
stay bleiben, verweilen; verspannen
Stay! (verbal command) Bleib! (Hörzeichen)
staying power Ausdauer
steadiness in retrieving Bringtreue
steady ruhig
steady (or indifferent) to gunshot schussfest
Steady! (verbal command) Langsam! (Hörzeichen)
steady temperament, of wesensfest
steal stehlen
steel chain/ collar Kettenhalsband
stench Gestank
step Schritt
step back zurückweichen
step obstacles zu überkletternde Geräte
step-by-step schrittweise
stereotyped movement Bewegungsstereotypie
stereotyped behaviour Verhaltensstereotypie
sterile steril, zeugungsunfähig
sterility Zeugungsunfähigkeit
sterilization Sterilisation
sterilize sterilisieren
steward Ordner, Steward
stick Stock
stick (protection work) Schlagstock (Schutzdienst)
stick of split bamboo (mondioring) Klapperstock (Ringsport)
stiffen versteifen
stiffness Muskelkater
still hunt Pirsch
stillbirth Totgeburt
stillborn totgeboren
stimulation from the helper Helferanreiz
stimulus Reiz
stimulus, aversive aversiver, unangenehmer Reiz
stimulus control Signalkontrolle
stimulus satiation Reizüberflutung
stimulus threshold Reizschwelle
stink stinken
stitch removal Nahtentfernung
stocky gedrungen, kompakt
stomach Magen

stony steinig
stool Kot, Stuhlgang
stool eating Kotfressen
stop Stirnabsatz
stop biting on command (protection work) Ablassen auf Kommando (Schutzdienst)
stop the fight (protection work) Kampf einstellen (Schutzdienst)
stop watch Stoppuhr
storm Sturm, stürmen
stormy stürmisch
stow away verstauen
stowage pocket Stautasche
straight steil; gerade, geradlinig
straight racing Whippetrennen, gerade Strecke
strain Strapaze, strapazieren; zerren; Zuchtstamm
strange fremd, ungewohnt, seltsam
stranger Fremde(r), Fremdperson
strangers' scent (or track) Fremdfährte
strangle strangulieren, würgen
strategy Strategie
stray streunen; streunend
stray animal herrenloses Tier
stray dog Streuner
streak Streifen
strenuous strapaziös
stress Stress
stress disease Stresskrankheit
stress indicator Hinweis auf Stress
stressed-out stressgeplagt
stress-free stressfrei
stressful stressig
stressors Stressoren (Reize, die Stress auslösen)
stretch strecken, sich strecken, sich recken
strict strikt, streng
strictness Strenge
strike schlagen
stripe Streifen
stripping (of dead hair) Trimmen (lose Unterwolle)
stripping tool Trimm-Messer
stroke kraulen, streicheln; Strich
strong stark
struggle against sich sträuben gegen
struggle for existence Existenzkampf
stubbly stoppelig
stubborn stur
stud agreement Deckvereinbarung
stud dog Zuchtrüde, Deckrüde
stud fee Deckgebühr, Decktaxe
studbook Zuchtbuch, Stammbuch
studdog class Nachzuchtgruppe

study studieren
study on Studie über
stuff ausstopfen
stuffy fleischig
stumble (over) stolpern (über)
stump tail Mutzschwanz
Stumpy-Tail Cattle Dog Stummelrutiger Cattle Dog
sturdy derb, widerstandsfähig, robust
style of leadership (agility) Führtechnik (Agility)
stylish elegant
Styrian Rough-Coated Alpine Hound Peintinger Bracke, Steirische Rauhaarige Hochgebirgsbracke
subject Thema
submission Unterordnung, Unterwerfung
submissive demütig, unterwürfig; sich unterordnen
submissiveness Unterwürfigkeit
submit sich unterordnen
subordinate rangniedriger, untergeordnet
subspecies Unterart
substantial substanzvoll
substantial (body) kräftig
substitute Ersatz
substrate Einstreu
subtle subtil
success Erfolg
successful experience Erfolgserlebnis
success rate Erfolgsquote, Erfolgsrate
successful erfolgreich
suck saugen, lutschen
suckle säugen
Sudan Greyhound Sudanwindhund
sudden plötzlich
suffer leiden, erleiden
suffering leidend
suggest vorschlagen
suggestion Vorschlag
suitability Tauglichkeit
sulky bockig
sultriness Schwüle
sultry schwül
Sumatra Wild Dog Batakenhund
summary procedure Schnellverfahren
superiority Überlegenheit
supple biegsam
supplementary food Ergänzungsfutter
support Hilfestellung
suppose vermuten
suppress unterdrücken
suppression Unterdrückung
surface Oberfläche

surprise attack (protection work) Überraschungsangriff, Überfall (Schutzdienst)
surrounding Umfeld
survival instinct Selbsterhaltungstrieb
susceptible (to an illness) anfällig (für eine Krankheit)
suspect (protection work) Verdächtige(r), Scheintäter(in) (Schutzdienst)
Sussex Spaniel Sussex Spaniel
suture line Naht
swallow schlucken, verschlucken
swayback Senkrücken
Swedish Drever Schwedische Dachsbracke
Swedish Elkhound Jämthund, Schwedischer Elchhund
Swedish Lapp Spitz Schwedischer Lappenspitz, Lapphund
Swedish Vallhund Vallhund, Westgotenspitz
sweet niedlich
swim schwimmen
swing finish schwungvoller (schneller) Abschluss (Übung)
swirl of hair Haarwirbel
Swiss Hound Schweizer Laufhund
switch umschalten
sworn enemy Erzfeind
symmetry Harmonie, Symmetrie
system Systematik
systematic systematisch

table Tisch
taboo Tabu, tabuisieren
tactile hair Tasthaar
tag Namensetikett, Namensschild
Tahl-Tan Bear Dog Tahl Tan Bärenhund
tail Rute, Schwanz
tail, gay fröhlich getragene Rute
tail, lashing schwingende Rute
tail, low set tief angesetzte Rute
tail, merry fröhlich bewegte Rute, Schwanzwedeln
tail, proud Ringelrute
tail chasing Schwanzjagen
tail gland Schwanzdrüse
tail set Rutenansatz
tail wagging Schwanzwedeln
take nehmen, aufnehmen, ergreifen
take a dog for a walk Gassi gehen
take a break Pause machen, pausieren
take loving care of liebevoll pflegen
take out for a walk spazieren führen
take part in teilnehmen an
take precautions Vorsichtsmaßnahmen treffen
take the responsibility for verantworten
take to one's heels Reißaus nehmen
taking readily to water wasserfreudig
Talbot Hound Talbot Laufhund
talent Talent
talented talentiert
talk reden
talk shop fachsimpeln
talkative lautfreudig, bellfreudig
tameness Zahmheit

tan kupferfarben, rostfarben; falb
tan markings loh
tangled verflochten
tangled (coat) verwirrt (Fell)
tape Band
taper sich verjüngen
tapeworm Bandwurm
target Zielpunkt
target stick Targetstick, Zeigestock
target stick holder Targetstickhalter(ung)
targeting berühren
tarsal joint Sprunggelenk, Tarsalgelenk
tartar Zahnstein
tassel Franse
taste schmecken
Tatra Mountain Sheepdog Owczarek Podhalanski, Tatrahund
tatter zerfleddern
tattoo Tätowierung, tätowieren
tawny falb, rostbraun
Tawny Brittany Basset Basset Fauve de Bretagne, Fahlroter Bretagner Niederlaufhund
Tawny Brittany Griffon Griffon Fauve de Bretagne
tax Steuer
team Gespann; Mannschaft
team captain Mannschaftsführer(in)
team classification Mannschaftswertung
team event Mannschaftswettbewerb
teamwork Teamarbeit, Zusammenarbeit
tear reißen
tear in pieces in Stücke reißen
teat Brustwarze
teats Gesäuge
teeter (agility) Wippe (Agility)
teeth Zähne, Gebiss
teeth chattering Zähneklappern
teeth, permanent bleibendes Gebiss
teeth, protruding vorstehende Zähne
teething Zahnwechsel
telepathy Gedankenübertragung
tell off abschnappen, abbeißen
tell others weitererzählen
Tellington Touch, TTouch Tellington Touch, TTouch
temper Temperamentsveranlagung
temperament Temperament
temperament test Wesensprüfung
temperament, of sound ... nervenfest
temperature Fieber; Temperatur

temporary vorläufig
temporary solution Notlösung
tempt verlocken
temptation Verlockung
tenacious hartnäckig
tenacity Hartnäckigkeit
tend hüten
tendency Tendenz
termite detection dog Termitensuchhund
terraces Tribüne (Stadion)
terrain Terrain
terrible furchtbar
Terrier Terrier
terrier appearance Terrierausdruck
terrier-like eye Terrierauge
territorial behaviour Territorialverhalten
territory Revier (eines Hundes)
territory, control of Revierkontrolle, -behauptung
test Prüfung
test condition Versuchsbedingung
test for evaluation a puppys' vitality Biotonustest
test of courage (protection work) Mutprobe (Schutzdienst)
test of proper use of voice Spurlautprüfung
testicle Hode
texture (coat) Struktur (des Haarkleides)
Thai Ridgeback Dog Thai Ridgeback
thaw Tauwetter
theory of evolution Abstammungslehre
therapy dog Therapiehund
therefore folglich
thermometer Thermometer
thesis These
thick fleischig, dick
thick (e.g. coat) dicht (z.B. Fell)
thigh Oberschenkel, Schenkel
thin mager
thin (coat) ausdünnen, effilieren (Fell)
think denken
thinkable denkbar
thinning shears Effilierschere
third eyelid Blinzhaut, Nickhaut
thirst Durst
thirsty durstig sein
thoracic vertebra Brustwirbel
thought process Denkprozess
thoughtless gedankenlos
thoughtlessness Gedankenlosigkeit
thrash prügeln, verprügeln, vertrimmen
threaten bedrohen, drohen
threatening bedrohlich, drohend

thresh out ausdiskutieren
threshold Reizschwelle
throat Kehle
throw werfen
throw chain Wurfkette
thumb Daumen
thunderstorm Gewitter, Unwetter
thundery gewittrig
Thuringian Shepherd Dog Thüringer Schäferhund
thymus gland Thymusdrüse
thyroid gland Schilddrüse
Tibetan Apso Lhasa Apso
Tibetan Bearded Dog Kyi Leo
Tibetan Mastiff Do Khyi, Tibet Mastiff
Tibetan Spaniel Tibet Spaniel
Tibetan Terrier Tibet Terrier
tibia Schienbein
tick Zecke, Holzbock
tick collar Zeckenband
tick tweezers Zeckenzange
ticked gestichelt, geschimmelt, getüpfelt
tie (in mating) Hängen (beim Deckakt)
tie off abschnüren
tie-out stake Anlegepflock, Anbindepflock
tight scissors bite Reibegebiss, knappes Scherengebiss
tighten up straffen
tightrope walk Gratwanderung
time factor Zeitfaktor
time gained Zeitgewinn
time pressure Zeitdruck
time-consuming zeitaufwändig, zeitraubend
time-out (in training) Auszeit (in Trainingssequenz)
time-saving zeitsparend
timid scheu, zaghaft
timidity Scheuheit
timing Zeitablauf
tinned food Dosenfutter
tiny winzig
tip Spitze
tip of the nose Nasenspitze
tip of the tail Rutenspitze
tipped ear hohes Kippohr
tire ermüden; Reifen
tire jump (agility) Reifen-Sprung (Agility)
tired müde
tiredness Ermüdung
titbit Leckerbissen, Leckerli, Belohnungshappen
titleholder Titelverteidiger(in)
to be able fähig sein
toe Zeh(e)
toe nail Nagel, Kralle, Klaue
toe pad Zehenballen
toe the line spuren (sich fügen)
toeing-in einwärts gedreht
tolerance Toleranz

tolerant geduldig, tolerant
tolerate dulden, tolerieren
tolling dog Lockhund
tongue Zunge
tonic Stärkungsmittel
tonsil (medical) Mandel (medizinisch)
tooth (or bite) check Gebissüberprüfung
tooth, (plural: teeth) Zahn
toothless zahnlos
top coat Deckhaar, Oberfell, Oberhaar; Grannenhaar
top dog Alphahund, Rudelführer, Kopfhund
top performance Spitzenleistung
top score Spitzenergebnis
topknot Schopf
topography Topographie
topskull Schädeldach
torment quälen
torn cruciate Kreuzbandriss
torsion Drehung
Tosa Inu Tosa Inu
touch anfassen, berühren, streifen
touchy empfindlich, heikel
tough (e.g. character) hart (z.B. im Charakter), zäh
toughen to abhärten (gegen)
toxic gift(halt)ig
toxin Gift
toy Spielzeug
toy dog Kleinhund
Toy Dachshund Zwergteckel
Toy Fox Terrier Toy Foxterrier, Zwergfoxterrier
Toy German Spitz Zwergspitz
Toy Mexican Hairless Dog Mexikanischer Zwergnackthund
Toy Poodle Zwergpudel, Toy Pudel
toys Spielsachen
track Rennpiste; Fährte, fährten
track racing Bahnrennen
tracking Fährtenarbeit
tracking collar Schweißhalsung
tracking dog Suchhund, Fährtenhund
tracking harness Fährtengeschirr, Suchgeschirr
tracking leash Fährtenleine, Schweißriemen, Suchleine
tracking off-lead freisuchend
tracking on the leash Riemenarbeit
tracking piece/ article Fährtengegenstand
tracking sign Fährtenabgangsschild
tracking test Fährtenprüfung
tracking test on a blood trail Schweißprüfung
tracklayer Fährtenleger(in)
tractability Führigkeit

tractable führig, leichtführig
traffic-sure companion dog verkehrssicherer Begleithund
trail Fährte, fährten; Rennstrecke
trailer Fährtenhund
train ausbilden, abrichten
trainability Trainierbarkeit
trainable erziehbar
trained to heel on leash leinenführig
trainer Trainer(in), Ausbilder, Abrichter
training Ausbildung, Abrichtung, Abführung
training aids Trainingshilfsmittel
training assistance dog Trainingsassistenzhund
training bargain Vertrag zur Ausbildung eines Hundes
training collar Erziehungshalsband, Dressurhalsband
training director Übungsleiter(in)
training equipment Trainingszubehör
training method Trainingsmethode
training sequence Trainingsphase, -sequenz
training session Trainingseinheit, Übungsstunde
training table Trainingstisch
traits Charakteristika
transform sich verwandeln
transition to übergehen zu
transition(al) period Übergangsphase
transmission range Sendebereich
transmitter Sender
Transsylvanian Hound Transsylvanischer Spürhund
trauma Trauma
traumatic traumatisch
travel reisen
travel guide Reiseführer
travel sickness Reisekrankheit, Reisübelkeit
Trawler Spaniel Trawler Spaniel
treasurer Schatzmeister(in)
treat Leckerbissen, Leckerli, Belohnungshappen
treat behandeln
treatise wissenschaftliche Arbeit, Abhandlung
treatment Behandlung
Treeing Walker Coonhound Treeing Walker Coonhound
tremble beben, zittern
trench mouth Mundfäule
trial Leistungswettbewerb, -prüfung
trial chairman (chairwomen) Prüfungsleiter(in)

trial grounds Wettbewerbsgelände
trial helper Schutzdiensthelfer(in)
trial judge Leistungsrichter(in)
trial paperwork Prüfungspapiere
trial phases Prüfungsabteilungen
trial regulations Prüfungsregelwerk
trial rules and regulations Prüfungsordnung
tricolour dreifarbig
Tricolour English Toy Spaniel Prince Charles Spaniel
tricoloured dreifarbig
trigger Auslöser, Auslöse-Reiz
trigger point druckschmerzhafter Punkt
trim trimmen
tripe Pansen
trophy Ehrenpreis, Trophäe
trot Laufschritt, Trab; traben, trotten
troublemaker Provokateur(in), Störenfried
trousered behost
truffle Trüffel
truffle dog Trüffelsuchhund
trunk Rumpf
trunk ventilator Heckbelüfter
trust Vertrauen, vertrauen
trust each other zueinander Vertrauen haben
trustful vertrauensvoll
trustworthy vertrauenswürdig
try out erproben
Tuareg Greyhound Tuareg Windhund
Tuareg Sloughi Azawakh
tucked-up aufgezogen
tucking of tail Schwanz einziehen
tuft Büschel, Schopf
tug zerren
tug toy Beißrolle, Beißwurst (Spielzeug), Zerrspielzeug, -seil
tug-of-war Lumpenzerren, Zerrspiel
Tulear Bichon Coton de Tuléar
tulip ear Tulpenohr
tumble purzeln
tumour Geschwulst
tunnel Tunnel
Turkish Hairless Dog Türkischer Nackthund
Turkmenian Greyhound Turkmenischer Windhund
turn Wendung
turn (off) abbiegen (nach)
turn inside/ outside Drehung nach innen/ nach außen
turn round sich umwenden
turn to sich zuwenden
turn-away-exercise Abwendeübung
turning away Körper wegdrehen

turning head away Kopf wegdrehen
turning manoeuvre Wegdrehbewegung
turning point Wendepunkt
Tweed Water Spaniel Tweed Water Spaniel
tweezers (pair of) Pinzette
two-day trial Zweitagesprüfung
type Typ
typey typvoll
tyrannize tyrannisieren
tyranny Gewaltherrschaft
Tyrolean Mountain Hound Österreichische Glatthaarbracke, Tiroler Bracke

ulcer Geschwür
umbilical cord Nabelschnur
umbilical hernia Nabelbruch
umbrella Regenschirm
unacceptable inakzeptabel
unasked unaufgefordert
unauthorized unerlaubt
unbalanced unausgeglichen, unausgewogen
unbearable unerträglich
unbroken ununterbrochen, unversehrt, ungebrochen
unclear unklar
uncomfortable unbehaglich
uncomplicated unkompliziert
uncomprehending verständnislos
unconfirmed unbestätigt
unconscious unbewusst
unconsidered unberücksichtigt
uncontrollable unkontrollierbar
uncontrolled unkontrolliert
undercoat Unterwolle
undergrowth Unterholz
underneath protection (protection work) Tiefenschutz (Schutzdienst)
undershot mouth (or jaw) Vorbiss
understanding verständnisvoll
undesirable unerwünscht
undesirable development Fehlentwicklung
undesired unerwünscht
undigested unverdaut
undisciplined undiszipliniert
undisturbed störungsfrei, ungestört
unease Unbehagen
uneven ungleichmäßig
unfair unfair
unfinished unfertig
unforeseen unvorhergesehen
unfortunately unerfreulicherweise
unfriendly unfreundlich

ungroomed ungekämmt
unhealthy ungesund
unhindered ungehindert
uniform einheitlich
unimaginative einfallslos
unintentional unabsichtlich, ungewollt, unfreiwillig
uninteresting uninteressant
unjust ungerecht
unkempt ungepflegt, ungekämmt
unkindness Lieblosigkeit
unknown unbekannt
unlearn verlernen
unloaded ungeladen (Waffe)
unmethodical unmethodisch
unmotivated unmotiviert
unnoticed unbemerkt
unobserved unbeobachtet
unplaced unplatziert
unpleasant unangenehm
unpredictable unvorhersehbar, unerwartet
unprepared unvorbereitet
unproblematic problemlos
unprotected schutzlos, ungeschützt
unpunished ungestraft
unqualified unfähig
unregistered dog nicht registrierter Hund
unreliable unzuverlässig
unripe unreif
unscrupulous skrupellos
unsteady unbeständig
unsteady to shot schusshitzig
unsuccessful erfolglos
untalented talentlos, unbegabt
untie losbinden
untrained ungeübt
unusual ungewöhnlich
unwanted ungewollt
unwillingly ungern
unyielding (e.g. charakter) hart (z.B. im Charakter)
upper arm Oberarm
upper jaw Oberkiefer
upper lip Lefze
upper thighbone Oberschenkelknochen
upright aufrecht
upsweep markiertes Kinn
uraemia Harnvergiftung
urethra Harnröhre
urinary incontinence Harnträufeln
urinary retention Harnverhaltung
urinate urinieren, harnen, Wasser lassen
urination Harnabsatz
urine Harn, Urin
usable verwendbar
use benutzen, gebrauchen
useful förderlich
useless nutzlos, ausgedient

uselessness Nutzlosigkeit
uterus Gebärmutter
utility Nutzen
utility (sport/ breeding) Gebrauchseigenschaft (Sport/ Zucht)
utility dog Gebrauchshund
utility training Gebrauchshundeausbildung
utilization as breeding stock Zuchtverwendung

vacation course Ferienkurs
vaccinate impfen
vaccination Impfung, Schutzimpfung, Auffrischungsimpfung, Wiederholungsimpfung
vaccination certificate Impfbescheinigung
vaccination record (card) Impfpass
vaccine Impfstoff
Vaghari Hound Vaghari
vagina Scheide
valley Tal
value judgement Werturteil
values Wertvorstellungen
variable variabel
variation Variation
variegated mehrfarbig gescheckt, bunt gefleckt, bunt gescheckt
variety Varietät, Schlag (Zuchtrichtung)
vary variieren
vehement ungestüm
veiled verschleiert
vein Vene
Vendeen Griffon Griffon Vendéen
venture wagen, sich getrauen
verbal command Hörzeichen
verbal correction verbale Korrektur, verbale Einwirkung
vermifuge Wurmmittel
vermin hunting raubzeugscharf
versatile vielseitige Person
versatility Vielseitigkeit
versatility trial Vielseitigkeitsprüfung
vertebra (plural: vertebrae) Wirbel
vertebral column Wirbelsäule
vertebrate Wirbeltier
vestibule Vorhof
vet Tierarzt, Veterinär(in)
veterans class Altersklasse, Seniorenklasse

veterinarian (us) Tierarzt, Veterinär(in)
veterinarian on site Platztierarzt
veterinary surgeon Tierarzt, Veterinär(in)
viable lebensfähig
vice-president Vize-Vorsitzende(r)
vicious bösartig (Tier)
viciousness Bösartigkeit, Bissigkeit
victorious siegreich
victory rostrum Siegertreppchen, -podest
vigilance Wachsamkeit
vigilant wachsam
violence Gewalt
violent gewalttätig
violent temper Jähzorn
virus Virus
visible sichtbar
visual visuell
vitality Vitalität
vitamin content Vitamingehalt
vitamin deficiency Vitaminmangel
vitamin preparation Vitaminpräparat
vitamin(e) Vitamin
vivacious temperamentvoll
vocal cord Stimmband
vociferous bellfreudig, lautfreudig
voice Stimme, Stimmlage; Waidlaut
voice, soft leise Stimme
voluntariness Freiwilligkeit
voluntary freiwillig
vomit sich erbrechen, kotzen
vote (on) abstimmen (über)
voting Abstimmung
v-shaped (ear) v-förmig (Ohr)
vulva Vulva, Nuss

W

wag wedeln
wagon barrier Hundeschutzgitter, Hundeschutznetz (Auto)
waist Taille
wait warten
wait for abwarten
walk Schritt, gehen; Spaziergang, spazieren
walker Spaziergänger(in)
wall hurdle (agility) Mauer (Agility)
wallow (in mud/ faeces/ carrion) wälzen (im Schmutz/ Kot/ Aas)
wanderer Wanderer, Wanderin
wanted erwünscht
warm up wärmen
warmth Wärme
warn warnen
warning Verwarnung, Warnung
warning sign Warnschild
washed out verwaschen
watch anschauen
watch over wachen über
watchdog Wachhund
watchdog, chained Kettenhund
watchful wachsam
watchfulness Wachsamkeit
water Wasser
water dog Wasserhund
water jump (agility) Wassergraben (Agility)
water shortage Wassermangel
Water Spaniel Wasserspaniel
water work Wassersuche
watering eye Triefauge
water-repellent wasserabstoßend
wavy gewellt, wellig
way of acting Handlungsweise
way the lips meet Lefzenschluss
waylay someone jemandem auflauern
weak schwach
weakness Schwäche
wean absäugen, entwöhnen
weaning absäugen, absetzen (Welpen von der Muttermilch)

weather Wetter
weather conditions Wetterbedingungen
weave (agility) Slalom (Agility)
weave poles (agility) Slalom-Stangen (Agility)
webbing Schwimmhaut
webbing between toes Zwischenzehenhaut
weigh (e.g. words) abwägen (z.B. Worte)
weight Gewicht
Weimaraner Weimaraner Vorstehhund
well-behaved wohlerzogen
well-groomed gepflegt
well-known allbekannt
well-proportioned ausgewogen
well-proportioned head wohlproportionierter Kopf
well-tried altbewährt
Welsh Collie Welsh Collie
Welsh Corgi Cardigan Welsh Corgi Cardigan
Welsh Corgi Pembroke Welsh Corgi Pembroke
Welsh Gray Herder Grauer Walisischer Hütehund, Welsh Gray Herder
Welsh Hound Welsh Hound
Welsh Red Herder Roter Walisischer Hütehund, Welsh Red Herder
Welsh Springer Spaniel Welsh Springer Spaniel
Welsh Terrier Welsh Terrier
West Country Harrier West Country Harrier
West Highland White Terrier West Highland White Terrier
West Siberian Laika Westsibirische Laika
Westphalian Hound Westfälische Dachsbracke
wet (dog) food Feuchtfutter (oder -nahrung)
wetness Nässe
wheaten weizenfarben, semmelfarben
wheel dog Schlittenhund unmittelbar vor dem Schlitten
wheel round umschwenken
whelp werfen (Geburt)
whelping box Wurfkiste
whelping report Wurfmeldung, Geburtsprotokoll
whimper jammern
whine jaulen, wimmern, winseln
whip (protection work) Peitsche (Schutzdienst)
whip tail Peitschenrute
whip-lash Peitschenhieb
Whippet Whippet
whipworm Peitschenwurm
whirl Haarwirbel
whiskers Bart, Schnurrhaare

whisper flüstern
whistle Pfeife, pfeifen, Hundepfeife; Pfiff
white weiß
whole foods Vollwertkost
whole point of the exercise Zweck der Übung
wholecoloured einfarbig
whorl Haarwirbel
will to achieve Leistungswille
willing willig
willing worker arbeitswilliger Hund
willingness to heel on leash Leinenführigkeit
willingness to retrieve Bringfreude
willingness to work Arbeitsfreude, Arbeitswilligkeit
win Sieg, siegen
wind force Windstärke
windpipe Luftröhre
wing dog Schlittenhund unmittelbar hinter Leittier
wing of nose Nasenflügel
wink at someone jemandem zublinzeln
winner Sieger(in)
winner's certificate Siegerurkunde
winter break Winterpause
wire coat Drahthaar
wire crate Gitter-Transportbox
Wire Fox Terrier Drahthaar Foxterrier, Rauhaar Foxterrier
wire netting Maschendraht
wire-coated drahthaarig
wirehair Drahthaar
wirehaired rauhaarig, drahthaarig
Wirehaired Dachshund Rauhaardackel
Wirehaired Hungarian Pointer Drahthaariger Ungarischer Vorstehhund
Wirehaired Pointing Griffon Französischer Rauhaariger Vorstehhund, Korthals Griffon
Wirehaired Vizsla Vizsla Drahthaar
wisdom Weisheit
with a stick and a carrot mit Zuckerbrot und Peitsche
with each other miteinander
with full force mit voller Wucht
with nose to the ground mit tiefer Nase
with the hair mit dem Strich
withers spot Nackenfleck
without a leader führerlos
without comment kommentarlos
without complaining klaglos
without gaps lückenlos
without lustre glanzlos
without plan planlos

without refinement ohne Adel, plump
without result ergebnislos
wobble wackeln
wolf Wolf
wolf down verschlingen
wolf grey wolfsfarben, wolfsgrau
wolf hybrid Wolfshybride, Wolfsmischling
wolf sable hellbraun mit schwarzen Haarspitzen, grau gewolkt
wooded area Waldgebiet
woof wuffen
Woolly-Haired Griffon Griffon à Poil Laineux
wooly hair Wollhaar
Woolyhared Griffon Wollhaariger Griffon
words of farewell Abschiedsworte
work Arbeit, arbeiten
work against entgegenwirken
work hard for sich erarbeiten
work record book Leistungsheft
work towards hinarbeiten auf
working breeds Gebrauchshundrassen
working certificate Gebrauchshundprüfungsnachweis, Abrichtungskennzeichen (AKZ)
working clip jugendliche Schur
working dog Arbeitshund, Sporthund
Working Terrier Working Terrier
world champion Weltmeister(in)
world championship Weltmeisterschaft
world dog show Welthundeausstellung
worm Wurm, entwurmen
worm infestation Wurmbefall
wormer Wurmmittel
worming Entwurmung, Wurmkur
worn out abgearbeitet
worrying beängstigend
worth reading lesenswert
wound Verwundung, Wunde
wounded verwundet
wrench Abschiedsschmerz
wrinkle Runzel
wrinkly faltig
wrong falsch
wrong decision Fehlentscheidung
wrong diagnosis Fehldiagnose
wrong drop (tracking) falsch verwiesen (Fährtenarbeit)
wrongly fälschlicherweise
Wurttemberg Pointer Württemberger Kurzhaariger Vorstehhund

XY

x-ray Röntgenbild, röntgen

yap kläffen
yard Hof
yawn gähnen
yell schreien, anbrüllen
yellow spots Porzellanscheckung
yellowish grey lederfarben
yellow-orange fahlrot
yelp anbellen, blaffen; Schrei, schreien
yelp of pain Schmerzensschrei
yip at ankeifen
Yorkshire Terrier Yorkshire Terrier
young jung
young dog sleeve (protection work) Junghundarm (Schutzdienst)
youth champion Jugendmeister(in)
youth team Jugendmannschaft
youthful jugendlich
Yugoslav Hound of the Save Valley Savetalbracke
Yugoslavian Mountain Dog Jugoslawischer Gebirgslaufhund
Yugoslavian Mountain Hound Jugoslawische dreifarbige Bracke, Jugoslawische Gebirgsbracke
Yugoslavian Sheepdog Jugoslawischer Schäferhund
Yugoslavian Tricolour Hound Dreifarbiger Jugoslawischer Laufhund

Zanzibar Dog
Sansibar Jagdhund
zero latency ohne Verzögerung (unmittelbare Reaktion)
zoonosis Zoonose

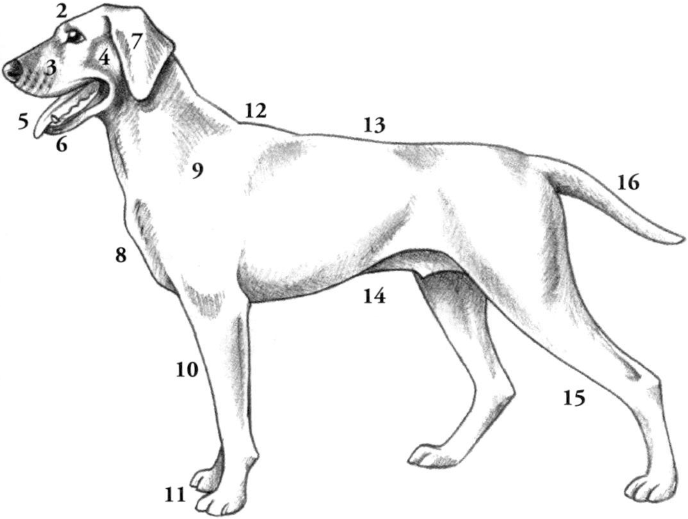

1 Nase / nose
2 Auge / eye
3 Schnauze, Fang / muzzle
4 Wange / cheek
5 Zunge / tongue
6 Lippe / lip
7 Ohr / ear
8 Brust / chest, breast
9 Schulter / shoulder
10 Vorderlauf / front leg
11 Pfote / paw
12 Widerrist / withers
13 Rücken / back
14 Bauch / belly, abdomen
15 Hinterlauf / hind leg
16 Rute / tail

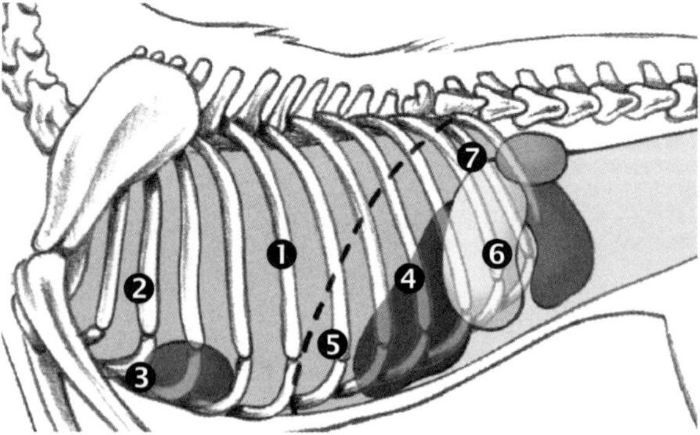

❶ = Zwerchfell / diaphragm
❷ = Lunge / lung
❸ = Herz / heart
❹ = Magen / stomach
❺ = Leber / liver
❻ = Milz / spleen
❼ = linke Niere / left kidney

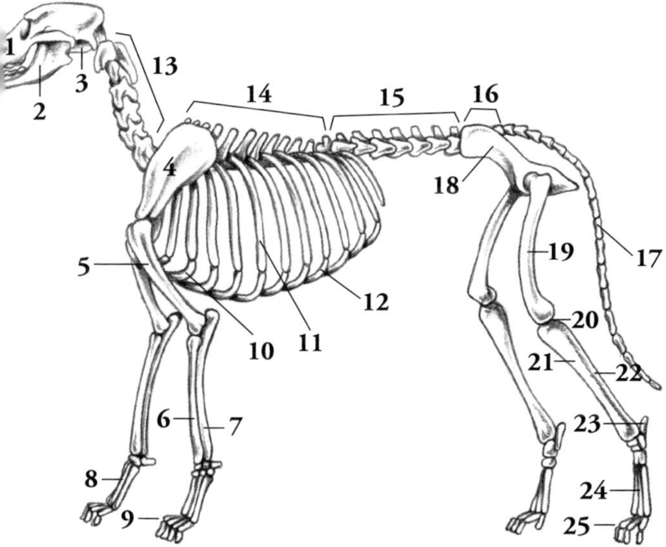

Oberkiefer / upper jaw, maxilla
Unterkiefer / lower jaw
Kehlkopf / larynx
Schulterblatt / shoulder blade
Oberarmknochen / humerus
Speiche / radius
Elle / ulna
Vordermittelfußknochen / metacarpus
Zehenknochen / phalanges
Brustbein / breast bone
Rippe / rib
Rippenknorpel / false rib
Halswirbel / cervical vertebrae

14 Brustwirbel / thoracic vertebrae
15 Lendenwirbel / lumbar vertebrae
16 Kreuzbein / sacrum
17 Schwanzwirbel / caudal vertebrae
18 Becken / pelvis
19 Oberschenkelknochen / upper tighbone
20 Kniescheibe / patella, kneecap
21 Schienbein / tibia
22 Wadenbein / fibula
23 Fersenbein / heel bone
24 Hintermittelfußknochen / metatarsus
25 Zehenknochen / phalanges

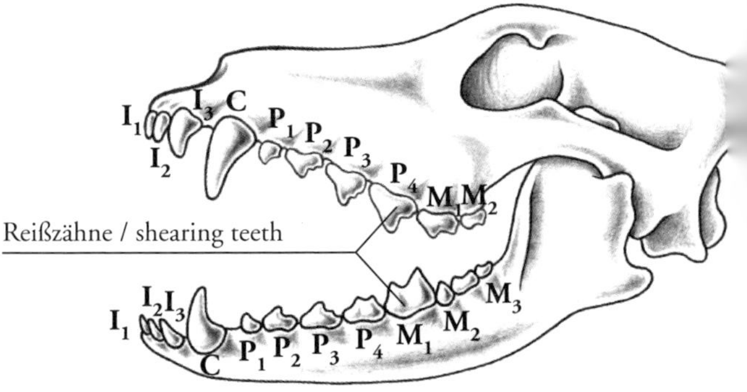

I = Incisivus / Schneidezahn / incisor
C = Caninus / Hakenzahn / canine tooth
P = Prämolar / Vorbackenzahn / pre-molar
M = Molar / Backenzahn / molar